Sketches for the
NORTH AMERICAN REVIEW

Sketches for the

NORTH
AMERICAN
REVIEW

by

HENRY
ADAMS

Edited by

EDWARD
CHALFANT

ARCHON BOOKS : 1986

© 1986 by Edward Chalfant. All rights reserved
First published 1986 as an Archon Book,
an imprint of The Shoe String Press, Inc.,
Hamden, Connecticut 06514

Printed in the United States of America

The paper in this book meets the guidelines for
permanence and durability of the Committee on
Production Guidelines for Book Longevity
of the Council on Library Resources.

Library of Congress Cataloging-in-Publication Data
Adams, Henry, 1838–1918.
Sketches for the North American review.

1. United States—Civilization—Book reviews.
2. Harvard University—History—18th century—Book
reviews. 3. Education, Higher—United States—History—
Book reviews. 4. History—Book reviews. 5. Adams,
Henry, 1838–1918. I. Chalfant, Edward, 1921–
II. Title.
E175.5.A2A25 1986   973   86–10901
ISBN 0–208–02115–9 (alk. paper)

CONTENTS

v

PREFACE

The sketches by Henry Adams brought together in this book may appeal to the reader as valuable statements of their author's ideas and feelings concerning issues fundamental in education, literature, and history. In two ways the sketches may be surprising. Although written by an inveterately political member of America's most conspicuous political family, they avoid direct allusion to contemporary politics. And they reveal themselves as always *personal*—a quality that publication in the old *North American Review* does not usually suggest.

The first sketch—the word is Adams's—was published in the ponderous Boston quarterly in January 1872. Much later, wanting to include it in his *Historical Essays* (1891), Adams made revisions and deletions. Excising the passages most related to himself, he effected a metamorphosis. What was personal he changed into something impersonal.

Here Sketch 1 is reprinted in its original form for the first time. All the others are reprinted for the first time except Sketch 4, which was suppressed and here is first published. Sketch 22 has not till now been attributed to Adams and in that sense also is wholly new.

The main consideration is that after a century of neglect some ostensibly separate writings are brought from the shadows and offered for what they assuredly are: a loosely knit, yet coherent series; and thus a book, new though old, by one of America's established writers.

Henry Adams was born in 1838 in Boston and proved exceptionally purposive. While a schoolboy, he settled upon a fourfold ambition. He meant to be the leading American politician of his time; he aspired to become a great writer; he wanted to live in Washington; and he hoped to travel over much of the globe. Not divergent, his objects were complementary. Not excessive, they comported with his unfailing energy, very evident powers of mind, and talent for practical management.

He lost no time getting started. At Harvard, he published an article when a freshman. Ten weeks after graduating, he left for Europe. When he returned two years later, he could speak fluent German and good French. His father, then a congressman, required his serving in Washington as private secretary. The son responded by doubling as secret journalist. His unsigned newspaper reports from the capital to the *Boston Advertiser* during the secession crisis, and later, after his father was made minister to England, his anonymous weekly dispatches as London correspondent of the *New York Times* during the *Trent* Affair—when a world war seemed to start, yet was averted, in a measure through his influence—made the son an important, though unrecognized, political power when a mere genius of twenty-three. They also brought their author to the end of one life, leaving him to attempt a second.

In 1866, after an interval of silence and fresh preparations in London, young Adams began to supply ambitious articles to the *North American Review*, at first anonymously, then signed. In 1868, he moved to Washington. He contributed also to British magazines, the *Edinburgh Review* and the *Westminster Review*, and wrote systematically for a New York weekly, the *Nation*. For two years, by writing often and to a purpose, by avoiding office, and by allying himself with capable persons in office and not in office, he led the forces determined to introduce good national government of a kind not wanted by President Grant.

For Adams, whether to be more a politician or more a writer had long been a question. As it happened, his efforts as a political leader—indeed all his efforts without exception—were cut across terrifically by the death of his elder sister from lockjaw, an occurrence he watched to the end from her bedside through twelve nights and thirteen days. Changes ensued. After much hesitation, on September 21, 1870, though it meant leaving Washington, he accepted the editorship of the *North American Review*. A few days later he also accepted a five-year appointment as assistant professor of history at Harvard. And on October 24 or 25 he changed his name. Originally Henry Brooks

Adams (also Henry B. Adams, H. B. Adams, and H. B. A.), he dropped the Brooks and began to sign himself as Henry Adams (and H. A.).

Editing and teaching were interim occupations he would soon have to leave, but they helped him reach a decision. Henceforward he would be a politician only limitedly, a writer unlimitedly.

The *North American Review,* founded in 1815, was incomparably the country's most prestigious magazine. Published quarterly, it appeared in January, April, July, and October. Typical issues contained as many as six articles and ten critical notices. Two issues comprised a volume and if bound together would bulk as a good-sized book.

Adams's responsibility as editor began with the issue for January 1871. At first, his duties as editor-teacher were so crushing that he could not have written anything for the magazine even if much inclined. Late in 1871, two things coincided: he wanted to write, and a looming issue was short of copy. In his words, ". . . my staff of contributors suddenly broke down and left me sprawling."

Earlier the writer of many full-length articles, he had sometimes reacted against the article form as unsuited to his abilities and overheavy. He felt drawn to a lighter form, something writers were calling sketches. As he understood the term, sketches were flexible as to length. They could end in a few lines. Just as easily, they could continue for many pages. And now, as editor, he confronted a fearful chasm of empty space.

The January 1872 issue appears to have lacked two articles and two or more critical notices. Unexpectedly, a manuscript arrived from England. Sent by Francis Turner Palgrave, it was an article about an Elizabethan poet, Thomas Watson (twenty-two pages). In three desperate weeks, Adams himself completed a long sketch (thirty-seven pages) and two short ones (seven pages). The chasm (sixty-six pages) was bridged.

For the April 1872 issue, Adams wrote a fourth sketch, had it set in type and was ready to print it, but at the urging of James R. Osgood, the magazine's publisher, suppressed it—creating a ten-page, last-minute gap. To fill most of the gap, Adams wrote three small sketches. To fill the rest, he accepted or solicited a critical notice by a young Harvard teaching colleague, Thomas Sergeant Perry.

Thus, in the space of three months, partly under pressure of circumstance, partly out of desire, the hard-driven editor-teacher produced seven sketches and made a new beginning as a writer.

In July 1872, when he had edited seven issues and started work on an eighth, Adams went off on a year-long wedding journey to Europe and Egypt. His editorship was suspended, not stopped. William Dean Howells completed the editing of the issue for October 1872. Perry, as interim editor, brought out five issues, through January 1874. Before resuming work as editor, Adams asked Henry Cabot Lodge, one of his former students, to join him as assistant editor. Adams and Lodge edited eleven issues, from April 1874 through October 1876.

The labor of editing a magazine so voluminous was considerable. In 1870–1872, Adams edited 38 articles and 59 critical notices, excluding those in the issue completed by Howells. In 1874–1876, he and Lodge edited 56 articles and 117 notices. The totals for Adams in his eighteen issues were 94 articles and 176 notices.

As viewed by readers and subscribers, the *North American Review* was largely anonymous. The names of its editors were not disclosed. The names of the writers of articles were usually given (only at the end of the article), yet many articles were published unsigned. The names of the writers of notices were never given. An occasional notice bore the writer's initials or last initial; the vast majority were anonymous.

Always resourceful, Adams took advantage of the rules about names to achieve a personal object. Readers of the magazine must have seen that the fifth article in the January 1872 issue was signed "Henry Adams." (The article was his first sketch: "Harvard College. 1786–87." Also it was the first of his writings signed with the name he would have when famous.) But if the same readers saw that a notice in the issue for January 1874 was initialled "H.A.," they could not know for a fact that the Henry Adams of 1872 had reappeared as the H. A. of 1874. Still less could they know that the 1874 notice was the eighth sketch of a series that Adams was writing for the magazine. And they had no grounds at all for suspecting that, always adding sketches as notices, and never again with his initials, the editor would extend the series until twenty-odd sketches were written, as many as twenty-two had appeared in print, and he could account himself the author of a book, artfully hidden, very nearly anonymous, yet almost entirely published.

Adams had agreed to edit the magazine and teach at Harvard on condition that at his convenience he would again move to Washington. He decided that the October 1876 issue, scheduled to appear just prior to the centennial election, would be "very political." An article intended to appear in the issue, unsigned, was written by his brother Charles. (See Attributions, no. 32.) The proprietors of the magazine were apprised of the article's political tendencies and ventured objections to Henry. Seizing the objections as a pretext, Adams broke off his editorship of the magazine. Lodge also resigned. As a result, below the table of contents, the issue displayed a Publishers' Notice:

> The editors of the 'North American Review' having retired from its management on account of a difference of opinion with the proprietors as to the political character of this number, the proprietors, rather than cause an indefinite delay in publication, have allowed the number to retain the form which had been given to it, without, however, committing the Review to the opinions expressed therein.

Another article in the editors' last issue reviewed a book by Hermann von Holst, a German historian, newly translated and published as *The Constitutional and Political History of the United States.* Two names were printed at the end of the article: Henry Adams and H. C. Lodge. Most readers who saw the names presumably thought them the names of writers who had collaborated to produce the article. But the publishers' notice at the front of the issue used a plural, "editors." So an unusual question could be asked. Were the names a simple declaration that the signers had collaborated as writers of the article, or were the names also, or instead, indications that Henry Adams and H. C. Lodge were the unnamed "editors" who had "retired"? The question merited a reply; for conceivably the true authorship of the article— although it was followed by two names—had not been revealed.

The loss of Adams and Lodge as editors ended the magazine's chances of continuing as a ponderous quarterly. It was quickly sold to another publisher and transformed to a popular monthly.

In 1877, presumably on his own initiative, William Cushing, a former librarian, began compiling an *Index to the North American Review.*

Volumes I–CXXV. 1815–1877, to include both an Index of Subjects and an Index of Writers. When his work was finished, Cushing wrote a preface, dated July 1878, in which he made bold to say, ". . . on every side I have met with encouragement and assistance. The fullest sources of information, in regard to the past and present writers, have been opened to me by the past and present editors, by the late and present publishers. I am able to furnish the names of the writers of nearly all the principal articles; and of nearly all the critical notices. . . ."

That Cushing ever talked with Adams about indexing problems seems doubtful. Adams had vacated his Boston house in May 1877 and moved to Washington the following autumn. It appears, however, that Adams, to the limits permitted to himself, cooperated with the indexer by mail, or by mail at one remove, through Lodge. Emphatically, there were limits. For example, there is evidence that Adams, readying the July 1876 issue, had obtained a notice from a writer on condition that the secret of his or her authorship be kept from all other persons.

Cushing's *Index to the North American Review* proved a helpful resource, accurate in the main, but sometimes in error, and rather often in error in its entries relating to Adams. Both its Index of Subjects and its Index of Writers ascribed things to Adams which he is known not to have written. One was the July 1876 notice whose authorship he had vowed to keep secret.

Adams acquired a copy of the *Index,* presumably when issued. In the Index of Subjects, he crossed out two entries attributing notices to himself and wrote "Brooks" (meaning his younger brother) next to one of the cancelled entries. He also corrected an entry by replacing "Lea" with "Lodge." In the Index of Writers, he crossed out five attributions of notices to himself and one attribution of a notice to William James. But he did not search the copy from start to finish, looking for entries he might need to cancel or correct. He simply made the markings listed above and kept the copy on the shelves of his Washington library.

The exact list of Adams's writings for the *North American Review* during his editorship (and Perry's) has long been needed but has not been easy to settle. The sketches published here correspond to a list for which I am solely responsible. The list adds to and subtracts from the list that can be gathered from Cushing's *Index*. It also differs from lists published by modern authorities and from case-by-case judgments made in print by modern editors.

A detailed statement of my grounds for concluding that Adams wrote just these twenty-three sketches, no more and no less, is given at the back of the book, in Attributions and Facsimiles.

PART ONE
1872

1

HARVARD COLLEGE 1786–87

H enry Adams went to Harvard and at graduation in 1858 ranked in the middle of his class. A student's rank was calculated by subtracting penalty points for misconduct from academic points won in courses. An excellent but increasingly restive student, Adams accumulated points of both kinds in impressive numbers. His conduct when a senior strayed so far from desired norms that, having *him* for a problem, the college authorities did not investigate, much less punish, an act of extreme revolt by a person or persons unknown (manifestly Adams at his most defiant)—the secret printing and extensive distribution of a seemingly official but thoroughly false, inverted rank list of the senior class.

After a twelve-year absence, the alumnus returned as a member of the faculty. He arrived with "peculiar ideas," as he called them, including ideas about the place the student should be accorded in education, and ideas about student revolts, why they occur, and how they can be minimized, as opposed to repressed.

This long first sketch is the only surviving, extended statement of Adams's educational principles as felt and held by him when at work as a college teacher. Their tendency was revolutionary. It so remains.

The merits of the sketch grow more apparent when it is read in conjunction with the chapters "Harvard College" and "Failure" in *The Education of Henry Adams*. It also gains in interest when read together with an essay he completed in 1859 but never published. The essay appears in full in the *American Historical Review* 53 (October 1947):59–64, under the title "Henry Adams Reports on a German Gymnasium."

Edward Everett, whose "Autobiographical Fragment" is quoted towards the start of the sketch, was married to Adams's mother's sister

Charlotte and was president of Harvard when Adams—then a small child—was first brought to the campus. Coming back as a teacher, Adams lived in the house in which he had visited the Everetts long before.

The unnamed student whose college diary is quoted in the later portions of the sketch is Adams's grandfather, John Quincy Adams.

Henry Adams himself kept a diary while a collegian. He read and burned it in 1888, for reasons the sketch may help to suggest.

—*North American Review* (January 1872); signed "Henry Adams"—

1. *Old Cambridge and New.* By THOMAS C. AMORY. Reprinted from the New England Historical and Genealogical Register. Boston: J. R. Osgood & Co. 1871.
2. *Edward Everett's College Life: An Autobiographical Fragment.* Old and New, July and August, 1871.

MR. AMORY'S little work contains some curious and not uninteresting details of local history, all the more welcome because it is not an easy matter for the historian to pursue small game of this kind through the forests of manuscript in which it is their custom to hide; and any one who will undertake the labor, or happens to know the secret places of forgotten and curious facts, has a right to claim the historian's gratitude, even though the actual result of the sport is not precisely rich. Cambridge to the world at large is a place of limited importance, no doubt, and even in the eyes of Boston, her neighbor, is only a considerable suburb, which contains an University; but the principle of solidarity in modern society extends even to suburbs, and Cambridge has some right to claim that neither Massachusetts nor America would have been the better for losing Cambridge from their roll of cities. Nature has not been prodigal to her; art has added but few attractions to the small number of those that nature conferred; but she is, nevertheless, one of the largest cities in the Commonwealth, and she contains its only considerable school of knowledge. Her history is therefore a fair subject for more than local interest.

Nevertheless, to the great mass of persons who know Cambridge only by name, it is the College and not the town which lends the subject such interest as it has. Indeed, under the most flattering light, the public or popular concern in the College itself, or in its sister at New Haven, is by no means deep, and the traveller who undertakes to cross the continent soon reaches the limits beyond which the two Universities, if mentioned at all, present only vague ideas to the listener. Yet such general interest as there is attaches itself to the University, and as the small circle of cultivated readers is reached, this interest becomes very decided, and extends to matters which are apparently trivial, and certainly have only a very slight historical or literary value. This feeling was curiously shown in the attention which Mr. Everett's reminiscences excited, as they were printed in the course of last year. Mr. Everett himself belonged to the present century. He took his degree in 1811, and there are graduates in plenty who could amplify his short sketch indefinitely. Yet the public seemed to feel a certain amount of active interest in the little account, extracts from which may without harm be quoted, of student life and manners in the first decade of the century:

I was thirteen years old in April, 1807, and entered as freshman the following August, being the youngest member of my class. I lived the first year with my classmate, Charles P. Curtis, in a wooden building standing at the corner of the Main and Church Street. It was officially known as the 'College House,' but known by the students as 'Wiswall's Den,' or more concisely, 'The Den,' whether from its comfortless character as a habitation, or from some worse cause, I do not know. There was a tradition that it had been the scene of a horrid domestic tragedy, and that it was haunted by the ghosts of the Wiswalls; but I cannot say that during the twelvemonth I lived in the Den this tale was confirmed by my own experience. We occupied the southwest corner chamber, up two flights of stairs,—a room about fourteen feet square, in which were contained two beds and the rest of our furniture, and our fuel, which was wood, and was kept under the beds. Two very small closets afforded a little additional space; but the accommodations certainly were far from brilliant.

A good many young men who go to college are idlers, some worse than idlers. I suppose my class in this respect was like other classes; but there was a fair proportion of faithful, studious students, and of well-conducted young men. I was protected in part, perhaps, by my youth from the grosser temptations. I went through the prescribed studies of the year—which were principally a few books of Livy and Horace for the Latin, and Collectanea Græca Majora for the Greek—about as well as most of the class; but the manner in which the ancient languages were then studied was deplorably superficial. It was confined to the most cursory reading of the text. Besides the Latin and Greek languages, we had a weekly recitation in Lowth's English Grammar, and in the Hebrew grammar *without points*; also in arithmetic and history, the last from Millot's compend as a text-book. In all these branches there was an entire want of apparatus, and the standard compared with that which now exists was extremely low. And yet, in all respects, I imagine a great improvement had taken place in reference to college education over the state of things which existed in the previous generation. The intense political excitement of the Revolutionary period seems to have unsettled the minds of men from the quiet pursuits of life.

President Webber was at the head of the University when I entered it, having succeeded to President Willard, who died in 1804. . . .

President Webber was a man of great worth, but destitute of popular gifts. He was a person of tradition and routine, and never attempted to say a word to the students except from a manuscript prepared beforehand. He could not be said to be popular with the young men, but it was simply from the want of the art of kindly intercourse. I remember going to his office in my freshman year to ask leave of absence for one night, that I might be at home for some family gathering, as I did not like to have to return to Cambridge at a very late hour. I found the whole academic corps assembled in the President's office,—a circumstance which did not diminish my trepidation at being there for the first time. I modestly stated my request and the reason. I had never asked a favor nor incurred a penalty; and I had never passed an hour away from the college without permission. I received my answer, however, in the monosyllable "No," without the addition of a word to soften the flat refusal. Such was the tone of authority in those days.

The mode of life of students in Cambridge is greatly changed since my day. We then lived in commons; the five classes assembled daily for the three meals in the Commons Hall, where the tutors and other parietal officers occupied an upper table. Till the year 1806, the evening meal was not even served in the hall, but was received by the students at the kitchen window, and conveyed to their rooms. The disagreeable nature of this operation in bad weather in a New England winter may easily be conceived. This practice was done away with, and supper, like the two other meals, provided in the hall, the year before I entered college. The tables were served by beneficiary students, according to the custom formerly existing in the English colleges; and I believe it may with strict truth be added, that the said position of the "waiters," as they were called, was in no degree impaired by performing this office for their fellow-students. Although commons were attended with some inconveniences and evils, I have regretted that some other remedy could not have been found than entire discontinuance. The rooms were furnished in a very simple style. I do not recollect that there was a carpet, a window-curtain, a sofa, or an easy-chair in any student's room; and nearly all the young men brought their own water from the pumps, and trimmed their own lamps. A little luxury in this respect crept into the higher classes. One or two persons got their living about college as general boot-blacks. Charles Lennox, a respectable colored man, became in this way, I have heard, the richest man of his complexion in the State. He used to bring in his bill so much for brushing *bootes*.

The practice of fagging, borrowed from the English schools, or rather, perhaps, growing out of that amiable propensity in human nature which leads the strong to find pleasure in oppressing the weak, prevailed to some extent in the last century at Cambridge. A member of the freshman class was obliged to take off his hat in the presence of members of the higher classes, and to do their errands if required. As a check on the abuse of this latter obligation, each freshman placed himself under a member of the senior class, who was called his senior; and it was a lawful excuse for not obeying the orders of any other student, that you were doing an errand for your senior. These practices in my time were obsolete, though it was still not unusual for a freshman to have "his senior," usually some family friend, to whom he could go in case of need for a word of advice.

I was considered, I believe, as taking rank among the best scholars in the class; although there was no branch in which I was not equalled, and in several was excelled, by some one of my classmates, except, perhaps, metaphysics.

I have mentioned metaphysics as a study in which I succeeded. I mean, of course, only that I prepared myself thoroughly in the textbooks. Watt's Logic was the first book studied in this branch; not a very inviting treatise compared with that of Archbishop Whately, but easily comprehended, and not repulsive. The account of the syllogistic method amused me; and the barbarous stanzas describing the various syllogistic modes and figures dwelt for a long time in my memory, and have not wholly faded away. Locke's "Essay on Human Understanding" came next. This was more difficult. We recited from it three times a day the four first days of the week; the recitation of Thursday afternoon being a review of the rest. We were expected to give the substance of the author's remarks, but were at liberty to condense them, and to use our own words.

At the close of the junior year I received the appointment of English orator at the public exhibition. This appointment, according to the usage then prevailing, implied that I was considered by the faculty one of the three first scholars in the class. I called my subject the "Prejudices of Criticism," a not very significant phrase, borrowed from the phraseology of that time prevalent at college.

I passed the winter vacation of this year at college, principally employed in miscellaneous reading. Among other standard works, I read Gibbon's "Decline and Fall" with considerable care, with a considerable portion of Burke. The gorgeous style of the latter, and the stately eloquence of Gibbon and Johnson, caught my youthful fancy, and pleased me more than the simple diction of Goldsmith and Addison. These last I had always read with pleasure; but I thought the three great masters I have just named were rather to be imitated as models of style; an error which it took me some years to discover and correct.

During my senior year I relaxed a little from my studious habits, though I did not fall into serious neglect of my college duties, still less into any vicious indulgence. But I had become weary of the restraints of college life, and the natural restlessness of the age I had reached (seventeen) rendered me impatient of academic confinement and routine. I was in some danger of going astray.

In August, 1811, I took my degree, and delivered the valedictory oration of the class on Commencement Day. I called my subject "Literary Evils," an unmeaning phrase, like that which I chose as the subject of my exhibition oration. It was, I suspect, an inferior performance. Not much can be effected, even by a mature mind, in a set discourse of only twelve minutes in length, of which some portion had to be given up by the valedictory orator to the enumeration of some of the chief benefactors of the College,—a practice borrowed from the "commemoration," of the English universities, and now discontinued at Harvard. Our class was the first to which these English orations had been assigned, and it was some years before the example was followed. An entire change in the arrangement of the literary exercises of Commencement Day has since taken place, and there is still room for great improvement. At present, they are greatly too numerous, and the time devoted to them necessarily too long. The average character of these juvenile efforts is now vastly beyond the standard in my time.

This is certainly entertaining, so far as it goes, but one cannot help wishing it went further. For the large and increasing class of instructors, or persons interested in the improvement of instruction in this country, there could be few more entertaining and suggestive books than a history of instruction at Harvard College; an account, not of the numbers of students, nor of the gifts of donors, but of the processes tried, the experiments that failed, the discipline enforced, the customs observed, and, above all, the steady improvement in scholarship, if any such can be shown to have existed. One wishes to know with what standard the College started, and to what extent this standard has been raised or lowered. In fixing once for all the facts of the case, whatever they may be, and in ascertaining precisely what direction the College has followed during its two centuries and a half of activity, some light might perhaps be thrown on the very disputed question of the future. Since its foundation the College has vastly altered its character, and there is every reason to suppose that it will continue to experiment with new methods and in new directions as rapidly as is safe. There is all the more reason for bearing in mind that its history is of no small importance as illustrating the growth of

American society and as indicating its future progress. Both as a social and as an educational question, therefore, the matter is of considerable interest.

Such a story, however, to be well told, should come directly from first sources, and, with the exception of the College records, first sources are not easily reached. The College records, too, have the disadvantage that they tell a somewhat stiff and often ludicrously formal tale of boys' experiences and petty discipline, without in the least entering into boys' feeling. For after all it is primarily with students that education deals, and the opinion of students is therefore an essential part of all successful education. One wishes to know what the student, at any given time, thought of himself, of his studies and his instructors; what his studies and his habits were; how much he knew and how thoroughly; with what spirit he met his work, and with what amount of active aid and sympathy his instructors met him in dealing with his work or his amusements. The past brings down traditions of solid learning and careful training in the branches of study it assumed to deal with. One would like to know how such learning was gained, the methods and the instruments by which great results were reached. In short, one cannot but feel that one's self-esteem is a little at stake in the question whether the present generation, in making what it calls its progress, has sacrificed anything which was once useful to its predecessors, and this too, quite aside from the further question whether such a sacrifice, if ever made, was a matter of necessity or of mere recklessness.

If it were possible by some chance to disinter from the repositories of old manuscripts a series of students' diaries throughout the seventeenth and eighteenth centuries, from which, by any careful process of sifting out the chaff, a certain continuity of thought and experience could be discovered, the greatest difficulty would be overcome. Unfortunately, students' diaries are apt to be so feeble productions that the writers, if they ever think to read them in later years, commonly put them in the fire. Yet feeble as they are, they represent the most important part of any educational system, and their place can by no means be taken by mere reminiscences, no matter how entertaining or extensive the latter may be. A skilful instructor ought, perhaps, to derive as many ideas from the absurdities or extravagances of the scholars who are in his charge, as he does from their better qualities;

and, above all, no instructor can well be allowed to forget the fact, which, nevertheless, is extremely apt to be forgotten in practice, that the teacher exists for the sake of the scholars, not the scholars for the sake of the teacher. No system of education can be very successful which does not make the scholar its chief object of interest; a principle which may sound like a truism, but which, in fact, will be found to have been rarely put in practice on any great scale, and which, in the daily work of education, is the most difficult of all principles to act upon. In the great majority of cases the teacher is, in his own eyes, the most important part of a school; the institution or school or system itself ranks next, and the scholar comes last of all. To reverse this order of things in an historical treatment of the subject may seem trivial enough to grown men who look upon a great and influential corporation like Harvard College in the same light as a railway or a banking corporation, with a history which is thoroughly economical, made up of charters, deeds, and statistics of passengers carried, discounts effected, boys educated, and stock watered; but it is, nevertheless, the true historical method, if there were but the means of carrying it out.

Unfortunately, as has been already said, the means are wanting. But it is not only the means which are wanting. The work itself could only be done to advantage by some one peculiarly constituted. Attempts without number have been made to use college life as a groundwork for fiction, and the result has almost if not quite invariably been failure, for the reason that the field of interest is too narrow, and that the attempt to enlarge it by introducing forced situations is more fatal to success than the narrowness of the field itself. The same difficulty would be found in a more practical treatment of the same subject. The details are numerous and fatiguing; the possible combinations few and simple; the treatment itself must make atonement for the want of incident, and such treatment could only come from a master critic who could employ his labor to more effect in matters of wider and deeper interest. The student must probably, therefore, remain content to have no history which shall deal with education from his stand-point.

Nevertheless, such material as exists, which can throw light on the movement of high education in America, ought not to be wasted. No doubt the family records of more than one household in New England contain papers that might be of service in following out this path of inquiry; but one such manuscript record at least lies before us, and offers a curious and extremely characteristic picture of the education which was given at Cambridge towards the close of the last century. The record in question is a student's diary for fifteen months in the years 1786–87; years, it will be remembered, of great depression in America, immediately following the peace with Great Britain, but preceding the establishment of a responsible national government. The winter was famous for the outbreak and forcible repression of Shays' rebellion, which was the principal subject of interest in Massachusetts, and threatened for a time to affect Cambridge itself. The student in question was a young man in his nineteenth year, who came late to the University, and joined the junior class on the 15th March, 1786. As will be seen, he had a fair share of youthful crudities, but he appears to have been as free from extreme prejudices as could reasonably be expected from a young man of his age, while his manner of looking at things occasionally indicates a mind which had come into closer contact with grown and educated men than with people of his own age. It is perhaps almost unduly mature.

In the present days of ever-increasing severity in examinations for admission to college, it is interesting to inquire what the requisites were in the last century. The student here gives, it is true, no indication of what examination was required for entrance into either of the two lower classes. He applied for admission to the junior class, and not only that, but for admission in the third term of the junior year, when more than half of the year's work was done. His examination, therefore, indicates the minimum required by the College after about three years of college education. The examination itself appears to have been a very formal proceeding, and although the proportion of absolute rejections was smaller then than now, yet admission was far from a matter of course. In this particular instance the applicant appears to have had a special examination as he applied for admission at a time when no one else wished to enter. He tells his own story, as follows:

15 *March*, 1786. Between 9 and 10 in the morning I went to the President's, and was there admitted before the President, the four tutors, three professors, and Librarian. The first book was Horace, where Mr. J——, the Latin tutor, told me to turn to the Carmen sæculare, where I construed three stanzas and

parsed the word *sylvarum,* but called *potens* a substantive. Mr. J——, the Greek tutor, then put me to the beginning of the fourth book of Homer. I construed—lines, but parsed wrong ἀλλήλους. I had then παραβλήδην given me. I was then asked a few questions in Watts's Logic by Mr. H——, and a considerable number in Locke on the Understanding, very few of which I was able to answer. The next thing was geography, where Mr. R—— asked me what was the figure of the earth, and several other questions, some of which I answered, and others not. Mr. Williams asked me if I had studied Euclid and arithmetic, after which the President conducted me to another room and gave me the following piece of English to turn into Latin, from the World: "There cannot certainly be an higher ridicule than to give an air of importance to amusements, if they are in themselves contemptible and void of taste; but if they are the object and care of the judicious and polite and really deserve that distinction, the conduct of them is certainly of consequence." I made it thus: "Nihil profecto risu dignior quam magni æstimare delectamenta, si per se despicienda sunt atque sine sapore. At si res oblatæ atque cura sunt sagacibus et artibus excultis et revera hanc distinctionem merent, administratio eorum haud dubie utilitatis est." I take it from memory only, as no scholar is suffered to take a copy of the Latin he made at his examination. The President then took it, was gone about ¼ of an hour, returned and said, "You are admitted"; and gave me a paper to carry to the steward.

Certainly the examination was not a very difficult one, and the candidate, according to his own account, does not appear to have made a very brilliant figure at it. Setting aside Watts and Locke, which are no longer so important a part of the liberal education as they formerly were, one may perhaps say that the freshman of our day would think himself the happiest of beings if he could escape with no more severe an examination than this. But the most remarkable fact of all is, that this examination, so far as the classics are concerned, represents not the minimum but the maximum of requirements, not for the junior year, but for the entire college course. Homer, Horace, Terence, and Cæsar were all that the student attempted to study. With the junior year, instruction in the classics ended. As evidence of the condition of classical studies in the University at this time the following entry would seem to be very significant:

July 5, 1786. Mr. J—— gave us a piece of Latin to make; the first the class have had since I have been here. This is the last week that we attend the Latin tutor, and last week we closed with Mr. J—— (Greek). In the senior year there are no languages studied in college. It is very popular here to dislike the study of Greek and Latin.

All that the student could do in college, at least in the direction of classical acquirements, was therefore limited within a very narrow margin, which is perfectly represented by the examination described above. Another extract will illustrate this fact:

> *May* 10, 1786. We finished the Andria of Terence this morning. The class began it last February. I went through it at Haverhill in three evenings. However, it must be said that they study it only one week in four, and that week only four mornings, but even in that way it has taken thirteen lessons to go through this one play. We recite afternoons the Latin week in Cæsar, but I have had nothing to say this week. The class is so numerous that he (the tutor) cannot hear more than one half of them recite at once, and so he takes turns.

It seems tolerably clear, therefore, that where students dropped the classics at Cambridge in the last century, there students begin the study in the present one. If this be the case, an interesting question rises as to how and where the last generation, or any preceding generation in America, got its classical knowledge, if it had any. Cambridge was its best school, and at Cambridge the classics were unpopular and neglected. Homer and Horace or Terence and a simple sentence in Latin composition represent all the classical knowledge that Harvard gave; and it is quite clear that beyond the simple construing of the text and the application of the elementary rules of grammar, nothing was even attempted.

In regard to mathematics, the same relative position seems to have been held. Euclid and arithmetic are no further advanced as mathematics than Homer and Horace as classics, if indeed they are so far. But mathematics were continued through the senior year, and apparently with comparative energy. Any other requirement, with the exception of logic and metaphysics, seems to have been unknown, unless geography were something more than the mere form which the single question repeated in the diary would imply.

So far, then, as the standard of knowledge was concerned, it was low enough; and to judge from the account of the student himself, his success in satisfying even this low standard was not so brilliant as it might have been. Yet the best acquirements of the highest scholars in his class appear to have been no greater. At all events there was no one of sufficient superiority, among the fifty graduates of his year, to prevent him from carrying away an English oration at his Commencement, a prize commonly given only to the best scholars.

The examination being over, the new student was fairly a member of the College. The first matter of interest is naturally his studies. One who is familiar with the elaborate system of instruction now in use, is curious to know the steps which have led up to it. And so far as the student himself is concerned, his information is reasonably exact. He did not appear at the college exercises until a week after his admission, when he went to the President.

March 22. Immediately after prayers I went to the President, who said, "You may live with Sir Ware, a Bachelor of Arts." I made a most respectful bow, and retired.

To persons who have forgotten this use of the title *Sir,* another extract may be of interest:

July 19. Commencement Day. The new Sirs got quite high in the evening, at Derby's chamber, and made considerable of a noise.

Recitations now began. For one week the class recited in Euclid. The following week it recited in Homer and the Greek Testament; the third week, in Locke; the fourth, in Terence and Cæsar. This was the round of studies, and when the four weeks were passed, the process was begun again. But the weeks were classed as mathematical, metaphysical, Greek, and Latin weeks, and no two of these subjects were ever recited at the same time.

There appear to have been six recitations in these branches every week. On Mondays and Wednesdays, both morning and afternoon; on Tuesdays and Thursdays, only in the morning. Friday was a leisure day for the whole College, so far as recitations were concerned. On Saturdays there was one early recitation in Doddridge's Divinity, a work which appears not to have been a favorite text-book. This seems to have been all the work of the College in respect to recitations. In addition to this, however, there were frequent lectures, both philosophical and doctrinal, which the students of all classes seem to have attended, and there were also literary exercises, as well as a regular exercise in declamation.

As the description of a single day, the following is sufficiently clear:

May 3, 1786. Wednesday and Monday are our two busiest days in the week. This morning (Wednesday) at 6 we went into prayers, after which we immediately recited (Homer). This took us till 7¼. At 7½ we breakfasted. At 10 we had a lecture on Divinity, from Mr. Wigglesworth. It was upon the wisdom of all God's actions, and justifying those parts of Scripture which some have reproached as contrary to justice. At 11 we had a philosophical lecture from Mr. Williams upon the mechanical powers, and particularly the lever and the pulley. At 12½, dinner. At 3, an astronomical public lecture upon the planet Mercury, a very circumstantial account of all its transits over the sun's disk. At 4 again we recited (Greek Testament), and at 5 attended prayers again, after which there are no more exercises for this day, but we are obliged in the evening to prepare our recitation for to-morrow morning. This I think is quite sufficient employment for one day, but the three last days in the week we have very little to do; Thursdays and Saturdays reciting only in the morning, and Fridays a philosophical lecture.

A modern student would not think this work very severe, for except the two recitations there is nothing which requires preparation. Perhaps the most curious part of the old arrangement is the very subordinate place filled by recitations, and it is certainly interesting to hear a student in 1786, who has but seven recitations a week, finding fault with the system in language like this:

September 4, 1786. As we have no metaphysical tutor here at present, we supposed that for the ensuing fortnight we should have no reciting. But the government have determined that we shall continue to attend Mr. R——. This is not an agreeable circumstance. A person who does not belong to the University and hears only the word reciting, naturally concludes that the scholars are an idle set of fellows, because they are always averse to recitations. Now the fact is just the contrary. A person fond of study regards the time spent in reciting as absolutely lost. He has studied the book before he recites; and the tutors here are so averse to giving ideas different from those of the author whom they are supposed to explain, that they always speak in his own words and never pretend to add anything of their own. Reciting is indeed of some service to idle fellows, because it brings the matter immediately before them and obliges them at least for a short time to attend to something. But a hard student will always dislike it, because it takes time from him which he supposes might have been employed to greater advantage.

A change in the recitations occurred in the senior year. Greek and Latin were entirely dropped, and during the whole first quarter the seniors recited in mathematics alone, because the tutor in metaphysics had resigned, and his place had not been filled. Only on the 3d October did the new tutor make his appearance and begin upon Burlamaqui's Natural Law, after which the two studies alternated during the rest of the year. The lectures were continued, and a new course, "very dry," was added, upon language. The principal professor would seem, however, to have not satisfied the more zealous students, if the following extract can be trusted:

April 5, 1787. At 11 this forenoon Mr. Williams gave us the second philosophical lecture. It was upon the incidental properties of matter, and, excepting very few deviations, was expressed in the same terms with that we had last year upon the same subject. Indeed, whether the professor's time is taken up by other studies, or whether he is too indolent to make any improvements in his lectures, it is said he gives every year the same course, without adding or erasing a line.

April 7. Mr. Williams gave us this forenoon a lecture upon motion, the same which we heard a twelvemonth past upon that subject.

The fourth year appears, therefore, to have been principally occupied by the study of mathematics. Indeed, except for reading Burlamaqui and writing a large number of literary disquisitions, of a somewhat stereotyped and academic class, for college societies and public occasions, it is difficult to see that even the best students had any other employment at all. After the winter vacation, that is, after the middle of February, afternoon recitations were dropped in the senior year, and the class had but five recitations a week for nine weeks, at the end of which recitations entirely ceased.

This analysis of the College studies leads naturally to the conclusion, which is enforced by every word of this diary, that, for the ordinary enjoyments of university life, the last century was the golden age of the College. It was hard, indeed, if the most modest capacity could not manage to maintain itself upon such a level. This seems to have been the impression which prevailed among the students themselves, for the writer of this diary, in speaking of a classmate who was in his twenty-fifth year, says:

He was, as he says himself, too old when he entered the University. From fourteen to eighteen I should suppose the best age for entering. The studies which are pursued here are just calculated for the tender minds of youth.

In comparison with the present system, the simplicity of the older one seems marvellously attractive. One cannot detect a sign of unreasonable coercion on the part of the College government. An examination of any kind within the college career was still a thing unheard of among our happy ancestors. Rank was apparently unknown, except so far as it was vaguely intimated in the assignment of parts at exhibitions. These parts, if the President is to be believed, were the *only* incentive to study; at least such is the inference from the following curious entry:

April 11, 1787. I went down this morning to the President to know the determination of the corporation with respect to a private Commencement, and was told that the petition of the class was rejected, because they supposed that *if public Commencements were lain aside, there would be no stimulus to study among the scholars,* and they are afraid that by granting our petition they might establish a precedent which the following classes would take advantage of, and claim as a right what we only request as a favor. Another reason which Mr. Willard said had weight, although the gentlemen did not choose to avow it publicly, was the fear of offending the future Governor by depriving him of that opportunity to show himself in splendor and magnificence.

Here is another extract, delightful in its patriarchal simplicity. It was the student's first day in college:

March 23, 1786. I did not hear the bell ring this morning, and was tardy at prayers. Every time a student is tardy at prayers he is punished a penny, and there is no eluding that law; so that a student must prefer not attending prayers at all to being half a minute too late.

The instructors appear to have trusted only their general impressions in awarding distinctions. Misdemeanors, absences, and other shortcomings were punished by fines. As for the recitations themselves, here is a picture of them:

June 13, 1786. This reciting in Locke is the most ridiculous of all. When the tutor inquires what is contained in such a section, many of the scholars repeat the first two lines in it, which are very frequently nothing to the purpose, and leave the rest for the tutor to explain, which he commonly does by saying over again the words of the author.

In regard to vacations and permissions of absence, there was no rigidity in the College law. In April the students had two weeks holiday by law, but in practice at least three. On the 13th July the summer vacation began, and closed by law on the 16th August, lasting five weeks, but recitations were only resumed on the 21st. There were two weeks more in October, with the same liberal margin. And in the middle of December, 1786, the supply of wood fell short, and as none could be obtained from the country, the students were sent home and enjoyed a vacation of eight weeks, till February 7th. Recitations began on the 12th. On the 23d "about half the class" had arrived. Thus in the course of the year the College had seventeen weeks of actual vacation, and twenty-one weeks of freedom from all required exercises. Add to this a very liberal interpretation of the rule of attendance, and an equally liberal practice in regard to leaves of absence, and it cannot be disputed that the actual working terms of the College were by no means unreasonably long or severe. In point of fact, when the exercises were most regular, there were many interruptions, and the amount of work accomplished would seem, from a modern point of view, to have been but small.

In proof of these statements, the following extracts will be sufficient:

April 26, 1786. Put my name in at the buttery. At the end of each vacation every scholar must go in person and give his name to the butler. Any scholar who stays away after the expiration of the vacancy, unless he gives good reasons for it, forfeits 1 *s.* 6 *d.* every night.

April 27. No reciting this day, nor indeed this week. The scholars that live near Cambridge commonly come and enter their names in the buttery, and then go home again and stay the remainder of the week.

April 28. About half the college are now here. The bill at prayers is not kept till the Friday after the vacation ends.

May 1. We recite this week, etc.

August 17. The scholars are coming in very fast.

August 19. Almost all the college have got here now, and the new monitors, who must always belong to the junior class, took their seats yesterday.

August 21. We recite this week, etc.

December 12. The government this morning determined that if more than half the students should be destitute of wood, the college should be dismissed. The President went to Boston to consult the corporation upon the subject, and he informed Little this evening that the students would be permitted to disperse to-morrow morning.

December 13. This morning, immediately after prayers, the President informed us that the vacation would begin at present, and be for eight weeks, and hinted that the spring vacation might on that account be omitted.

But the spring vacation was not in the least shortened by the hint.

Perhaps it is no concern of the public to inquire how the student occupied these eight weeks. He had a right to do what he pleased with them. Nevertheless, since it is possible that the extreme exertions which were evidently not made in term-time may have fallen on the vacation, it is worth the while to ask how the most distinguished students of the oldest standing occupied their two months of winter vacation. The particular student now under consideration remained in college rooms to devote his time to his work, with less interruption than was otherwise possible.

As I thought I should be able to study much more conveniently here than anywhere else, I obtained leave to remain in town. Bridge proposes staying likewise, and we shall live together. Bridge engaged for us both to board at Professor Wigglesworth's.

Other young men remained, no doubt for the same purpose, since their names occur afterwards on the list of parts at Commencement, attached to English orations and other unusual honors. Immediately afterwards, however, an entry occurs which is calculated to raise some interesting doubts in the reader's mind:

December 18, 1786. The young ladies at Mr. Wigglesworth's dined at Judge Dana's. I went down there with Bridge to tea, and passed the evening very sociably. The conversation turned upon divers topics, and among the rest upon love, which is almost always the case when there are ladies present.

Nowhere in this diary is love mentioned as one of the College studies; but if it is always discussed when there are ladies present, these young gentlemen would seem during this vacation to have devoted far more attention to it than ever they had paid to Locke or Euclid. The next day, however, a slight improvement in tone is visible:

December 19. Several of the class still remain, and until they are gone it will be impossible for us to study much. As they expect to go every day, they are rather dissipated, and more or less make us so.
December 20. I have been rather more attentive to-day, and have written considerably.

After this spark of energy, however, comes a fearful relapse. Descriptions of young ladies recur with alarming frequency, while, except for a single reference to Montesquieu, there is by no means any indication of absorbing mental application.

December 22. Miss —— is but eighteen, rather giddy and unexperienced. She has a very fair complexion and good eyes, of which she is sensible. Her face is rather capricious than beautiful, and some of her features are not handsome. Of this she is not so well apprised. Her shape is not inelegant, but her limbs are rather large. She is susceptible of the tender sentiments, but the passion rather than the lover is the object of her affection.

December 26. Mason finally took his leave and left us to ourselves, so that we shall henceforth be able to study with much less interruption than we have hitherto done.

December 27. In the evening we went down with Mr. Ware and Freeman to Judge Dana's. We conversed, and played whist, and sung till 10 o'clock. The ladies seem to have settled that we are to be in love; but ideas of this kind are very common with the ladies, who think it impossible to live without love.

Exemplary young man! And yet it would be instructive to learn what is the meaning of a succession of remarks like these:

January 17, 1787. After tea we went down to Mr. Dana's. Miss E—— was there, and Miss J—— with her. Bridge accompanied this lady home, and after they were gone I had a deal of chat with Miss E——, who has a larger share of sense than commonly falls to an individual of her sex. We conversed upon divers subjects, but I can never give anything but general accounts of conversations, for I cannot always keep this book under lock and key, and some people have a vast deal of curiosity.

January 22. Almy [the young gentleman no doubt meant to write Miss Almy E——] has a larger share of sense than commonly falls to the lot of her sex, and that sense is cultivated and improved, a circumstance still more uncommon.

March 2. I went to take tea at Mr. Pearson's. I got seated between Miss E—— and Miss H——, but could not enjoy the pleasures of conversation, because the music was introduced. Music is a great enemy to sociability, and however agreeable it may be sometimes, there are occasions when I should wish it might be dispensed with.

Perhaps it is best to quit this subject here, since the vacation has already expired, and the student has returned to the labors of five recitations a week. Besides the Spirit of Laws, he had read, so far as can be gathered from his diary, Watson's Chemical Essays, Sheridan's Lectures on Elocution, a volume of the Idler, and some algebra, in two months. He had also developed an uncommonly strong fancy for the study of female character,—a study not embraced in the College curriculum, either then or afterwards.

The 7th of February began the new term. On the 12th recitations began, one every day, except Friday. On the 15th there was a ball, at which it need hardly be said that Miss E—— heads the list of ladies. The young gentlemen, among whom were most of the first scholars, retired to bed "at about 4 o'clock," and "rose just before the common bell rang for dinner, quite refreshed, and not more fatigued than I commonly am." In fact, the dances have now become nearly as frequent as the recitations. On the 23rd, "about one half the class are here." On the 27th, "almost all our class have arrived." Among other lectures, on March 5th, "Professor P—— gave a lecture with which he concluded his observations upon the article. I did not hear many of them"; but the same evening there was a meeting of the ΦBK at Cranch's chamber, at which a dissertation was read, of which the text is here preserved, on the extremely erudite question, "Whether love or fortune ought to be the chief inducement to marriage." This essay is done with much calm reflection and elaborate knowledge of the human heart, but is not precisely a college exercise. On the 7th March he went to Haverhill, probably to obtain relief from the severe pressure of recitations, and returned on the 10th. On the 12th the parts were distributed for the next exhibition, and he received an English "Conference," with Freeman and Little, upon the Comparative Utility of Law, Physic, and Divinity.

March 14, 1787. Was employed almost all day in thinking upon the subject of my Conference. Wrote a few lines with much difficulty. Did not like the subject. Wished the Conference to the Devil.

Little and Freeman, it seems, were of the same mind. After a week's labor, however, the Conference was written, and the next week was devoted to the voluntary work of calculating the elements for a solar eclipse for May 15, 1836. This was also for an exhibition.

March 30. I have been somewhat idle for several days, and expect to continue so till the exhibition is over, for so long as that is before me I can pay very little attention to anything else. I found this to be the case last fall, and do now still more so, but thank fortune I have only one more trial, at the worst, of this kind to go through, which will be at Commencement, unless we should obtain a private one. Distinctions of this kind are not, I think, very desirable; for besides the trouble and anxiety which they unavoidably create, they seldom fail of raising the envy of other students. I have oftentimes witnessed this with respect to others, and I am much deceived if I have not lately perceived it with respect to myself.

April 9. This is the last week on which our class attend recitations.

If such were the laborious duties of the most distinguished scholars, one would like to know what was done by those students who were not remarkable for scholarship; but on this point no certain information is given, beyond allusions to gunning, fishing, and an occasional "high-go."

Meanwhile a difficulty had occurred:

August 26, 1786. Immediately after prayers we had a class meeting for the purpose of choosing a Valedictory Orator, and Collectors of Theses. When the votes were collected it was found that there was no choice. A second attempt was made, equally fruitless. It was then resolved that the choice of an Orator should be deferred, and that the class should proceed to that of the choice of Collectors. The one for Technology, Grammar, and Rhetoric was first balloted. Abbot 2d was chosen. The second Collector, for Logic, Metaphysics, Ethics, Theology, and Politics, was then chosen. Fiske was the person. The Mathematical part fell to Adams, and the Physical to Johnstone. The meeting at about 7 o'clock was adjourned till Monday evening, when we shall proceed to the choice of an Orator.

August 28. After prayers the class met by adjournment. The second ballot was between Freeman, Little, and Waldo. The third was between Freeman and Little, who finally carried it by a considerable majority. The class then all went to his chamber, but did not stay there more than an hour.

August 31. We had a class meeting immediately after prayers. The committee of the class that was appointed to inform the President of the choice for an Orator, etc., reported that the President had not given his consent to have the Oration in English, because he thought it would show a neglect of classical learning. I motioned that the vote for having it in English should be reconsidered, but there was a considerable majority against it. It was then voted that the President should be informed that the class had determined to have an English Oration or none at all. The former committee all declined going again. Johnstone, Fiske, and Welch were chosen, but declined. It was much like Æsop's fable of the mice, who determined to have a bell tied round the cat's neck; they were all desirous that it should be done, but no one was willing to undertake the performance of it. The meeting was finally adjourned till Monday next.

September 12. We had a class meeting after prayers for determining the matter concerning a Valedictory Oration. By dint of obstinate impudence, vociferation, and noise, the minority so wearied out those on the other side that several of them went out, after which a vote was passed ratifying the proceedings of the last meeting. Johnson, Sever, and Chandler 3d were then chosen as a committee to inform the President of the proceedings in the class.

September 18. We had a class meeting after breakfast. The committee that was sent to inform the President of the proceedings of the class, informed that he had said he feared he should be obliged to direct the class to have the Oration in Latin. Notwithstanding this, it was voted by a majority of two that the class should still persist.

The result was that the President carried his point in so far that there was no Class Day. In consequence of this, the members of the class began to leave Cambridge long before the 21st of June, the usual day for separation. The parts for Commencement were distributed on the 17th May:

May 24, 1787. Our class having no College exercises to attend to, and many of them having now finished their parts for Commencement, are generally very indolent. Riding and playing and eating and drinking employ the chief part of their time.

Long before Class Day the graduating students were scattered in every direction, only to return on the 18th July to Commencement. Thus, to sum up the result of the half-year since the 13th December, the students who were now to take their degrees had attended recitations at the rate of five per week, for nine weeks, and had further prepared exercises for one exhibition and Commencement. They had listened to one course of lectures, which they had for the most part already heard, and another on "the parts of speech," which the best of them thought a mere waste of time. And they dispersed in May, without the faintest conception that there could be such a thing in the student world as an examination for degrees.

One or two more extracts, to illustrate the stringency of rules during term-time, must be admitted:

May 4, 1786. No reciting this morning, on account of last night's class meeting. This is a privilege that all the classes enjoy, and I am told there have been in our class fellows so lazy and so foolish as to call a class meeting merely for that purpose.

Naturally, class meetings were very frequent.

April 10, 1786. No reciting this day, because the government met to examine the reasons of those scholars that are absent, or have been within the last two quarters.

September 22. Mr. R—— sent for me this morning, informed me that the exhibition was to come on next Thursday, and offered to excuse me from recitations till then, in case I was not prepared, as the time that had been given for getting ready was so short. But, as it happened, I was not in need of more time.

October 9. No reciting. Mr. B—— is engaged to preach several Sundays at Hingham, and does not return early enough for the next morning recitation.

These extracts need not be multiplied. The rules were not more rigidly applied in regard to required exercises than they were in other respects, and neither instructors nor students considered themselves to be under any very inflexible law.

Students who lived under so mild and beneficent a government as this should have had no just cause of complaint, unless it were that the means of the College did not reach far enough to satisfy all the requirements of a liberal education. They might, indeed, urge that Euclid and Burlamaqui were only dry nutriment to satisfy the hunger of a whole year, but they could scarcely maintain that it was a step-mother's hand which, when they cried for bread, threw them these husks. This leads naturally to the further subject of the relations between the teachers and the taught. There seems to have been no obvious reason why, under a system so nearly voluntary, a thorough accord should not exist between the instructors and their best scholars. And if such a harmony was wanting, it may be of some practical value to inquire what the causes were which stood in its way, and whether the fault, if there was a fault, lay with the older or the younger men.

The President, Mr. Joseph Willard, was a graduate of the year 1765, and therefore still a comparatively young man. Many instructive hints as to his character are scattered through this diary, as for example the following:

> It is against the laws of the College to call any undergraduate by any but his Sir name, and I am told the President, who is remarkably strict on all those matters, reproved a gentleman at his table for calling a student Mr. while he was present.

Again:

> *March* 24, 1786. After prayers I declaimed, as it is termed; two students every evening speak from memory any piece they choose, if it be approved by the President. It was this evening my turn, and I spoke from "As You Like It": "All the world's a stage," etc. When I came to the description of the Justice, in fair, round belly with good capon lined, tutors and scholars all laughed, as I myself truly represented the character. But the President did not move a feature of his face. And indeed I believe it is no small matter that shall extort a smile from him when he is before the College.

> *September* 10, 1786. Cranch and myself dined at the President's. He is stiff and formal, attached to every custom and trifling form, as much as to what is of consequence. However, he was quite sociable; much more so, indeed, than I should have expected.

A little portrait of the President in the pulpit:

February 18, 1787. The President preached in the afternoon, when we were improved by a very laborious encomium upon Moses. Whatever the President's literary talents may be, he is certainly not an elegant composuist nor a graceful orator.

June 21, 1786. Class Day. This day the seniors leave college. There is no recitation in the morning, and prayers are deferred till 10 o'clock. The class then went down in procession two by two with the Poet at their head, and escorted the President to the chapel. The President made a very long prayer, in which, in addition to what he commonly says, he prayed a great deal for the seniors; but I think he ought to get his occasional prayers by heart before he delivers them. He bungled always when he endeavored to go out of the beaten track, and he has no talent at extempore composition.

April 6, 1786. Fast Day. The President preached two sermons; that in the afternoon especially I thought excellent. No flowers of rhetoric, no eloquence, but plain common sense, and upon a liberal plan. But the President has by no means a pleasing delivery. He appears to labor and struggle very much, and sometimes strains very hard; and making faces, which do not render his harsh countenance more agreeable.

The description is evidently true to the life, and certainly indicates no ill-feeling towards the President. There is no indication throughout this diary that the President was disliked by the students, or that he failed in any way to maintain the dignity of his position. But it is clear that a man cast in such a mould was not likely to throw much life or much novelty into the system over which he presided. He was one of those men already mentioned, in whose eyes it was not the students whose interests stood first; nor, to do him justice, was it merely his own importance which filled his thoughts; it was the institution, the University, as one of the most important corporations in the Commonwealth, on which his thoughts were bent, and the students, who are quick to feel such distinctions, responded with respect and indifference. He was, after all, an excellent representative of the old New England school, which lost its hold, as a clerical body, on American education, before it had time to give an American Arnold to Harvard College.

But the President seems to have had little immediate connection with the undergraduates. The burden of labor fell almost entirely on the four tutors, and yet it may be doubted whether even the tutors were obliged to perform so much work as would seem very alarming to the most lightly burdened tutor of the present day. Six or seven hours a week in the recitation-room, and the simplest instruction on the letter of the text-book, appear to represent the full extent of their duties, over and above the charge of the College discipline. Under these circumstances it might be supposed that a considerable opportunity for usefulness was open to the four tutors, and that at least one or two of them might have impressed the students with some appreciable degree of sympathetic activity. One may therefore feel some interest to know what the relations were between the students and their tutors; and on this point there is a great quantity of information:

May 1, 1786. The Greek tutor is a young man; indeed much too young (A.B. of 1782), as are all the tutors, for the place he occupies. Before he took his second degree, which was last Commencement, he was chosen a tutor of mathematics, in which he betrayed his ignorance often. Last fall he changed departments, and took up the Greek. His own class, the freshmen, were the first that laughed at him in that. He has improved since that, but still makes frequent mistakes. It is certainly wrong that the tutors should so often be changed, and be so young as they are. It would be better to choose a person immediately after he has taken his degree, than as they do; because when a youth leaves college he is obliged to turn his attention to other studies, and forgets a great deal of what he studied at college, whereas when he has lately graduated he has all fresh in his mind. The Doctor affects a great deal of popularity in his class, and with the help of the late disagreement between the classes, he has pretty well succeeded, but he does not seem to care what the other classes think of him.

May 2. Our tutor gave us this morning a most extraordinary construction of a passage in Homer. Abbot 1st was beginning to construe the 181st line of the 6th Book,

Πρόσθε λέων, ὄπιθεν δὲ δράκων, μέσση δὲ χίμαιρα,

he said: a lion before; but the Doctor corrected him by saying it meant superior to a lion. Abbot immediately took the hint and made it: superior to a lion, inferior to a dragon, and equal to a wild boar.

An account of the metaphysical tutor is still less flattering:

15 *May*, 1786. We recite this week to Mr. H—— in Locke. This is, upon the whole, the most unpopular tutor in College. He is hated even by his own class. He is reputed to be very ill-natured and severe in his punishments. He proposes leaving College at Commencement, and I believe there is not an individual among the students who is not very well pleased with it. One of my classmates said the other day, "I do not believe it yet; it is too good news to be true." Such are the sentiments of all the students with respect to him.

The writer passes on to the mathematical tutor:

May 22, 1786. We recite this week to our own tutor, in Gravesande's Experimental Philosophy. This gentleman is not much more popular than the rest of the tutors. He is said to be very prejudiced and very vindictive. He is liked in general by the class, however, and this may be a reason why I have not heard as much said against him as against the others.

He closes the list with a blast of indignation:

May 8. We recite this week in Terence and Cæsar to Mr. J——. This is the tutor of the oldest standing in the College; he is very well acquainted with the branch he has undertaken, and persons that are not students say that he is much of a gentleman. But it seems almost to be a maxim among the governors of the College to treat the students pretty much like brute beasts. There is an important air and a haughty look that every person belonging to the government (Mr. [Professor] Williams excepted) assumes, which indeed it is hard for me to submit to. But it may be of use to me, as it mortifies my vanity, and if anything in the world can teach me humility, it will be to see myself subjected to the commands of a person that I must despise. Mr. J—— is also accused of having many partialities and carrying them to very great length, and moreover that those partialities do not arise from any superior talents or virtues in the students, but from closer and more interested motives. There are some in our class with whom he has been particularly severe, and some he has shown more favor than any tutor ought to show to a student. I wish not his favor, as he may prize it too high; and I fear not his severity, which he can never display if I do my duty.

Some light is thrown on the "interested motives" by the following:

May 3, 1786. We had after prayers a class meeting about making a present to our tutor. It is customary at the end of the freshman year to make a present to the tutor of the class, but it has been delayed by ours to the present time, and many would still delay it and lay it wholly aside. The custom, I think, is a bad one, because it creates partialities in a tutor, because it increases the distinction between the wealthy and the poor scholars, because it makes the tutor in some measure dependent upon his class, and because to many that subscribe it is a considerable expense; but the salaries of the tutors being so low, and it having been for many years an universal custom, I am sorry to see our class so behindhand, and several who could well afford it and have really subscribed meanly endeavoring to put off the matter from quarter to quarter till they leave College.

A year later the writer has become aware that there is another side to the question. Speaking of one of his classmates, he says:

His spirit he discovers by relating how many times he has insulted the President and the tutors, particularly Mr. R—— (the class tutor). He damns

Mr. R—— for being partial towards those who have always treated him with respect, and against those who have always made it a practice to insult him.

In short, it is quite evident that the relations between instructors and scholars were far from satisfactory. Thoroughly cordial these relations never could be and never can become so long as any means of coercion or any connection with college discipline remain in the hands of the instructors. To be "subjected to the commands of a person," rarely teaches humility and almost inevitably breeds ill-feeling. The duty of giving instruction, and the duty of judging offences and inflicting punishment, are in their nature discordant, and can never be intrusted to the same hands, without the most serious injury to the usefulness of the instructor. This evil was conspicuous at the time now under attention. Gentle as the rein was, and mild as were the punishments, an invincible hostility between students and instructors was one of the traditional customs of the College, and the one which created most annoyance to both divisions of the University, the teachers as well as the taught.

There is perhaps a certain amount of practical interest in this matter still. The question as to the allotment of responsibility for such a state of things as these extracts describe, is one worth considering in connection with all systems of education, since it leads directly to the problem, so difficult to solve, how the necessary friction between young and old, students and instructors, can be reduced to the lowest possible point. That young men of twenty or thereabouts are not always distinguished for courtesy and good-breeding, is a fact that no one will question; but that the habit of instruction and the incessant consciousness of authority tends to develop extremely disagreeable traits in human character, especially wherever character naturally inclines towards selfishness, is another fact which is better known to young men than to old. Between these two influences it is natural that incessant annoyance should be generated, and it is equally natural that each party should invariably throw the blame on the other.

Nevertheless, after setting aside exceptional cases of individual character, which make themselves disagreeably prominent both in old and young, and which can be controlled by no law, something is always due to the assistance or discouragement which the system itself offers to the development of discordant influences. And in the last century the system was radically a wrong one. It was a system which, while perhaps more liberal in its forms than anything which has succeeded it, rested on an assumption of social superiority such as invariably galls to the quick every one who is subjected to it. This assumption was due in part perhaps to the fact that the instructors had commonly belonged to that clerical body which in the early history of New England formed what one may almost call a caste, and which stood towards the public in something like the same insulated and dominating attitude which it assumed towards the young; but it was also in part due to the fact that in regard to the student there existed, not only the consciousness of social superiority, but the consciousness of power to enforce obedience. The jealousy of this assumption, backed as it was by force, naturally created a spirit of opposition in the students' minds, and the records of the College show how persistent the attempt was, on the part of the students, to break down the social barrier. Generation after generation followed the same course. Rebellion after rebellion broke out among the undergraduates. And it was only in proportion as the College government began to concede and act upon the principle that the student was in all respects the social equal of the instructor, entitled to every courtesy due to equals, that these disorders began gradually to subside. Even then, however, the question of discipline remained a source of incessant uneasiness, and the instructor who was known as a strict disciplinarian, who in other words attempted to combine his duty of acting as police-officer, judge, jury, and executioner, with his duties of instruction, necessarily sacrificed no inconsiderable share of his usefulness as instructor, in consequence of the same jealousy in the students' minds.

That the spirit of insubordination so persistently exhibited was not due to any mere distinctions of age, or to any peculiar hostility to the instructing body as such, is proved by the fact that it was by no means shown in conflicts with the instructors alone. Another series of extracts will illustrate this point:

August 21, 1786. This afternoon, after prayers, the customs were read to the freshmen in the chapel. They are read three Mondays running in the beginning of every year, by the three first in the sophimore class, who are ordered to see them put in execution.

March 27, 1786. After prayers the senior class had a class meeting, in order to check the freshmen, who, they suppose, have taken of late too great liberties. By the laws of the College all freshmen are obliged to walk in the yard with their heads uncovered, unless in stormy weather, and to go on any errand that any other scholar choses to send them, at a mile distance. But the present freshmen have been indulged very much with respect to those laws, and it is said they have presumed further than they ought to have done.

March 28, 1786. After prayers, Bancroft, one of the sophomore class, read the customs to the freshmen, one of whom (McNeal) stood with his hat on all the time. He, with three others, were immediately *hoisted* (as the term is) before a tutor, and punished. There was immediately after a class meeting of the freshmen, who, it is said, determined they would hoist any scholar of the other classes who should be seen with his hat on in the yard, when any of the government are there.

June 14, 1786. The freshmen, by their high spirit of liberty, have again involved themselves in difficulties. The sophimores consider themselves as insulted by them, and in a class meeting, last evening, determined to oblige all the freshmen to take off their hats in the yard, and to send them. There has been a great deal of business between them to-day. Mr. H—— has had several of them before him.

June 15, 1786. The struggle between the freshmen and sophimores still continues. They have been mutually hoisting one another all day.

July 12, 1786. The freshmen carry their enmity against the sophimores a great deal too far. They injure themselves both in the eyes of the other class and in those of the government. This afternoon, while Cabot was declaiming, they kept up a continual groaning and shuffling and hissing, as almost prevented him from going through.

The freshmen ultimately carried their point and established their right to complete social equality; but they were obliged to struggle violently both against the College system and against their immediate masters. These disorders committed by them were but a repetition, as against a different authority, of still greater disorders on the part of older classes, in their attempt to establish their own social rights as regarded the College government.

It is true that the manners of the time were far from polished. A glimpse of students' amusements is furnished by the following:

March 22, 1786. As we passed by Milton Hall, we saw the ruins of the windows. On the 21st of March the junior sophister class cease reciting at 11 in the forenoon. They generally, in the evening, have a frolic. Yesterday they had it at Milton Hall, and as they are not by any means at such times remarkable for their discretion, we saw many fractures in the windows of the hall they were in.

March 15, 1786. The sophimore class had what is called in College an highgo. They assembled all together in the chamber of one of the class, where some of them got drunk, then sallied out and broke a number of windows for three of the tutors, and after this sublime manœuvre staggered to their chambers. Such are the great achievements of many of the sons of Harvard! Such the delights of many of the students here!

The manners indicated by these extracts were certainly rude enough. But it does not appear that such offences were looked upon as extremely heinous by the College government or by public opinion. And it is plain from other facts that the severity of discipline in the College was by no means such as to explain the ill-will between the students and the government. Although the students undoubtedly considered this discipline as very annoying at the time, they learned afterwards to accept, without a murmur, punishments which, in the last century, would have been thought monstrous; and this submission was due principally to the fact that the old antipathy to the government was beginning to subside. Had they supposed that they were still treated as a body with the old haughtiness, the modern discipline, made necessary by an extreme compactness of organization such as no European University knows, would not have been accepted at all. The old punishments, so far from being severe, were remarkably light, notwithstanding the loud complaints against them. A number of amusing passages will show this to have been the case. As mentioned above, certain members of the College had, on the night of March 15, 1786, indulged themselves in a very drunken disturbance in the College grounds:

March 23, 1786. After prayers the President read a paper to this effect: That on the evening of the 15th it appeared the sophimores had assembled at the chambers of one in the class, and had behaved in a tumultuous, noisy manner; that at length they sallied out and were very riotous, to the disturbance and *dishonor* of the University. But as their conduct till then had been such as deserved approbation, and was submissive, and as they early shew a proper repentance for their fault, having presented an humble petition to be forgiven; therefore it had been voted that no further notice should be taken of it, but it was hoped the students would not abuse the lenity of the government, but rather show that they were deserving of it. The freshmen, who are always as a class at variance with the sophimores, thought the government had been partial; and the consequence was that Mr. ———, the tutor of the sophimore class, and who was supposed to have favored them, and to have been the means of saving them from severe punishment, had four squares of glass broken in his windows. Such was the effect of the lenity which was to induce the students to do their duty.

A more curious case, which showed a considerable sense of humor on the part of our ancestors, was the following:

May 23, 1786. This morning a number of the seniors were sent for by the President to go to his house at 8 o'clock. They went, and the parts were distributed thus: Thompson, English Oration, A. M. Champlin, Latin Oration, A. M. Fowle and Gardner, 2d, each a Poem. Blake, English, and Andrews 1st, Latin Orations, P. M. Harris, Dwight, Hubbard, and Parker, a Conference. Bigelow and Crosby, Lowell and Taylor, Loring and Sullivan, Forensics. Lincoln and Warland, a Greek Dialogue. Bradford, Norton, Simpkins, and Wyeth, respondents in Syllogistics, and all the rest opponents to the same. These Syllogistics are very much despised by the scholars, and no attention seems to be paid to them by the company at Commencement. The scholars in general think that the government, in giving them those parts, write on their foreheads DUNCE in capital letters. Notwithstanding this, some of the most learned men in the country had Syllogistics when they graduated here. The good parts, as they are called, are more numerous this year than they have ever been. Before this there has been only one English and one Latin Oration, and no Poems. It is a doubt whether they intend to establish this as a precedent or whether it is only a distinguished favor to the present class, who pretend to be the best class for learning and genius that ever graduated here. It is said that the parts have been exceedingly well distributed, and all the College are pleased. However that may be, the syllogists all got together this evening and drank till not one of them could stand straight, or was sensible of what he did. A little after 9 they sallied out, and for a quarter of an hour made such a noise as might be heard at a mile distant. The tutors went out and after a short time persuaded them to disperse. Mr. —— had two squares of his windows broke.

May 24. It is feared that some bad consequences will ensue from the highgo of the syllogists last evening. Borland, it seems, was the most active of them all; he collared Mr. —— and threw an handful of gravel in his face, and was rather disrespectful to Mr. ——. He went this morning to the former to make an apology for his conduct, but was told it could not be received, as the matter was already laid before the government. Thus those fellows play the tyrants here; they have no regard, no allowances for youth and circumstances. They go out when they are almost certain of being insulted, and then bring the scholar for a crime of which he knew nothing under public censure. They cannot with any face say that a scholar ought to be so severely punished for depriving himself of his senses. For there are here in College persons who have seen —— as much intoxicated as Borland was yesterday and behaving quite as ill. But compassion is too great a virtue ever to be admitted into the breast of a tutor here. It is supposed, however, that Borland's punishment will not be very severe, because it requires an unanimous vote among the governors of the College to punish a student, and they are said to be at such variance one with the other that they can very seldom all agree.

May 25. Government met and were assembled almost all this day to determine what punishment to inflict upon Borland. He was informed of it in the evening, and the class petitioned that it might be mitigated, but probably without much success.

May 26. This morning after prayers Borland was called out to read an humble confession, signifying his repentance of his conduct, etc. The President read the votes of the government; the affair was stated, and it was said that Borland had insulted, in a flagrant manner, two of the governors of the University: whereupon it was voted, that he read a confession; and secondly, that he be degraded to the bottom of his class, and that he take his place there accordingly. The other scholars were warned by this example not to run into such excesses, and to behave respectfully. I wanted, I think, neither of these warnings, but the event has warned me to alter my opinion concerning ——. I thought him the best of the tutors, but now I do not think he is a jot better than the rest.

Six weeks afterwards Borland was restored to his regular place in class.

This is certainly a proof that the spirit of liberty in the Americans of the last century has not been underrated. No student of a later day would have dreamed of calling such a penalty severe. Any undergraduate of the nineteenth century who indulged in the agreeable but dangerous amusement of collaring an unpopular tutor and rubbing gravel in his face, would have accepted the extremest penalty of the law without a murmur, recognizing the fundamental principle of society, that no man can violate the law and enjoy it at the same time, can eat his cake and have it too. And further the notion that drunkenness is anything but an aggravation of the offence hardly commends itself to modern New England.

Such difficulties were by no means uncommon under this *régime*. But it is fair to say that they appear occasionally to have been due in no small part to the instructors themselves. The following seems to have been such a case:

May 31, 1786. Election Day. There is a custom among the scholars here which some of the classes follow and others do not. It is choosing a Governor and Lieutenant-Governor for the class. They commonly take some rich fellow who can treat the class now and then. The seniors this morning chose Champlin Governor, and Lowell Lieutenant-Governor. The Lieutenant-Governor treated immediately, and they chose their other officers. At commons they all went into the hall in procession. Thomas, who was appointed Sheriff, marched at their head, with a paper cockade in his hat, and brandishing a cane in his hand instead of a sword. He conducted the Governor and Lieutenant-Governor to their seats, made his bow, and retired to the other table, for which Jackey H—— punished him four shillings. However, he performed his part so well that the spectators were much pleased and clapped their hands. H—— happened to see Baron, the junior, clapping, and sent orders for him to go to him after commons. Baron, not happening to go before 2 o'clock, was punished five shillings for impudence, and four for disobedience. That is the way these modest tutors tyrannize over us. As there was a little noise in the hall, H—— struck the handle of his knife three times on the table to still it, but instead of that almost every knife in the hall was struck on the table three times. At last the tutors rose, and as they were going out about half a dozen fellows hissed them. They were enraged, turned round and looked as if they would devour us, but they did not discover one person, which made them look silly enough. When they turned their backs again, there was nothing but hissing and groaning and clapping hands and stamping heard in the hall, till they got into the yard, where a few potatoes were sent out to meet them.

A difficulty of such a kind would, probably, in later times, have been avoided by a little good-nature and forbearance on the part of the tutor. But it made little difference to the student whether he was in the right or the wrong. The true grievance lay in the assumption of social superiority; in the fact that the College government set itself in a position of semi-hostility to the students, and refused to acknowledge them as entitled to active assistance and sympathy. The manner, not the act, of discipline, was the cause of the evil. Hence the mildest punishments were made a cause of as much complaint as the most arbitrary vexations.

March 14, 1787. The junior class being displeased with the distribution of parts for exhibition, so far as respected their class, assembled this evening at Prescott's chamber and made a great deal of noise.

March 17. The government met this forenoon to make inquiries concerning the noise at Prescott's and at Wier's chamber.

March 19. This morning, the juniors Prescott and Wier were publicly admonished for having had riotous noises at their chambers last week. The sentence is considered all over College as uncommonly severe, and by many as wholly unmerited, at least on the part of Prescott.

March 22. In consequence of the late severity of the College governors there has been, yesterday and this day, a subscription paper handed about among all the classes, to promote a meeting of the whole College to-morrow evening in the chapel, every person having a pipe, a glass, and a bottle of wine, and there to convince the government that the students are possessed of 'a noble spirit, a spirit which shall nip the bud of tyrannical oppression.' They will get as drunk as beasts, and probably break every tutor's windows in College. This absurd and ridiculous plan has found so many votaries, that a large majority of every class, except ours, have already subscribed; but I am happy that in our class there are but few who have joined the association, and, as it is to take place only upon condition that there be a majority of every class, the plan will most probably fail.

At the risk of serious injury to the dignity of history, already gravely compromised by this sketch, the fact of the extreme leniency of the government in the punishment inflicted in this case must be shown by a final extract from the diary so often quoted. Some verses, which are not absolutely contemptible, represent all the facts, and the general impression made by the different members of the government on the students, more exactly than anything which the regular entries of a prosaic diary can be expected to supply. The verses in question are entitled

LINES UPON THE LATE PROCEEDINGS OF THE
COLLEGE GOVERNMENT.

BY A STUDENT.

The government of College met,
And Willard ruled the stern debate.
The witty J—— declared
That he had been completely scared.
"Last night" (says he) "when I came home
I heard a noise in Prescott's room.
I went and listened at the door,
As I have often done before.
I found the juniors in a high rant;
They called the President a tyrant;
They said as how I was a fool,
A long-eared ass, a sottish mule,
Without the smallest grain of spunk;
So I concluded they were drunk.
From Xenophon whole pages torn
As trophies in their hats were worn.
Thus all their learning they had spread
Upon the outside of the head;
For I can swear without a sin
There's not a line of Greek within.
At length I knocked, and Prescott came;
I told him 't was a burning shame
That he should give his classmates wine,
And he should pay an heavy fine.

Meanwhile the rest grew so outrageous,
That though I boast of being courageous,
I could not help being in a fright,
For one of them put out the light,
And 't was, as you may well suppose,
So dark I could not see my nose.
I thought it best to run away
And wait for vengeance till to-day.
For he 's a fool at any rate
Who'll fight when he can rusticate.
When they found out that I was gone,
They ran through College up and down,
And I could hear them very plain
Take the Lord's holy name in vain.
To Wier's chamber they repaired,
And there the wine they freely shared.
They drank and sung till they were tired,
And then they peacefully retired."
When this Homeric speech was said,
With drawling tongue and hanging head,
The learned Doctor took his seat,
Thinking he'd done a noble feat.
Quoth Joe: "The crime is great, I own.
Send for the juniors one by one!
By this almighty wig I swear,
Which with such majesty I wear,
And in its orbit vast contains
My dignity, my power and brains,
That Wier and Prescott both shall see
That College boys must not be free!"
He spoke, and gave the awful nod,
Like Homer's Dodonean God.
The College to its centre shook,
And every pipe and wineglass broke.
Williams, with countenance humane,
Which scarce from laughing could refrain,
Thought that such youthful scenes of mirth
To punishments should not give birth.
Nor could he easily divine
What was the harm of drinking wine.
But P——, with an awful frown,
Full of his article and noun,
Spoke thus: "By all the parts of speech,
Which with such elegance I teach,

By all the blood which fills my veins,
By all the power of Handel's strains,
With mercy I will never stain
The character which I maintain.
Pray tell me why the laws were made,
If they are not to be obeyed."
J—— saw 't would be in vain t' oppose,
And therefore to be silent chose.
R——, with his two enormous eyes
Enlarged to thrice their common size,
And brow contracted, staring wild,
Said government was much too mild.
"Were I" (said he) "to have my will,
I soon would teach them to be still.
Their wicked rioting to quell,
I'd rusticate, degrade, expel;
And rather than give up my plan,
I'd clear the College to a man."
B——, who has little wit or pride,
Preferred to take the strongest side;
And Willard soon received commission
To give a public admonition.
With pedant strut to prayers he came,
Called out the criminals by name:
Obedient to his dire command,
Before him Wier and Prescott stand.
"The rulers, merciful and kind,
With equal grief and wonder find
That you should laugh, and drink, and sing,
And make with noise the College ring.
I therefore warn you to beware
Of drinking more than you can bear.
Wine an incentive is to riot,
Destructive of the public quiet.
Full well your tutors know this truth,
For sad experience taught their youth.
Take then this friendly exhortation!
The next offence is rustication."

This sketch of the historical development of the College has already been drawn out too far, and most readers will probably be of the opinion that it deals with the subject in too trivial a manner, and from too low a stand-point. Yet one may fairly doubt whether it is possible in any other way to obtain a correct idea of the gradual steps by which the standard of high education in America has been slowly raised; and it is certainly the fact that, in this age, when instruction has become a science, any person who attempts to deal with the education of young men in actual practice, without attempting in some degree to understand their motives and susceptibilities, runs great danger of neutralizing the whole effect of his most conscientious exertions.

HENRY ADAMS.

2
FREEMAN'S 'HISTORICAL ESSAYS'

Adams lived seven years in England, from his twenty-third to thirtieth year. Being son of the American minister and a principal, though unofficial, member of the legation, he became acquainted with many of the leading British politicians and met a large number of British editors, writers, artists, and scientists. Long experience taught him balanced views of the English, both critical and appreciative.

When he went back to Massachusetts as editor and professor at thirty-two, he found Boston and its adjoining communities still fairly content and assured in self-submission to English ideas, manners, and customs. He saw, too, that American undergraduates might accord greater credence to English authors merely because they were English.

Today it is difficult to guess how many of Adams's students knew their teacher was editing the *North American Review,* and how many studied issues for evidence that he also was writing for the magazine. But students who made such studies could have found evidences aplenty. This unsigned sketch appears in the same issue as Adams's signed "Harvard College. 1786–87." The signed sketch is a manifesto advocating one sort of college education and identifying the chief deficiency of another. The unsigned sketch is a second manifesto. A signal to British writers that they will not enjoy uniform approbation in Boston, it chaffs one of the reigning monarchs among the English historians. To compound the impertinence, it chaffs him in an all-but-English manner.

If any of Adams's students credited the second manifesto to their teacher, they presumably understood it as directed in part at themselves, encouraging them to keep their self-respect, become good learners, and hope in time to write better books than their English rivals.

—*North American Review* (January 1872); unsigned—

Historical Essays. By EDWARD A. FREEMAN, M. A., Hon. D. C. L., late Fellow of Trinity College, Oxford. London: Macmillan & Co. 1871. pp. 406.

MR. FREEMAN stands in the very front rank of living English historians. He is a legitimate successor of Hallam, Palgrave, and Grote. Any book coming from him is therefore sure to attract attention and to receive its full share of approval. Every library which has any pretensions to merit must possess it, and the literary man who neglects to examine it does so at his imminent peril.

Having said so much, we have said all that is required in recommendation of this book, the contents of which are rather necessary to an elementary education than to the attainment of any very advanced knowledge. There is little or no original investigation in these essays, and as for speculation or novel theory, Mr. Freeman cannot be charged with rashness of experiment in this direction. More than half the volume concerns points of continental history, and Mr. Freeman's special grievance, as appears here, is that French ideas of continental history are utterly distorted, and that Englishmen, and we may add Americans, are profoundly ignorant of anything except French ideas. This is not a very lofty aim for an historian of Mr. Freeman's rank; if he stops to fight with elementary ignorance and to teach his readers their alphabet, he is not likely ever to do much more. The audience which requires to be taught that Burgundy and Guienne were once independent of Normandy and Paris, is not likely to grasp more than a very few such facts, and will not advance far into the study of real difficulties. As the best example of more serious work of the same kind, the essay on Kirk's Charles the Bold will probably most interest American readers. In three other essays, *passim*, Mr. Freeman assaults the French "Empire" with much success, but with a very vicious temper. As usual with his controversial work, he ends in producing a feeling of reaction against himself and his very just though rather commonplace ideas. That France has grown wholly at the expense of her old neighbors is naturally true; she must have done so or not have grown at all. That she has covered many very infamous violations of international comity with a special excuse of a quite imaginary national unity, is as true as it is that the German "Reich" (since Mr. Freeman objects to the word "Empire" in a narrow sense) habitually covered very ugly transactions with its Eastern neighbors under the veil of religion, and exacted tributes or annexed territory solely in the interests of Christ and the Church. But a passage like the following is altogether bungling and inartistic in effect; it would drive even a German into remonstrance, and fail to rouse anything but a laugh in the most sensitive of Frenchmen:

> When Louis Napoleon Buonaparte first expressed his wish to become master of Savoy, the word selected for the occasion was the verb "révendiquer," and the actual process of annexation is expressed by the noun "réunion" and the verb "réunir." At first sight this seems very much as if a burglar who asked for your money or your life should be said to "révendiquer" the contents of your purse, and afterwards to effect a "réunion" between them and the contents of his own. According to all etymology "*ré*vendiquer" must mean to claim back again something which you have lost, and "*ré*union" must mean the joining together of things which have been separated after being originally one. Now undoubtedly in modern French usage the particle "re" has lost its natural force, and "réunion" has come simply to mean "union." . . . . It is a most speaking fact that in any language "réunion" should have come to mean the same as "union." It could only have come to do so in the language of a country where a long series of fraudulent or violent "unions" had been ingeniously passed off as lawful "réunions."

Here is an ingenious etymological theory, much livelier at any rate, if not better founded, than many of its author's favorite historical notions. But in the first place, even if it is assumed that Mr. Freeman's philology is equal to the very best German standard, one must still remonstrate against one wilful, malicious, and unjustifiable calumny of "Louis Napoleon Buonaparte," a calumny which must add a considerable sting to the sufferings of that unfortunate man. The literary style of the ex-Emperor has often been sharply criticised, as it possibly deserved, but it certainly passes the limits of fair play when Mr. Freeman actually ventures to make the Emperor responsible for Mr. Freeman's own French. We will risk a heavy stake on the assertion that the Emperor never used the word "révendiquer," and that no one but an Englishman not very much at home in French, nor very well fitted for philological theorizing, would ever have put the word in a Frenchman's mouth.

But setting aside such trifles as accents, which Englishmen have for many centuries agreed to despise, it still seems a little surprising that Mr. Freeman should ever have committed himself to such a statement as the one quoted above. It is surprising because there is in English history a curious anecdote with which Mr. Freeman must be perfectly well acquainted, which bears on this very point. The story is told of Harry Marten the regicide, who in the fervor of republicanism spoke of England, in full Parliament, as "*restored* to its ancient government of Commonwealth." Marten was at once attacked for ignorance of the English language and of history, with as much temper as if he had been a French Emperor and Mr. Freeman his critic, and as he was neither Emperor nor historian nor philologist, but only a wit, he fell back on an authority which Mr. Freeman might also consult to advantage. "There was," he said, "a text which had often troubled his spirit concerning the man who was blind from his mother's womb, but at length whose sight was *restored* to the sight *which he should have had.*"

Barring Mr. Freeman's most inveterate prejudices, he is, when there is neither a French Emperor to abuse nor an Anglo-Saxon king or earl to worship, a hard student and an honest workman. That he is or ever can be a great historian, in any high sense of the word, is difficult to believe. He has read the great German historians, and he probably admires them, but he has certainly failed to understand either their method or their aims. He shows only a limited capacity for critical combinations, and he has a true English contempt for novel theories. In spite of his labors, the history of the Norman Conquest and an accurate statement of Anglo-Saxon institutions still remain as far from realization as ever. Yet Americans owe him some love, if only because he was not one of their English enemies in days when they had few English friends.

A few slight errors in this volume require correction. Page 190: "King *Charles* was succeeded by his son Lothair," should read, "King *Louis*";—Louis d'Outremer. Mr. Freeman comes near treating Mr. Kington as unfairly as he does the Emperor Napoleon. Page 297: "In 1210 Frederick was elected king; two years later, Otto, in Mr. [Kington] Oliphant's words, 'rushed on his doom.'" The words are indeed Mr. Kington's, but the date belongs to Mr. Freeman. Frederick II. had the ill fortune to be three times elected king, but never in the year 1210. The election here meant is that of 1212, from which Frederick dated the years of his reign. Again, p. 186: "In 888 Charles the Fat was deposed," and "in 963 Otto the Great finally annexed the Roman Empire and the Italian Kingdom to his own Teutonic crown." Charles the Fat was deposed in 887, and setting aside the fact that Otto did not "finally" annex the Italian Kingdom to his Teutonic crown, but that the Italians continued after him to dispose of their own crown as in the case of Ardoin of Ivrea in 1002, the date itself is incorrect. Otto the Great was crowned Emperor on the 2d of February, 962.

3

MAINE'S 'VILLAGE COMMUNITIES'

The assignment Adams accepted as a starting teacher was to perform all of Harvard's instruction in medieval history and medieval institutions. Skilled in obtaining books and unafraid of books written in difficult German, he made a discovery shocking and tempting to himself: the English historians had confused, inaccurate ideas of seven centuries of English history, from the Saxons' arrival till the Norman conquest; and German historians were publishing data and ideas which might permit a clarification of English history during those centuries by anyone willing and able to pursue the German lead.

The sketch takes its title from the first book of the three to which it responds, and Sir Henry Maine was an English writer for whom Adams felt great respect. But the book which so affected Adams was the third: Rudolph Sohm's *Die Altdeutsche Reichs- und Gerichtsverfassung,* or rather its first volume. Sohm (1841–1917) was slightly younger than Adams. The German's work accordingly could appeal to the American as heralding great achievement in history by persons in their generation. Adams's copy of the book, preserved in the Henry Adams Library at the Massachusetts Historical Society, shows signs of keen appreciation and hard study.[1]

Similarly, this sketch may show signs of hard work. It possibly was the first sketch to be drafted. Writing it, Adams went a long way towards establishing the dominant themes of his series.

---

[1] A folded sheet of thin paper, inserted in the copy, bears a set of notations in Adams's handwriting titled "Earliest Constitution." See Appendix B.

—*North American Review* (January 1872); unsigned—

1. *Village Communities in the East and West.* Six Lectures delivered at Oxford by HENRY SUMNER MAINE, Corpus Professor of Jurisprudence in the University. London: John Murray. 1871. pp. 226.
2. *Agricultural Communities of the Middle Ages.* From the German of E. NASSE. Translated by H. A. OUVRY. Published by the Cobden Club. London: Macmillan & Co. 1871. pp. 100.
3. *Die Altdeutsche Reichs- und Gerichtsverfassung.* Von DR. RUDOLPH SOHM, ord. Professor an der Universität Freiburg i. Br. Erster Band. Die Fränkische Reichs- und Gerichtsverfassung. Weimar: Hermann Böhlau. 1871. pp. 588.*

THERE are many indications that a new historical school must soon develop itself in England, with new methods and with a deeper basis than has yet been required of English historical students. It is clear that the old school is practically worn out, and in spite of various false starts and much premature theorizing, that the new one sooner or later will run its course and triumph. It is now some years since Sir Henry Maine in his "Ancient Law" sketched out with great breadth and boldness one principal path which the new student would be obliged to follow; and as Sir Henry dealt with legal conceptions, so a French writer whose work has been translated into English and widely read—M. de Coulanges in his *Cité Antique*—has followed a somewhat similar method with forms of religious worship. Sir John Lubbock has in his turn struck into a promising path, though in a very slipshod manner, and has traced society back, on sound critical principles, to a very early stage, in which war figures as the great civilizer. All these are, however, only tentative sketches, outlines of a vast scheme which must inevitably lead to nothing less than the entire reconstruction of historical literature.

Sir Henry Maine's six lectures delivered at Oxford last year aim at illustrating one corner of this immense canvas. Having laid down the principle that the family was the great source of personal law, and that groups of families cultivating land in common—the village communities of undeveloped society—are the great source of proprietary law, he proceeds with a sound sense of critical method, to show what

*As printed in the *North American Review*, "Reichs- und" incorrectly appears as "Reichs-und" (E. C.).

these village communities are, and he describes the system as it actually exists in India, where it was a part of his duty as a judge to
recognize and study it. The same work, so far as concerns the traces
of the same communal system in Germany, has been elaborately done
by a school of German jurists of whom Von Maurer is perhaps the
most eminent.

The mere fact that English historians have always known and recognized the early existence of a communal system, does not prevent
this new movement from shaking the foundations, if there were any,
of the old historical method. Practically neither lawyers nor historians
in England ever succeeded in getting beyond the manor as the source
of land law. They stopped at William the Conqueror and what they
called the feudal system, and assumed that there was here a break of
legal and historical continuity. If they were not too thoroughly convinced both of the merits of English law, and of the merits of English
historians, to feel any slight sense of mortification, one would suppose
that this translation of Nasse's Mediæval Communities would be likely
to stimulate it. Here is a plodding, obscure, and far from lively German, who collects English materials which have been lying under the
eyes of Englishmen for six centuries undisturbed, and by means of
these he puts a new face on English history and law. That all his facts
were well known before he wrote, does not alter the case at all. No
English lawyer or historian has ever used them with any effective
comprehension of their value. The Englishman has accepted feudal
law; he has, very unwillingly but at last frankly, accepted Roman law
as modifying feudal law; but he still does battle with desperate energy
against the idea that Germans as such, before they were either feu-
dalized or Romanized, had an actual system of personal and proprietary law of their own, a system as elaborate, as fixed, and as firmly
administered by competent and regular courts, as ever was needed to
guarantee security of person and property in a simply constructed,
agricultural community. From these laws and this society, not from
Roman laws or William the Conqueror's brain, England, with her
common-law and constitutional system, developed; and from similar
laws by a similar process with a similar result, Rome had developed
before her; as every society which is based on the principle of contract
always has and always must have developed.

English literature has yet to learn that these points of historical science have already been worked out into formulas by German minds, and that there is a mass, one may even say a library, of German books, all of which bear more or less directly on the history of England, and none or few of which have ever been utilized for the explanation of that history. The latest and in some respects the most remarkable of all these works is that of Professor Sohm of Freiburg. Since the publication of Professor Waitz's "Constitutional History" some thirty years ago, although there has been a great amount of active investigation in this field, only two works have achieved any very distinguished success. The first of these was the "History of Benefices" or the origin of Feudalism, by Dr. Paul Roth, Professor at Marburg, in which some of Waitz's theories were roughly and decisively upset. This work dealt principally with the military side of the German constitution down to the tenth century. The second is the work of Dr. Rudolph Sohm, which concerns more immediately the early German system of administering justice, and which has appeared so recently that its exact place in literature cannot yet, at least at this distance, be precisely fixed. To any one who has struggled with early feudal institutions as expounded by writers like Hallam and Guizot, or even by Eichhorn and Waitz, these books of Roth and Sohm produce somewhat the same impression as flashes of lightning in an extremely dark night.

The question cannot but rise in an English reader's mind, why no such works as these, equally thorough and equally broad, have ever been produced in England. Certainly it is not because the Germans had any advantages at the outset, for English historical literature was vastly in advance of the German until a comparatively recent time. We believe that there is an obvious explanation of this difficulty if it is looked at as a purely professional question. These German works are the works of jurists rather than of historians, and there never has been a time when the training of an English lawyer admitted of the possibility of such speculations. No doubt this was an advantage in some respects. It implied that English law had maintained itself in a course of development little disturbed from without; that it was jealous of foreign ideas and external influence; that it frowned upon unpractical theorizing. An Austin was a solitary and not a welcome apparition to the English bar. Perhaps it was well for the common law that it should have grown in this practical and healthy way; that it should have drawn assistance from the civil law only by stealth, and without acknowledgment of its thefts; that it should have created a close corporation of lawyers who knew nothing but law, and only the common law at that. But for history the disaster was enormous. In proportion as Englishmen have made themselves good lawyers they have become bad historians. The whole fabric of the common law rests on a quantity of assumptions which as history are destitute of any sound basis of fact, and these assumptions have decisively influenced the ideas even of those English historians who, technically speaking, knew no law. Just as in the Middle Ages history was appropriated by monks, who wrote with minds controlled and permeated by religious assumptions which color and distort their works from beginning to end, and which have now to be carefully strained away before a residuum of fact can be reached, so in later times the study of history in England, so far as it was legal,—and perhaps the most practical part of history is the development of law,—fell into the hands of a class of men whose purely historical knowledge and faculty for historical criticism were of the most limited kind, and whose minds were hopelessly imbued with common-law fictions. In Germany the case was different. German law may be very inferior as a science to English law; it may have been warped and biassed by its connection with Rome, and its development may not have been spontaneous and healthy. But the German lawyer was also a jurist, and his study of codes, rendered necessary as it was by his situation, has forced him to develop a faculty for comparison and criticism, for minute analysis and sweeping generalization, such as no Englishman, except perhaps Austin and Maine, has ever dared to conceive. It is evident that this state of things is now rapidly passing away in England, and it may be that in the process of overthrow the English law will suffer; but even if this prove to be the case, some compensation may be drawn from the chance that English critical literature will spring into new life, and that English history will perhaps at last be written.

4

TAYLOR'S 'FAUST'[1]

Goethe, whom he read in German, affected Adams as a model in connection with something of the utmost importance to himself: learning how to manage in life. Thus, in a letter to his brother Charles, written in Berlin on December 21, 1866, he praised Goethe as "a great practical genius as well as a great poet."

This never-before-published sketch is Adams's only extended statement about Goethe as a poet, and is the fullest statement by Adams about the translation of poetry—a literary problem he knew at first hand and many times attempted to solve.[2]

The sketch, too, concerns sensuous allurement.

On February 27, 1872, after a bachelorhood lasting into his thirty-fifth year, Adams became engaged. If he had not begun writing the sketch by that fateful moment, he must have begun soon after.

One wonders whether the suppression of the sketch when in page proof resulted solely from a suggestion to Adams by the magazine's publisher (see Attributions, no. 4) or both from that suggestion and an agreement between Adams and his wife-to-be, Marian Hooper, alternatively known as Clover. In view of their writings about each other, she is easily imagined to have seen the proofs.

---

[1]Published by permission of the Massachusetts Historical Society, from Adams's copy of the proofs, signed "By Henry Adams" in his handwriting, and bound in a volume in the Henry Adams Library titled *Critical and Literary Papers*.
[2]Examples of Adams's efforts as a translator of poetry are most readily found in his *Esther*, chapter 5, and his *Mont-Saint-Michel and Chartres*, *passim*.

—intended for the *North American Review* for April 1872; suppressed—

Faust. A Tragedy. By JOHANN WOLFGANG VON GOETHE. First and Second Parts. Translated in the original Metres by BAYARD TAYLOR. Boston: James R. Osgood & Co.

No great poet, of ancient or modern times, has suffered more from translators than Goethe. About thirty-five versions, of the First Part of Faust, preceded Mr. Taylor's translation, each one of which was chiefly remarkable for the author's facility at blundering through the poet's words into a misconception of his meaning. Let one example suffice: we might give a hundred. It is taken from Gower's translation. Wagner, the pedantic famulus of Faust, warning his master against having anything to do with the spirits, says that,

> Sie hören gern, zum Schaden froh gewandt,
> Gehorchen gern, weil sie uns gern betrügen,
> Sie stellen wie vom Himmel sich gesandt,
> Und lispeln englisch, wenn sie lügen.

Misled by the look of *englisch,* Gower rendered the last two lines in this ludicrous manner:

> They feign their native home the sky,
> Assume a false gentility,
> And *lisp in English* where they lie.

If this blunder has no equal in English, it may be matched by that of a French translator of Faust, who mistook *gar* for a proper name in the line,

> Heisse Magister, heisse Doctor gar,

and accordingly rendered it, as we should write in English,

> I am called Magician, I am called Doctor Gar!

Hayward gave the first translation of the First Part of Faust which lays any claim to scholarship; and he, in forsaking poetry for prose, transgressed a fundamental law of translation. Utterly wanting in poetic intention, Mr. Hayward failed to catch the subtler graces of the original, and his Faust bears the same relation to Goethe's that a geologist's map does to a landscape by Turner. No man ever read it with pleasure. One of the best English versions, previous to Mr. Taylor's, was that of Mr. Charles T. Brooks. It was the first in which a conscientious attempt was made to reproduce the rhymes and metres of the original, without sacrificing sense and spirit; but while we admit its general accuracy, the reader is painfully conscious of its lack of poetic fidelity, of its frequent infelicities of expression, and of its occasional lapses into downright vulgarity, for which no warrant can be found in the original. Let us take a few examples.

When Faust, spurned by the Earth Spirit, and overwhelmed by mortification and despair, resolves to die, he exclaims:

> Hier ist es Zeit, durch Thaten zu beweisen
> Dass Manneswürde nicht der Götterhöhe weicht,
> Vor jener dunkeln Höhle nicht zu beben,
> In der sich Phantasie zu eigner Qual verdammt,
> Nach jenem Durchgang hinzustreben,
> Um dessen engen Mund die ganze Hölle flammt;
> Zu diesem Schritt sich heiter zu entschliessen,
> Und wär' es mit Gefahr, in Nichts dahin zu fliessen.

These vigorous lines are but faintly echoed in Mr. Brooks's translation:

> Now is the time to show by deeds *of wonder*
> That manly greatness not to godlike glory yields;
> Before that gloomy pit to stand, unfearing,
> Where fantasy self-damned in its torment lies,
> Still onward to that passway *steering,*
> Around whose narrow mouth hell-flames forever rise;
> Calmly to dare the step, *serene, unshrinking,*
> Though into nothingness *the hour should see thee* sinking.

The words we have placed in italics are added either to fill out the line or to make a rhyme, and every one lowers the tone of the passage. Compare Taylor's rendering:

> 'T is time, through deeds this word of truth to thunder:
> That with the height of Gods Man's dignity may vie!
> Nor from that gloomy gulf to shrink affrighted,
> Where Fancy doth herself to self-born pangs compel,—
> To struggle toward that pass benighted,
> Around whose narrow mouth flame all the fires of Hell,—
> To take this step with cheerful resolution,
> Though Nothingness should be the certain, swift conclusion!

We question the propriety of translating *zu beweisen* by "this word
of truth to thunder," and Goethe says nothing of a pass *benighted.*
Neither translator has rendered the concluding line correctly. Here
Martin's version is more accurate, if not remarkably poetical:

> Serene, although the risk before thee lay,
> Into blank nothingness to melt away!

Mr. Brooks's translation is open to a graver charge than that of
weakness. It is frequently low in tone and sometimes even vulgar.
Goethe portrays Faust as a rich and noble nature, sometimes partly
but never wholly obscured, who, having run the circle of human
knowledge, throws himself in despair into the whirl of earthly passion
and enjoyment. Such a man could never address the tempter in words
like these:

> I laid no snare for thee, *old chap!*
> Thou shouldst have watched and *saved thy bacon.*
>
> *Some pin 's loose* in your head, *old fellow!*
>
> And fetch me some new jewels, *old chap!*

Faust often addresses Mephistopheles in terms of fierce contempt, but
never descends to low familiarity.

The task to which Mr. Taylor set himself, more than twenty years
ago, was one from which the boldest might have shrunk without in-
curring the charge of cowardice. It was to translate the whole of Faust
in the original metres,—to reproduce the poem line for line, measure
for measure, rhyme for rhyme, preserving not merely the exact sense
and tone of every passage, but every peculiarity of rhythm. This had
never been done in English, with any poem of equal length. There
are German translations in which a similar task has been attempted
with marvellous success; but the German language is so much more
flexible than our own, that these examples cannot, we think, have
given Mr. Taylor much encouragement. We cannot help thinking that
he encumbered himself needlessly, and that he lays too great stress
on the literal imitation of every line. That the translation should reflect
the general features of the original, admits of no doubt; but it does
not follow that every line of the translation should be of the exact
length of the original. Freedom, born of consummate art, is one of
the chief characteristics of Goethe's versification, especially in Faust,

where the nature of the subject required a wildness, an abrupt and open fantastic variety and changefulness of rhythm. To reproduce these features is, indeed, incumbent upon the translator who aims to give a faithful impression of the original; but to copy slavishly the measure of every line, and the very order of the rhymes, is a devotion to principle which approaches fanaticism. If a German line of ten syllables can be given in an English line of six or eight, or *vice versa*, in passages where irregular measures are employed, the translator's duty would seem to be rather to the meaning than to the measure; and had Mr. Taylor, who adheres with wonderfully few exceptions to the rule of literal imitation, allowed himself more liberty in this respect, he would have lessened the labor and drudgery of his task, without detracting from the essential merit of his work. Yet we cannot but admire the courage and the patience with which he faces the obstacles in his way. As a daring rider in a steeple chase would not ask to have the gates swung open and the bars let down, Mr. Taylor exults in overcoming difficulties from which a timid man would shrink. That he is not always successful, must be allowed. Here and there a halting line, an ungraceful inversion, a weak rendering, jars upon the ear of a sensitive reader; but as a whole the work is a great achievement in this kind of translation.

To form a correct idea of Mr. Taylor's success in overcoming the difficulties of rhythm and meaning which Faust presents, one must compare his work, not only with the original, but with the efforts of other translators. We could not, perhaps, select a better passage for such a comparison than the mysterious and sublime song of the Earth-Spirit:

> In Lebensfluthen, im Thatensturm,
> Wall' ich auf und ab,
> Webe hin und her!
> Geburt und Grab,
> Ein ewiges Meer,
> Ein wechselnd Weben,
> Ein glühend Leben,
> So schaff' ich am sausenden Webstuhl der Zeit,
> Und wirke der Gottheit lebendiges Kleid.

Mr. Taylor's version is very close and spirited:

> In the tides of Life, in Action's storm,
> A fluctuant wave,
> A shuttle free,
> Birth and the Grave,
> An eternal sea,
> A weaving, flowing
> Life, all-glowing,
> Thus at Time's humming loom 't is my hand prepares
> The garment of Life which the Deity wears!

Carlyle has given a paraphrase rather than a translation, but adheres closely to the spirit of the original:

> In Being's floods, in Action's storm
> I walk and work, above, beneath,
> Work and weave in endless motion!
> Birth and Death,
> An infinite ocean;
> A seizing and giving
> The fire of the Living:
> 'T is thus at the roaring loom of Time I ply,
> And weave for God the garment thou see'st Him by.

Mr. Brooks departs still further from the original, and by changing *time* to *destiny*, in the last line but one, shows that he had no spiritual comprehension of this magnificent outburst. We add his translation, that our readers may compare it with the original and with that of Mr. Taylor:

> In life's tide currents, in action's storm,
> Up and down, like a wave,
> Like the wind, I sweep!
> Cradle and grave—
> A limitless deep—
> An endless weaving
> To and fro,
> A restless heaving
> Of life and glow,—
> So shape I, on Destiny's thundering loom,
> The Godhead's live garment, eternal in bloom.

"*Like* a wave," "*like* the wind,"—how commonplace and prosaic beside the original:

Wall' ich auf und ab,
Webe hin und her!

Equally happy is Mr. Taylor's translation of the passage in which
Faust, disgusted by the flattery of the peasant folk who crowd about
him and hail him as their friend and benefactor, gives utterance to
that yearning of unrest which every thoughtful person has at some
time felt, but which finds its perfect expression only in the poet's
words:

O happy he, who still renews
The hope, from Error's deeps to rise forever!
That which one does not know, one needs to use;
And what one knows, one uses never.
But let us not, by such despondence, so
The fortune of this hour embitter!
Mark how, beneath the evening sunlight's glow,
The green-embosomed houses glitter!
The glow retreats, done is the day of toil;
It yonder hastes, new fields of life exploring;
Ah, that no wing can lift me from the soil,
Upon its track to follow, follow soaring!
Then would I see eternal Evening gild
The silent world beneath me glowing,
On fire each mountain-peak, with peace each valley filled,
The silver brook to golden rivers flowing.
The mountain-chain, with all its gorges deep,
Would then no more impede my godlike motion;
And now before mine eyes expands the ocean
With all its bays, in shining sleep!
Yet, finally, the weary god is sinking;
The new-born impulse fires my mind,—
I hasten on, his beams eternal drinking,
The Day before me and the Night behind,
Above me heaven unfurled, the floor of waves beneath me,—
A glorious dream! though now the glories fade.
Alas! the wings that lift the mind no aid
Of wings to lift the body can bequeath me.
Yet in each soul is born the pleasure
Of yearning onward, upward and away,
When o'er our heads, lost in the vaulted azure,
The lark sends down his flickering lay,—
When over crags and piny highlands
The poising eagle slowly soars,

> And over plains and lakes and islands
> The crane sails by to other shores.

This passage is one of the most beautiful in the First Part of Faust, and it is not extravagant praise to say that the translation preserves the music of the verse, and the suggestiveness that breathes through every line.

As an example of Mr. Taylor's treatment of a peculiarly difficult task, take his rendering of the remarkable chant or chorus known in German as the *Einschläferungslied,* or Lullaby. It is, says Mr. Taylor, "one of the few things in the work which have proved to be a little too much for the commentators, and they have generally let it alone. By dropping all philosophical theories, however, and applying to it only the conditions of Poetic Art, we shall find it easily comprehensible. Faust is hardly aware (although Mephistopheles *is*) that a part of his almost despairing impatience springs from the lack of all enjoyment of physical life; and the first business of these attendant spirits is to unfold before his enchanted eyes a series of dim, dissolving views—sweet, formless, fantastic, and thus all the more dangerously alluring—of sensuous delight. The pictures are blurred, as in a semi-dream; they present nothing positive, upon which Faust's mind could fix, or by which it might be startled: but they leave an impression behind, which gradually works itself into form. The echo of the wild, weird, interlinked melody remains in his soul, and he is not supposed to be conscious of its operation, even when, in the following scene, he exclaims to Mephistopheles:

> Let us the sensual deeps explore,
> To quench the fervors of glowing passion!"

Schwindet ihr dunkeln	Vanish, ye darkling
Wölbungen droben!	Arches above him!
Reizender schaue	Loveliest weather,
Freundlich der blaue	Born of blue ether,
Aether herein!	Break from the sky!
Wären die dunkeln	O that the darkling
Wolken zerronnen!	Clouds had departed!
Sternelein funkeln,	Starlight is sparkling,
Mildere Sonnen	Tranquiller-hearted
Scheinen darein.	Suns are on high.
Himmlischer Söhne	Heaven's own children
Geistige Schöne,	In beauty bewildering,

Schwankende Beugung	Waveringly bending,
Schwebet vorüber;	Pass as they hover;
Sehnende Neigung	Longing unending
Folget hinüber, etc.	Follows them over.

We cannot quote the rest. The work must indeed have been what Mr. Taylor calls it, a "head and heart breaking task," but it is done with spirit and faithfulness.

Let us now turn to the crucial test of the poet, if not of the translator. We have a right to require much from the poet who offers to render Goethe's Gretchen into English. Indeed the true worshipper of Goethe must always shrink from this coarse laying of strange hands on one of the most delicate creations of the human mind, as a sort of profanation which may be necessary but must be painful. Gretchen is essentially German. She cannot be made English. Her charm vanishes as soon so she is made to speak in English. Let us take the lines to which every lover of Goethe must always turn in testing a new translation:

> Denkt ihr an mich ein Augenblickchen nur,
> Ich werde Zeit genug an euch zu denken haben.

> Think but a little moment's space on me!
> To think on you I have all times and places.

In a note on this passage Mr. Taylor says:

These two lines are literally: "Think but a little moment's space on me; I shall have time enough to think of you." I have been obliged, by the exigency of rhyme, to express the latter phrase in different words; yet this is one of those instances where *no* English words, though they may perfectly convey the meaning, can possibly carry with them the fulness and tenderness of sentiment which we feel in the original. *"Ich werde Zeit genug an euch zu denken haben"* suggests, in some mysterious way, a contrast between Faust's place in life and Margaret's, between the love of man and that of woman, which the words do not seem to retain when translated.

Mr. Taylor is perfectly right, and the only complaint we have to make against him is, that his prose is not only better translation but better poetry than his verse. "All times and places" is intolerable. Mr. Brooks's rendering is still worse:

> One little moment, only, think of me,
> I shall, to think of you, have ample time and leisure.

Martin is in this instance the better translator and the truer poet. He
is contented not to improve Goethe:

> A little moment, only, think of me;
> I shall have time enough to think of you.

No one but Goethe would have dared to write two such lines, or if
any other poet had attempted it, he would assuredly have lost their
startling effect. And the test of Goethe's genius is, that even his translators have not the courage to write what he wrote.

A parallel verse, expressing the same intensity of feeling in the same
simplicity or rusticity of language, is to be found in the last scene,
where Faust's passionate entreaty to Margaret, that she will fly with
him from the prison while there is yet time, is met by her wandering
answer:

> Oh weile!
> Weil' ich doch so gern, wo du weilest.

Martin renders this:

> Oh stay!
> I like so much to stay, love, where thou stay'st.

Mr. Brooks translates:

> Oh tarry!
> I tarry so gladly where thou tarriest.

Mr. Taylor's version runs:

> Delay now!
> So fain I stay when thou delayest.

The lover of the original can only turn from all these with a sigh, but
Mr. Taylor's translation is incorrect.

Let us turn to Margaret's song at the spinning-wheel, one of the
most tender and pathetic love lyrics ever written. Mr. Taylor makes
Gretchen talk of "*the bliss* in the clasp of his hand." The original says,
simply, "*sein Händedruck.*" Mr. Martin has used identically the same
academic formula. In fact, Mr. Taylor's rendering of this verse is the
same with Martin's. We must object, too, that "*Sein' edle Gestalt*" is
hardly well translated by "His noble size," and that the two last lines
of the following do not accurately represent the original:

Ach! dürfte ich fassen	Ah! dared I clasp him
Und halten ihn!	And hold and own
Und küssen ihn,	And kiss his mouth
So wie ich wollt',	To heart's desire,
An seinen Küssen	And on his kisses
Vergehen sollt'!	At last expire.

Translators have, of course, always failed in their rendering of this song. Mr. Brooks's failure is painful. For the sake of comparison we give Martin's version, which has spirit at least:

> Oh, if I might clasp him
> And keep him mine,
> And kiss him, kiss him,
> As fain would I,
> I'd faint on his kisses,
> Yes, faint and die.

We have but little space to deal with Mr. Taylor's still larger work, the Second Part of the poem. The task here proposed was yet more difficult than the earlier one. Not only are many scenes and passages of the Second Part hopelessly obscure, while others are trivial and apparently foreign to the purpose, but the poem as a whole sounds like a medley. Goethe kept it too many years in hand. His material accumulated too abundantly to be compacted into a work of regular design and grand simplicity. He appears to have been incapable of rejecting a thought or an image once presented to his mind, or of resisting the temptation to test all his poetical theories, whether romantic or classical, with a result which, to ordinary readers, strongly resembles a chaos. It is Mr. Taylor's principal claim to gratitude that he has made a determined effort to explain and simplify the poet's great ideas, and to make the work, so far as possible, intelligible to an English audience. In this path we shall not attempt to follow him, although we can cordially recommend his commentary to readers who have a real desire to form an opinion of their own as to the relative merits of this much-discussed Second Part,—a work which, whatever opinion we may hold upon it, deserves to be studied, if only to explain the mental condition of a typical artist.

As a translator Mr. Taylor has allowed himself more latitude in his Second Part than in his First. We are not disposed to quarrel with him on this account, holding as we do that the restraints of an exact metrical translation are somewhat pedantic, and that poetry means something more subtle than metre, however artistic the metre may be. But if exactness of rendering is sacrificed, it should be done only for the purpose of heightening the poetical effect; and there are occasional indications that Mr. Taylor, in this part of his work, has yielded not so much to the impulses of a poet as to a very natural and inevitable sense of fatigue. We cannot make the extracts necessary in order to do justice to Mr. Taylor; for that purpose a volume might easily be filled. But some idea of the translation may be drawn from the rendering of the two passages which connect most closely the Second with the First Part of Faust; that is to say, the death of Faust, and the appearance of Gretchen as a penitent in heaven. Faust, in the act of redeeming a waste of land from the sea, realizes his highest ideal, and dies.

> Solch ein Gewimmel möcht' ich sehn,
> Auf freiem Grund mit freiem Volke stehn.
> Zum Augenblicke dürft' ich sagen:
> Verweile doch, du bist so schön!
> Es kann die Spur von meinen Erdentagen
> Nicht in Aeonen untergehn.
> Im Vorgefühl von solchem hohen Glück
> Geniess' ich jetzt den höchsten Augenblick.

> And such a throng I fain would see,
> Stand on free soil among a people free.
> Then dared I hail the moment fleeing:
> 'Ah, still delay,—thou art so fair!'
> The traces cannot, of my earthly being,
> In æons perish,—they are there!
> In proud forefeeling of such lofty bliss,
> I now enjoy the highest moment—this!

More liberty has been taken with Gretchen's prayer, and we cannot candidly claim that the experiment is equally successful:

UNA PŒNITENTIUM	UNA PŒNITENTIUM,
(*sonst* GRETCHEN *genannt, sich anschmiegend.*)	(*formerly named* MARGARET, *stealing closer.*)
Neige, neige,	Incline, O maiden,
Du Ohnegleiche	With Mercy laden,
Du Strahlenreiche	In light unfading,

Dein Antlitz gnädig meinem
  Glück.
Der früh Geliebte,
Nicht mehr Getrübte.
Er kommt Zurück!

Thy gracious countenance upon my
  bliss!
My loved, my lover,
His trials over
In yonder world, returns to me in this!

5

HOWELLS'S *"THEIR WEDDING JOURNEY"*

Adams published two reviews of novels, one when a junior in college. Both concern American novels and show a preference for novels that are faithful representations of current experience. The first, in the *Harvard Magazine* 2 (December 1856): 440–441, dismisses *Paul Fane, &c.: A Novel*, by N. Parker Willis. The second is this sketch commending *Their Wedding Journey*, a first novel by William Dean Howells. The sketch reflects a situation thick with parallels. Adams was the new editor of the *North American Review*. Howells was the new editor of the *Atlantic Monthly*. Both magazines were published by James R. Osgood and Company. So was *Their Wedding Journey*. The novel came into Adams's hands when he and the person he wanted to marry were planning their wedding journey, or soon would. And Adams studied Howells's novel in part as a critic but principally as a writer who, in deepest secrecy, knew he would publish an explosive anonymous book in 1880, to be called *Democracy: An American Novel*. For Adams was nothing if not a planner, and with regard to his novel-to-be he could feel rather sure that a plan already arrived at would be carried out.

—*North American Review* (April 1872); unsigned—

Their Wedding Journey. By W. D. HOWELLS. Boston: J. R. Osgood & Co. 1872.

An interesting question presents itself to the cautious critic who reads this little book, and who does not care to commit himself and his reputation for sound judgment irretrievably to the strength of such a gossamer-like web: it is whether the book will live. Why should it not live? If extreme and almost photographic truth to nature, and remarkable delicacy and lightness of touch, can give permanent life to a story, why should this one not be read with curiosity and enjoyment a hundred or two hundred years hence? Our descendants will find nowhere so faithful and so pleasing a picture of our American existence, and no writer is likely to rival Mr. Howells in this idealization of the commonplace. The vein which Mr. Howells has struck is hardly a deep one. His dexterity in following it, and in drawing out its slightest resources, seems at times almost marvellous, a perpetual succession of feats of sleight-of-hand, all the more remarkable because the critical reader alone will understand how difficult such feats are, and how much tact and wit is needed to escape a mortifying failure. Mr. Howells has a delicacy of touch which does not belong to man. One can scarcely resist the impression that he has had feminine aid and counsel, and that the traitor to her sex has taken delight in revealing the secret of her own attractions, so far at least as she knows it; for Mr. Howells, like the rest of mankind, after all his care and study, can only acknowledge his masculine incompetence to comprehend the female character. The book is essentially a lovers' book. It deserves to be among the first of the gifts which follow or precede the marriage offer. It has, we believe, had a marked success in this way, as a sort of lovers' Murray or Appleton; and if it can throw over the average bridal couple some reflection of its own refinement and taste, it will prove itself a valuable assistant to American civilization.

6

KING'S 'MOUNTAINEERING IN THE SIERRA NEVADA'

Henry Adams and Clarence King met in the Rockies in the summer of 1871. In his *Education,* Adams says that King—like himself and "all their generation"—was "at that moment passing the critical point of his career."

The previous March, King had published a geological article in the *Atlantic*; and, in May, the magazine had begun to publish papers by King of another sort—installments of what Adams would later describe as "a book of sketches." So, when they met, King was far advanced in a project which Adams would want to match. This fact may help explain why, in the West, King instantly became the most valued and intimate of Adams's male American friends.

James R. Osgood and Company published King's sketches in book form the following January or February. Three editions sold rapidly; a fourth, with maps and additions, appeared in 1874. The book is now an American classic.

Four years King's senior, Adams loved and admired his friend but also wished anxiously to protect him. In this anonymous response to his friend's book of sketches, he verges on saying that sketches, while perhaps ideal to write and read, are often too dangerous to be signed; and he surely does say that King invited defamation by signing his. The consideration was not a small one. King's career would prove uncertain, always menaced, ultimately tragic. Adams's career, although he might seem to deny it, would be steadily successful and triumphant. The fact is there and has to be faced: the wrecked career was that of a signer; the triumphant career was that of a person slow to sign and often resolved to go unnoticed. So possibly Adams was right and in their generation Americans bent on having great careers courted fame, advertised themselves, and scored quick gains at extreme, even mortal, risk.

—*North American Review* (April 1872); unsigned—

Mountaineering in the Sierra Nevada. By CLARENCE KING. Boston: James R. Osgood & Co. 1872.

MR. KING is a kind of young hero of the American type. We do not mean to base this opinion of him upon this book, which, though agreeable reading enough, is but a trifle, and shows only the superficial qualities of a lively *raconteur.* To be appreciated it should be read in company with the five huge volumes now appearing, in which Mr. King, the dignified chief of the great national survey of the fortieth parallel, publishes the results of his long and indefatigable labors. As a matter of dignity, this book of sketches will rather injure than benefit Mr. King, who, like all persons in employ of government, must run the gauntlet of congressional criticism; and it would be interesting to know in point of fact whether the publication of these sketches in any way affected the opinions recently expressed in Congress of Mr. King's Report,—opinions in which even General Garfield, who should know better, allowed himself to angle for a little cheap popularity by denouncing what, next to the Coast Survey, is probably the most valuable and the best conducted undertaking our government has now in hand.

Of Mr. King, the man of science, we shall have occasion to speak at greater length when his Report is complete. The undertaking with which he is identified is unique in geological science. Its results must greatly affect geological theories, and may not improbably settle forever more than one difficult geological problem. But these results are not as yet published, and Mr. King's own deductions from the facts he has observed make no part of his mountaineering sketches. These are of the nature of monthly magazines, slight. They are written to amuse, or, if any instruction is intended, it is carefully concealed; and in fact they are amusing, although it must be agreed that mountain-climbers are apt to be monotonous on paper, and that, to enjoy their adventures, the reader should always have a series of exact stereoscopic views representing the adventurer in the act of performing all his most break-neck feats. Every impartial reader must wish to judge for himself in regard to the amount of danger at any special moment, and the photograph alone is to be trusted for the facts.

Artistically speaking, Mr. King's book errs perhaps in carrying sensationalism too far for effect. The truth is, that in work like that of Mr. King, the wonder always is that a day passes without accident. If he is not dragging or riding a mule up or down a perpendicular precipice, he is shooting at bears, getting struck by lightning, or catching rattlesnakes by the tail. There is no end to the forms in which life or health is risked in these adventures; yet however great the momentary dangers may be in these mountain ascents, they are not so wearing nor so fatal as the risks of the alkali plains or the river sinks, where health is surely undermined. The danger, therefore, loses its artistic effect by repetition. Even the actor becomes careless and breaks his neck at length from mere inattention, while the reader becomes distinctly sleepy. Perhaps it is for this reason, perhaps also because words convey at best so blurred and unsatisfactory a picture of natural scenery, that we have found more pleasure in Mr. King's studies of character than in his climbings. Perhaps, too, it is because Mr. King is a humorist, and has an evident relish for the type of humor in which the extreme West excels. The little sketch of "The Newtys of Pike," for example, is quite admirably done. Or for a very characteristic bit of description, we may stop a moment on the following, an extract from "Cut-off Copples's":

> With a look of despair the driver got off and laid the lash freely among his team; they jumped and jerked, frantically tangled themselves up, and at last all sulked and became stubbornly immovable. Meanwhile, a mile of teams behind, unable to pass on the narrow grade, came to an unwilling halt.
>
> About five wagons back I noticed a tall Pike, dressed in checked shirt, and pantaloons tucked into jack-boots. A soft felt hat, worn on the back of his head, displayed long locks of flaxen hair, which hung freely about a florid pink countenance, noticeable for its pair of violent little blue eyes, and facial angle rendered acute by a sharp, long nose.
>
> This fellow watched the stoppage with impatience, and at last, when it was more than he could bear, walked up by the other teams with a look of wrath absolutely devilish. One would have expected him to blow up with rage; yet withal his gait and manner were cool and soft in the extreme. In a bland, almost tender voice, he said to the unfortunate driver, "My friend, perhaps I

can help you"; and his gentle way of disentangling and patting the leaders as he headed them round in the right direction, would have given him a high office under Mr. Bergh. He leisurely examined the embedded wheel, and cast an eye along the road ahead. He then began in rather excited manner to swear, pouring it out louder and more profane, till he utterly eclipsed the most horrid blasphemies I ever heard, piling them up thicker and more fiendish till it seemed as if the very earth must open and engulf him.

I noticed one mule after another give a little squat, bringing their breasts hard against the collars, and straining traces, till only one old mule with ears back and dangling chain still held out. The Pike walked up and yelled one gigantic oath; her ears sprang forward, she squatted in terror, and the iron links grated under her strain. He then stepped back and took the rein, every trembling mule looking out of the corner of its eye and listening at *qui vive*.

With a peculiar air of deliberation and of childlike simplicity, he said in every-day tones, "Come up there, mules!"

One quick strain, a slight rumble, and the wagon rolled on to Copples's. . . .*

We betook ourselves to the office, which was of course bar-room as well. As I entered, the unfortunate teamster was about paying his liquid compliment to the florid Pike. Their glasses were filled. "My respects," said the little driver. The whiskey became lost to view, and went eroding its way through the dust these poor fellows had swallowed. He added, "Well, Billy, you *can* swear."

"Swear?" repeated the Pike in a tone of incredulous questioning. "Me swear?" as if the compliment were greater than his modest desert. "No, I can't blaspheme worth a cuss. You'd jest orter hear Pete Green. *He can exhort the impenitent mule.*"

It is pleasant to the Eastern man who lives in cities, who has no respectable mountains near him, and who cordially detests climbing them even when he is at their foot, to learn that the mountain-top is after all not an attractive spot even to the professional mountaineer. Persons who have, against their better judgment, been led to make one of these ascents must rejoice to hear their sensations expressed, by an authority like Mr. King, so well as they are in the following passage:

I always feel a strange renewal of life when I come down from one of these climbs; they are with me points of departure more marked and powerful than I can account for upon any reasonable ground. In spite of any scientific labor or presence of fatigue, the lifeless region, with its savage elements of sky, ice, and rock, grasps one's nature, and, whether one will or no, compels it into a

*As printed in the *North American Review*, "Copples's" incorrectly appears as "Copple's" (E. C.).

stern, strong accord. Then, as you come again into softer air, and enter the comforting presence of trees, and feel the grass under your feet, one fetter after another seems to unbind from your soul, leaving it free, joyous, grateful!

Mr. King has added to his mountaineering sketches a short concluding chapter on the people of California. His opinions on this subject will perhaps not be altogether gratifying to the Californians, although it is friendly enough. On one point, however, we are glad to find Mr. King express himself in terms very different from those which have been commonly used, even by Massachusetts travellers and writers who should have known better. Of all the mischievous precedents that have ever been set in America, that of the vigilance committees was the most dangerous. Its success has done more to shake faith in the supreme necessity of law and legal measures for the redress of society than any other single experience in American history. It is gratifying to meet with a man who is bold enough to express this opinion, and in whose mouth the opinion has unusual weight:

The vigilants quickly put out of existence a majority of the worst desperadoes, and by their swift, merciless action struck such terror to the rest that ever after the right has mainly controlled affairs. This was *perhaps* well. With characteristic promptness they laid down their power and gave California over to the constituted authorities. This was magnificent. They deserve the commendation due success. They have, however, such a frank, honest way of singing their praise, such eternal, undisguised, and virtuous self-laudation over the whole matter, that no one else need interrupt them with fainter notes.

Although this generation has written its indorsement in full upon the transaction, it may be doubted if History will trace an altogether favorable verdict upon her pages. Possibly to fulfil the golden round of duty, it is needful to do right in the right way, and success may not be proven the eternal test of merit.

That the vigilance committees grasped the moral power is undeniable; that they used it for the public salvation is equally true; but the best advocates are far from showing that with skill and moderation they might not have thrown their weight into the scale *with* law, and conquered, by means of legislature, judge, and jury, a peace wholly free from the stain of lawless blood. . . . Whether better or best the act has not left unmixed blessing.

Mr. King writes with characteristic spirit and energy, and his book will, we hope, create a wide and popular interest in the success of the great work on which he has been so long engaged.

7

HOLLAND'S 'RECOLLECTIONS OF PAST LIFE'

Sir Henry Holland, formerly physician to Queen Victoria, was an Englishman to whom Adams could feel a strong sense of indebtedness. The old doctor liked sharing his table. Inviting Adams to breakfast one day in 1863, he had brought the American together with a Cambridge undergraduate four years his junior, Charles Milnes Gaskell. They took a liking to each other, and a friendship began which would continue for fifty-five years, till Adams's death in 1918.

Meeting Gaskell led to Adams's making other close friends in England, including Gaskell's brother-in-law, Francis Turner Palgrave, a gifted critic, famous as editor of *A Golden Treasury of the Best Songs and Lyrical Poems in the English Language.*

On becoming editor of the *North American Review,* Adams urged Gaskell and Palgrave to write for the magazine. Palgrave supplied an article and Gaskell four notices. Perhaps mainly out of gratitude for their help, but also in payment of a long-standing debt, the American wrote and published this complimentary, unsigned sketch about aged Holland's *Recollections*—which Adams privately thought a bad book.

In the previous sketch relating to King, Adams shows fear of unguarded publication. Here he gently scolds the English physician for concealment, for not telling all he knew. This turnabout is as it should be. A tension between caution and boldness, and thus a contest between reluctance to tell the truth and determination to tell the truth at all costs, turns up everywhere in Adams's writings, as it did in his life. Its appearance in these sketches certifies how completely they are his.

—*North American Review* (April 1872); unsigned—

Recollections of Past Life. By SIR HENRY HOLLAND, Bart. Second Edition. London: Longmans, Green, & Co. 1872. [New York: Appletons.]

SIR HENRY HOLLAND's little book has, it appears, had a success in London. The second edition lies before us, and there is every reason to suppose that it will be, if it has not already been, followed by a third. Perhaps this success is, however, primarily as much due to the unusually large circle of acquaintance which the author enjoys as to the merits of the book itself. At least we are prepared to say that the personality of the author is the most noticeable part of his work, and that wherever he takes us—to London, Naples, Albania, Virginia, or Iceland—we are always distinctly conscious of Sir Henry's presence, and of something strongly marked in his manner of observing and reflecting; while, on the other hand, he prides himself with reason on the extraordinary number of his acquaintances in many parts of the world, so that one might risk the assertion that few or no men living could rival him in this respect. His book, therefore, as a picture of the man, if for no other reason, was sure of a wide circulation, even if it were limited to his personal friends.

It is as a picture of the man that we call attention to it, for all the critics have, we believe, agreed that the book in itself is disappointing, owing to the cautiousness of its author in refraining, not only from gossip and scandal, but from adverse criticism. Ali Pasha and Coleridge almost appear to be the only personages in regard to whom Sir Henry allows himself to indulge in something approaching fault-finding: the first having robbed him and attempted to make him an accomplice in murder; the second having committed the worse sin of talking too much, and talking German metaphysics at that. Here, therefore, are four crimes unpardonable in the eyes of the old English Court physician, and they are precisely the offences that one might have guessed in advance as likely to rouse the most vindictive feelings in the breast of the author. We say, therefore, with confidence that the book has one great charm, which consists in its exact reproduction of the entire personality of an English Court physician in the first half of this century. Sir Henry has made himself a typical man, and will figure in some historical novel, a few centuries hence, when our age has acquired that effect of romance which time always kindly gives to what is long dead and forgotten. We do not intend to describe him as he unconsciously describes himself in this book, though we refrain from doing so only because the canons of criticism have decided that such personal comments are out of place and impertinent, not because the result would be unfavorable to Sir Henry. He has, in fact, little to fear from attack. Through life he has, it is clear, carried his theories as a physician into practice as a member of society; he has observed, but not interfered with human nature; he has avoided dangers, not tempted them; followed society good-naturedly, with a smile covering a little well-concealed scepticism, but has not contradicted it; and in this way, leading a double life, half in the world of London, half in a larger world in his own mind, he has seen eighty-four years run by, and has made certain observations, of which he has collected a few of the most trifling and amused himself by giving them to society. Here is all he chooses to say. The rest, whatever it is, remains for the benefit of that other world of his in which he alone is actor and society at once. For ourselves we confess that we should prefer to know what he has not told, rather than what he has told. We would like to see a frank revelation of the cynical or the sceptical side of this keen and watchful courtier; to obtain a little insight into his mind when it worked, if ever it does work, in undress. Sir Henry is a man of very exceptional powers; he is a physician, and physicians of his stamp are more than other men obliged to be cautious, sceptical, and self-dependent; he has known London society long and well, and London society is a marvellous field for study: but in this volume he has not thought proper to tell much more than was already known to all mankind.

But if Sir Henry is doubly bound to secrecy, as a physician and as a courtier, there are men enough in England ready to meet the difficulty by supplying a little of the smaller kind of gossip which readers miss in this volume. The old school of table-talkers has vanished even in London before a generation which detests long stories and despises a man who is in what Mr. Disraeli calls his anecdotage. Even Macaulay was, towards the end of his life, near to being considered a bore. But there is still a class of diners-out whose business it is to be witty and scandalous, and who on this understanding are received in the character of tame cats in great country-houses. Sometimes these talkers are writers also, and it is one of these, we presume, who in the last number of the "Quarterly Review" furnishes an amusing article on Sir Henry's book, which should be read by every one who has an appetite for this kind of gossip, and has been disappointed by Sir Henry's professional cautiousness.

PART TWO
1874–1875

Henry Adams and Clover Hooper were high achievers. Their wedding journey to Europe and Egypt was planned to serve many purposes, one being that the husband should return much more a historian than he left. In that respect, their journey from its beginning was lucky beyond their hopes. Francis Parkman, whom Adams thought the best living American historian, was a passenger on their ship, accepted their gift of an airy berth in their upperdeck staterooms, and became a friend. Later, in Dresden, they crossed paths with George Bancroft, popularly thought to be the best of the country's historians, till then a stranger. A short while after, in Berlin, where he was United States minister, Bancroft declared Clover his "cousin" (she was related to his wife) and worked actively to expedite Henry's obtaining hard-to-get German books.

The fugitives wintered on a houseboat on the Nile, ascending the river to Abu Simbel. Adams read history and began intensive study of Anglo-Saxon. On their way back, in Paris, by some means that has not been traced, he formed cordial ties with two young French historians: Gabriel Monod, later cofounder of the Revue Historique, *and Marcel Thevenin, a medievalist supportive of the work of Rudolph Sohm, capable of writing authoritative critical notices in English, and eager to contribute to the* North American Review.

In London, English friends and acquaintances helped Adams plan a foray to Oxford. The foray turned into a festive welcome. Adams met "all the men I expected to see"—most importantly William Stubbs, who showed him the Anglo-Saxon manuscripts at the Bodleian—and "a number I did not expect to see"—most importantly Sir Henry Maine, who shortly dined the visitors in London as friends.

Restored to Massachusetts, the Adamses did not live in Cambridge. They took a temporary winter house in Boston, bought land on the North Shore at Beverly Farms on which to build a permanent summer home, and looked forward to eventual winter residence in Washington.

For several reasons, Adams could not return to the capital till President Grant was gone, and Grant was just beginning a second term. Compelled to find four years of satisfactory employment away from where he was going to live, Adams edited more issues of the North American Review, *again taught Harvard's courses in medieval history and medieval institutions, added a course in English history, initiated instruction in American colonial and United States history, and arranged to conduct a graduate seminar whose three members would be the first doctors of philosophy trained in history at Harvard. Simultaneously, he carried forward and completed this book of sketches; also, in the form of an essay so forbidding that few would read it, and fewer still would grasp what it said, or even sense what it was, he wrote a history of England. Given the choice of reading the sketches or the history of England, modern readers are better advised to read the sketches.*

Having gone that far, some readers may draw astonished enjoyment from reading the history, too. Titled "The Anglo-Saxon Courts of Law," it was published at Adams's expense in Essays in Anglo-Saxon Law *(Boston: Little, Brown, 1876). The volume includes his three students' doctoral essays. There have been several printings.*

8
FREEMAN'S 'HISTORY OF THE NORMAN CONQUEST'

E dward Freeman had disliked being chaffed by an anonymous reviewer in the January 1872 *North American Review* and had written complainingly to the editor about it. In this new sketch, the editor (and reviewer) gives the English historian something more grievous to complain about than light critical chaff. True, Adams does not declare that he will himself write a history of England. But he does something declarative enough. With evident confidence that he has firm grounds for his assertions, he overwrites the English historian's account of a medieval figure, Earl Godwine, with an opposite account of his own.

Adams presumably initialled his new offense for three reasons: to mark the resumption of his series of sketches; to separate his pages from the rest of the issue (edited by Perry); and to tell Freeman that both attacks on his books were the handiwork of the magazine's editor. Freeman read the initials as having that import and, in 1882, during a visit to the United States, upbraided Adams in person. Afterwards, Freeman wrote that his American critic (identified as "H. C. Adams") was "a mild man, with a somewhat overbearing wife."

—*North American Review* (January 1874); signed "H. A."—

The History of the Norman Conquest of England, its Causes and its Results.
By EDWARD A. FREEMAN, M. A., Hon. D. C. L., late Fellow of Trinity College, Oxford. Revised American Edition. Oxford. At the Clarendon Press for Macmillan & Co. New York. 1873.

A NEW edition of Mr. Freeman's great work, cheaper and more easily handled than the former, is a gift to the student of English history which he ought to value highly. The reader, too, will be flattered to find the new title-page announcing itself as introducing an American edition, a compliment to the solidity of American literary appetites which an American is bound to acknowledge.

The revised edition contains as yet only the four volumes which have already appeared in the larger form, and the revisions or alterations appear to be of little importance. Persons who have already provided themselves with the earlier imprint need not trouble themselves to discard it for the newer. The revised American edition is better suited for students and popular circulation, but the other remains the *édition de luxe*.

Perhaps at some future day, when the work is completed, this Review will be obliged to discuss it as carefully as its great merits deserve. Then will be the time for the reviewer to express a proper sense of the obligations which the public owes to Mr. Freeman. He had already written in the form of a child's history one of the most admirable books—it is not excessive flattery to say altogether *the* most admirable book—of its kind that exists in the language; and if any other language can boast its equal, its existence has not yet been properly made known. If this larger and more elaborate work on the same subject is far from attaining its aim so completely as the Early English History for Children, the fault is very largely due to the necessities of the case, which render equal success almost impossible. In one respect at least Mr. Freeman is here, too, a model. For carefulness in study this work is without a rival among English histories.

On the other hand, one may, perhaps, claim the right to confess a slight feeling of amused disappointment on examining this new and revised edition. The amusement is due to the fact that Mr. Freeman should have discovered in his revision so little to revise; the disappointment to the fact that he should have found nothing to improve. Not that any considerable change was possible or desirable. Mr. Freeman's prejudices, strong as they may be, are an essential part of the man, and his book would be tame without them. His patriotic enthusiasm for his Saxon ancestors, who were presumably the ancestors of New England as well, is an element of the book which has positive value, if only because it is a healthy reaction against the old tendency to consider everything good in civilization as due to Rome and Greece, to Cicero, to Homer, and to Justinian. Even if it were not so, enthusiasm such as his would still make a dull subject amusing. Most writers are appalled at the difficulties of inspiring enthusiasm for the English of the eleventh century, probably the only pure German race which was ever conquered twice in half a century and held permanently in subjection by races inferior to itself in wealth and power. To Mr. Freeman the difficulties are a stimulus, and no one would wish him to adopt that tone of impartiality which sounds more imposing in the mouth of Hallam, for example, than its actual merits perhaps really warrant. But most of Mr. Freeman's critics had long ago pointed out the unquestionable fact that the patriotic object at which he aims would be much more effectually reached if he would consent to put ever so slight a curb upon the really rampant vivacity of his enthusiasm, and moderate his pace a little, merely to keep his breathless followers in sight. It seemed reasonable to turn to the page which contains the well-known character of Alfred, in the hope that the opinions expressed there might have been somewhat affected by criticism. But the sentence still stands:

Aelfred . . . . is the most perfect character in history.

Might not Mr. Freeman have gained more converts by conceding a word here to his critics? "Perfect" is a strong term and liable to misconception. Mr. Freeman might, too, have considered his readers' feebleness of faith so far as to have limited the wide scope of the word "character." He might have compromised with his conscientious belief in consideration of his good intent, and declared that Alfred was the most perfect king that ever lived, which in an American edition would not have been taken ill; or he might have said that Alfred was the most perfect Englishman that ever lived, and this statement also would probably have sounded reasonable enough, at least to such Americans as still entertain a prejudice against their English relations; or he might have made an exception or two, if only to avoid shocking national susceptibilities; or, finally, he might have reflected that such sweeping assertions are liable to honest misunderstanding, and that there are characters in history which ought not, even by possibility, to be subjected to comparisons. But in spite of critics, Mr. Freeman adheres to his text. "In no other man on record were so many virtues disfigured by so little alloy." It is not from any wish to contradict this statement that one ventures to question its propriety. Mr. Freeman is as safe as though he made the same assertion about Alfred's progenitor Adam, or his other famous ancestor Woden. But although few English scholars will care to enter the lists in order to prove from the scanty pages of Asser and the Chronicle that Alfred was not the most perfect character in history, many will smile at what they will call the vivacity of Mr. Freeman's hobby, and will wonder that authors of his eminence should not know their art better than to undertake to browbeat their readers by sheer dogmatism.

This manner of dealing with history, innocent enough in the case of King Alfred, where no doubtful issues of morals are involved, becomes more serious when Mr. Freeman applies it to characters in regard to which the evidence is contradictory or adverse. Mr. Freeman has made it his duty to stand forward as the apologizer and eulogist of Earl Godwine, and Godwine's son Harold, characters which in themselves have claims to English sympathy strong enough to dispense with the dangerous aid of partisan advocacy. Mr. Freeman from the first has adopted towards these heroes a tone of adulation calculated better than any other possible expedient to inspire into his readers' minds a sentiment of scepticism, and perhaps, in particularly recalcitrant cases, a feeling approaching vindictive animosity towards the whole family, until the fact that one member of the house assassinated his cousin, and another killed his brother in battle, almost causes a sense of relief and satisfaction in the reader. No one would ask Mr. Freeman to change all this. Indeed, it is well to have the ablest advocacy employed on behalf of desperate cases. Mr. Freeman seems to consider it indispensable to Godwine's reputation to prove that he was not the great-nephew of Eadric Streona, the ideal and almost unimaginable miscreant and traitor of his age, whose ruin just preceded Godwine's rise to power. No one will complain of the elaborate special-pleading by which Mr. Freeman attempts to overthrow the genealogy, for he is honest enough to state the evidence so clearly and elaborately as to satisfy an ordinary reader beyond all reasonable doubt that the genealogy is correct. Again, among the many charges current in his own time against Harold is one that at some period of his life he promised William of Normandy to support his succession to the English throne, and swore an unusually solemn oath to William to that effect, which he afterwards broke without hesitation when he thought himself strong enough to seize the throne himself. Mr. Freeman defends his hero by another special plea which is curiously tortured and twisted, but disarms the critic by stating the evidence so elaborately that no one can possibly doubt as to the general bearing of the facts. A more serious question is whether Mr. Freeman has not allowed himself to overstate his case in regard to Harold's election as king. He is bent upon having it that Harold was elected king by the spontaneous voice of the people of all England, but it must be confessed that his case is a very lame one on his own showing. In the first place, the election, such as it was, took place before Edward's body was fairly cold, which in itself is a suspicious circumstance; in the second place, the authorities quoted by Mr. Freeman say not a word about that "great Gemot in London" which he imagines; in the third place, Florence declares that Harold was chosen "a totius Angliæ primatibus," which does not encourage the idea that the people were much consulted; and in the fourth place, Mr. Freeman calmly informs us that all the North of England, with the great Earls Edwin and Morkere, was in a state of passive resistance; in which case the inference is inevitable that Harold was elected by his own brothers and thanes, with the assistance of a part or all of the church, without opposition from the citizens of London. This seems to be all that can be proved about the matter, and it does not by any means justify the attempt to convert this election into a great and spontaneous uprising of the English people, whose influence in public affairs was at this time small enough, if one may judge from their behavior and their form of government. More objectionable, however, than any of the cases mentioned is Mr. Freeman's treatment of another point in the family history. This involves a charge of the most serious kind against the author; a charge of directly tampering with the moral aspects of his tale. He tells the story which once struck all Europe with horror, how, in the year 1036, in the short reign of Cnut's son Harold the Dane, Alfred the Atheling came to England and met his death. The Chronicle records the event in terms of unmistakable severity:

M.XXXVI.—In this year the innocent Aetheling Aelfred, son of King Aethelred, came hither and would go to his mother who sat in Winchester; but that Earl Godwine would not permit, nor other men also who could exercise much power; because the public voice was then greatly in favor of Harold; though it was unjust. But Godwine then impeded him, and in durance set him, and his companions he dispersed; and diversely some slew; some they for money sold, some cruelly killed, some they bound, some they blinded, some hamstrung, some scalped. No bloodier deed was done in this country since the Danes came and here made peace. . . . . The Aetheling yet lived, every evil they vowed him, until it was resolved that he should be led to Ely thus bound. As soon as he was near the land, in the ship they blinded him, and him thus blind brought to the monks; and he there abode the while that he lived. After that, he was buried, etc., etc.

King Harold died in the year 1040, and was succeeded by Harthaenut, his half-brother on the father's side, and half-brother to the murdered Atheling through his mother. Florence of Worcester continues the story, the Chronicle being silent:

He [Harthænut] was greatly incensed against Earl Godwine, and Lyfing Bishop of Worcester, for the death of his brother Aelfred, of which they were accused by Aelfric, Archbishop of York, and some others. . . . . Godwine, to obtain the king's favor, presented him with a galley of admirable workmanship, with a gilded figure-head, rigged with the best materials and manned with eighty chosen soldiers splendidly armed. . . . . Moreover, he made oath to the king with almost all the chief men and greater Thanes in England, that it was not by his counsel or at his instance that his brother's eyes were put out, but that he had only obeyed the commands of his lord King Harold.

The question of Godwine's complicity in this murder is one of only moderate importance to the world, and need not be discussed here, since Mr. Freeman discusses it quite sufficiently, and makes what may be truly called desperate attempts to clear his hero from the charge. But in doing this he was not obliged to resort to technical pleas as though he were an attorney. It was to be hoped, therefore, that in revising his work, he would, on sober consideration, omit the following passage:

Godwine's acquittal was as solemn as any acquittal could be. . . . . Godwine was acquitted after the most solemn trial which the jurisprudence of his own time could provide. He is in fairness entitled to the full benefit of that acquittal. The judgment of a competent tribunal is always worth something, though its worth may be overbalanced by facts or probabilities the other way. There are those who hold, in defiance of all fact and all reason, that Sir Thomas More and Anne Boleyn must have been guilty because English courts of justice pronounced them to be guilty. I am surely asking much less if I ask that Godwine may be held to be innocent because an English Court of Justice, whose verdict is outweighed by no facts or probabilities the other way, solemnly pronounced him innocent.

The allusion is peculiarly unhappy; so much so that one is inclined to wonder whether Mr. Freeman's sense of humor has not led him to laugh a little at his readers. Every one is familiar with the style of argument here mentioned, and every one knows what kind of judgment the public has with one accord passed upon the writers who have sinned in this way. But it is a fair question whether Mr. Freeman in the passage quoted has not surpassed the extravagance of all his predecessors. Indeed, one is a little puzzled to decide what most to wonder at in this short extract. Perhaps a lawyer, who knew a little of Saxon law, might think that the astounding legal ideas here advanced were the proper subject of criticism. Law is indeed Mr. Freeman's weakest point, and it is a matter of much regret that his books are so deficient in this direction as to make it necessary that some one—the duty belongs to Professor Stubbs—should go over the whole ground again. But to the reader who knows no law, the most surprising part of this extract will probably be its revelation as to Mr. Freeman's notion of his duties as an historian. Granting for the sake of argument that the German compurgation was equivalent to a modern acquittal, the question arises whether even a modern acquittal ought to bar the investigations of an historian. Most historical critics have gone so far as to assume not only that there can be no human sentence so solemn as to stand above the revision of posterity, but even that it is the special and conscientious duty of the historian to use all the resources of his skill and knowledge in analyzing the justice of precisely these sentences in order to redress an injury or inflict a punishment. This is the case even in regard to judgments pronounced by our own courts on principles of evidence best suited to establish truth. What then can be said of Mr. Freeman's grave attempt to silence doubt by appealing to the force of a technical oath, affecting in no way the moral bearings of the charge, and perfectly well understood, even in its own day, to have no such moral weight? If Mr. Freeman proposes to go through all mediæval history in this genial manner, acquitting every man from offence who has ever availed himself of the privilege of compurgation, he will end by offering to the public one of the most considerable lists of hardly treated ruffians and perjurers that has been seen even in this generation, to which the sight of rehabilitated criminals is so common. But the public patience will hardly last to the end of the list. Its judgment will be that the historian who resorts to such arguments has by the very act abdicated his high office and is no longer entitled to the name. He has become an advocate, and not a strong one.

H. A.

9

COULANGES'S 'ANCIENT CITY'

Judging from such evidence as has been found, Adams was a born historian who practically from infancy showed an unappeasable appetite for dependable knowledge about his fellow creatures, living, dead, or to come, in his family, his country, and the world. As he matured, he increasingly thought and acted with the help of historical research. Though adept at inquiries fixed on particular subjects, he tried constantly to widen the range of his interests. In 1870, when he changed the balances of his life and tilted from politics towards writing, desire to see what humans had done since they first evolved, to map the entire long course of past human experience, to infer what he and other human beings were probably driving at, became a ruling passion. What he most wanted to do as a general historian was to aid in the development of a satisfactory universal history, a credible account of all humanity.

At the time, even historians knew exceedingly little about the past. In consequence, reading their works had its terrors. As he says in sketch 3, Adams's intensified studies speedily led him into "an extremely dark night"; and in this sketch, published two years later, he looks at a darkness "impenetrably dense."

That he persisted as a historian can be explained in some measure by his confidence in himself as a finder or producer of light, but it seems mainly to be explained by his faith in the efficacy of intellectual cooperation. While prepared to be a historian alone, he preferred the prospect of being one capable historian among a great many, in various countries, working together.

Numa Denis Fustel de Coulanges was a French historian whose works had brought him world fame. By writing about the French historian's ideas, and those of a parallel thinker, Mariette Bey, Adams contrives in this sketch to outline the problem of universal history as conditioned by the very fragmentary, often merely speculative state of western historical knowledge in 1874. Along the way, Adams touches on ideas that would reappear in his much later writings, notably his *Mont-Saint-Michel and Chartres.*

—*North American Review* (April 1874); unsigned—

The Ancient City: a Study on the Religion, Laws, and Institutions of Greece and Rome. By FUSTEL DE COULANGES. Translated from the latest French edition by WILLARD SMALL. Boston: Lee and Shepard. 1874.

THE *Cité Antique* of M. de Coulanges has been so often referred to in the pages of this Review, that it seems now superfluous to enter into any elaborate discussion of its contents or its merits. Readers who are interested in prehistoric studies, who read Maine's "Ancient Law" and "Village Communities," and are on the watch for his forthcoming lectures, who are acquainted with Lubbock's "Origin of Civilization," M'Lennan's [sic] "Primitive Marriage," Tyler's [sic] "Early History of Mankind," Morgan's "Systems of Consanguinity," Müller's *Geschichte der Americanischen Urreligionen,* Bachofen's *Mutterrecht,* and similar works, must be assumed to have sufficient acquaintance already with the *Cité Antique.* If not, they should buy the book at once. It is indispensable for the study of the class of institutions with which it deals. Theology, law, and history are all touched so closely by this work, that no student in either branch can afford to neglect reading it.

M. de Coulanges has undertaken to show how the institutions of archaic Rome grew from, and were in every fibre permeated with, one great religious idea, the active force of this idea consisting in an intense realization of a life continued after death. His fundamental proposition is a simple one, and, so far as appears, indisputable. Religion in the condition here studied was, he says, purely domestic. The mystery of generation was to the ancient Roman what the mystery of creation is to our own age. The belief that generation was due entirely to males, that the female was only passive, receptive, and had no other share in it, caused the father to be alone regarded as the possessor of the mysterious spark of existence, and gave to him the peculiar sacredness which characterized the Roman *paterfamilias.* Hence came the extraordinary legal rights classified under the head of *patria potestas.* Each family, moreover, was an independent religious community, with a ritual of its own. The father was the priest. No member of another family could join in these ceremonies. Hence it resulted that the married daughter must pass into her husband's family; and cognatic relationship did not constitute membership in the Roman family. The mystery of generation incarnated in the *paterfamilias,* extending itself back to the deceased progenitor, gave as a necessary result the worship of ancestors. The mere fact of death was no interruption to the logic of their reasoning. The ancestor was in his tomb, hard by the house. His spirit lived there, a part of the family, invoked at every moment, interested in the welfare of the living, his hunger supplied by regular offerings, his power and his immediate presence unquestioned and undoubted. The domestic hearth was the altar; the fire upon it was perhaps regarded as the divine spirit of the ancestors. Their effigies stood about it, or about the atrium. Neglect of the worship, or failure to make the regular offerings, was therefore a crime like parricide. To allow the family to become extinct, so that no one should be left to carry on the worship and supply the offerings, was a compound of parricide and suicide. Naturally, therefore, the Roman fought *pro aris et focis,* and in defence of his Lares and Penates. Naturally, too, Roman law was intensely imbued with the logical consequences of this religious theory.

No doubt M. de Coulanges has grasped here an idea full of promise; and the manner in which he has developed it deserves the praise it has received. Nor is it a question of much importance whether he has or has not ridden his theory too hard. The object of a monograph like this is to throw its subject into strong relief, and to stimulate inquiry. But several years have passed since the book appeared; and now that its merits and its defects are tolerably well understood, it is natural that the student should begin to ask what further use can be made of the historical principle developed in it. The inquiry is interesting in various ways, but it has a peculiar interest in a legal point of view. The early history of law has never been written; indeed, it is safe to say that hardly an attempt has yet been made to collect, far less to study on any scientific system, the materials for such a history. The darkness which rests over the subject is as yet impenetrably dense.

Roman institutions have alone been studied with care, but they have necessarily been studied by themselves rather than as a part of a general subject. Hence Roman law has come to be regarded as the type and source of all law; and the history of Roman law appears to bound the ambition of the most curious student. When Sir Henry Maine raised a corner of the veil which covered, and still covers, comparative jurisprudence, and illuminated certain points of legal history by the light of Hindoo law, his lectures startled the public; yet even Sir Henry Maine is true, after a fashion, to the classical tradition. Roman law is to him, too, the pure, typical, legal history, to be illustrated rather than to be used for illustration, to be studied as the end rather than to be used as a subject for classification. It is true that he has, since the publication of his Ancient Law, shown a marked disposition to widen the range of his generalizations and studies. It is also true that however closely the professional lawyer may cling to his superstitious belief in the completeness of the law as he knows it, the public at large has become extremely curious and eager to follow a wider course of study, and is certain to find the means of gratifying this taste.

The Roman law is unquestionably the best, and almost the only satisfactory subject for scientific study to the student of legal history. Its advantages are obvious and undisputed, nor is it intended to dispute them here. Acquaintance with its history is no doubt a condition precedent to any scientific acquaintance with modern systems of law; but all this does not necessarily imply that Roman law is a final study. The more strongly all this is insisted upon, the more likely will the student be to assume what is not true,—that law is a sterile science, and offers but little variety in its forms of development. It is not even necessarily true that the archaic law of Rome was the truest type of archaic law; yet this is a matter of some importance as an element in legal history, and is worth an investigation. If deeper examination were to prove that Roman law as known to us in its archaic form was not pure archaic law, curious consequences might follow.

M. de Coulanges has described in a very lively manner the salient points of early Roman law, and has traced them back to their origin in the religious or superstitious ideas of the Roman citizen, as developed first of all in the Roman family. The evolution of law and society is to be studied, therefore, as proceeding from the Roman family and its family law. The Roman family, with all its extreme religious characteristics, its extravagant paternal authority, and its exclusion of cognatic relationship, is to be considered as the type of the family. It is to be assumed as the true Aryan type. All Aryan races sprang from an original Aryan society, in which the Roman family was the typical family. This is the usual assumption, and necessarily so; because unless this is assumed the value of Roman jurisprudence in breaking the fetters of the family organization will be less clear.

But as a matter of fact it is not altogether certain that the Roman family was the typical archaic family; and it is even quite conceivable that the extreme legal consequences which the Romans developed from their family system were nothing more than peculiarities of their own rigid logic and their local conditions. There are certain characteristics of the Roman family and its forms of worship which strongly suggest other than Aryan influences. They inspire an eager curiosity to know what was the organization of the Etruscan family, and its religious and philosophical mysteries. Etruscan law and society are still comparatively difficult to study; but there is one race of which something is really known, whose institutions seem to offer a clew of a certain sort, or at least indicate a possible clew. The influence of Egypt on the races which surrounded the Mediterranean in prehistoric times, the Etruscans among the rest, is far too much disputed to answer for the basis of any solid argument; but the institutions of Egypt are at least better known than those of any other contemporary race. They were not Aryan; and they existed in their perfection as many centuries before the rise of M. de Coulanges's Ancient City as the Ancient City existed before the time of modern New York. Egyptian law has been little studied, and is little known; but, happily, Egyptian religion is well preserved, and its very earliest form is peculiarly interesting, as furnishing a point of comparison with that of archaic Rome. Compare Mariette Bey, the first Egyptian authority of the time, with M. de Coulanges:

> Every complete funeral monument is divided in three parts: the exterior chapel; the pit, or shaft sunk vertically into the rock to a depth that varies between thirty and one hundred feet; and the mortuary chamber where the mummy reposes, at the foot of the shaft.
>
> The exterior chapel is composed of one or several chambers. Here at certain periods of the year came the relations, or perhaps the priests of a certain class, to perform the funeral rites in honor of the dead. The entrance fre-

quently has for door-posts bas-reliefs representing the standing image of the deceased, and for lintel a wide slab covered with an inscription in horizontal lines. This inscription always deserves to be read. It begins with an invariable formula of prayer, followed by a mention of the funeral gifts to be presented to the deceased at certain anniversaries throughout eternity. The list of these anniversaries is not at this earlier period so complete as it afterwards becomes. By the side of some feasts not well defined, there occur others which have a distinctly astronomical character. I will instance the twelve feasts of the first day of each month; the twelve feasts of the sixteenth day of each month; the feasts of the commencement of the seasons; and especially the two feasts to be celebrated at the first day of the sacred year and at the first day of the civil year, precious evidence that Egypt even then had established the true length of the year of three hundred and sixty-five and a quarter days. The representations that cover the walls of the interior have no less interest. Here the personality of the deceased is always prominent. One sees him surrounded by his family, assisting at different scenes; he hunts among the reeds; he presides over the field-work; servants bring him the produce of his farms; others immolate oxen at his feet. The furniture of the chambers where these representations of private life are figured is always as simple as possible; it consists only of tables for offerings, and stela. The first are votive. The offerings in sacred bread, wines, fruits, provisions, which must be brought in kind on the anniversaries mentioned above, appear here sculptured on the stone. The statues representing the deceased are, however, for the most part not in the open hall. At a little distance from the principal chamber the architects have concealed in the wall a sort of closet, walled in on all sides. In this corridor the statues were shut up. The usual custom was to hide these monuments for eternity, but sometimes a little rectangular opening in one of the walls of the principal chamber betrays a narrow duct leading to the hidden statues, used either to convey words which the statues were supposed to hear, or to serve as a passage for the smoke of incense. It is not impossible that the rectangular slits in the king's chamber of the pyramid of Cheops had this destination. The complete absence of figures of gods among the innumerable scenes represented on the walls of these early chapels is an anomaly peculiarly characteristic of the epoch.

All this reads like an extract from Coulanges, except that it describes a far more magnificent civilization. The pyramids themselves would appear to have been only the grandest emanation from this principle of ancestral worship. The pyramid was the rock within which the shaft was sunk and the mortuary chamber hidden. On the east side of the pyramid was the temple or chapel where at the fixed feasts offerings were brought. Mere vanity was not the motive which caused these prodigious monuments to be built. They are rather the emanations of the most intense faith that ever existed. They were the fortresses within which the monarch expected to dwell for eternity, protected by the magnitude of his own work, fed by regular offerings, and listening as when alive to the prayers or thanks of his subjects. But imposing as the pyramids are, they are not the most affecting evidence of this Egyptian creed. Among all the characteristic spectacles of that extraordinary land, the long line of tombs which dot and honeycomb the cliffs for hundreds of miles along the Nile is the most impressive, because of its incessant recurrence to rivet the same idea upon the mind. Of all races the early Egyptians must have been pre-eminently worshippers of the dead. "The Egyptians," says Mariette, "had no other domestic worship than that of their ancestors. They preserved about them, in their houses, the statues of their relations, which played the part of the Penates among the Romans."

All this is not advanced with the object of proving that the Romans obtained their family system from Egypt, but merely to show what kind of family system prevailed at least on one shore of the Mediterranean thousands of years before the Roman city existed, or at least is supposed to have found a name. The Egyptian worship thus described implies a complete system of law. We do not yet know whether the family law of the pyramid-builders was analogous to that of republican Rome, but Diodorus Siculus supplies one link in the chain when he says that, according to common belief among the Egyptians, the father was the sole author of his child's existence, the mother furnishing to it only nourishment and abode. The mystery of generation is the subject of the paintings in the third corridor of the tomb of Rameses VII. at Thebes, about contemporaneous with the siege of Troy.

Undoubtedly there is nothing in all this at all inconsistent with the idea that the same religious conception may at one period in the world's history have prevailed over a large part of Asia, Europe, and North Africa, embracing the Semitic and Aryan races in one legal and philosophical system. But the question is not so much whether one general system prevailed, as it is whether one particular race or tribe shall be considered as the type of that system, if it existed. The Egyptian philosophy was highly developed five thousand years ago. Either it was the same philosophy as that of the Aryans, in which case all Aryan races ought to have held it, or it was a development of its own, in which case the question rises, why the Romans so nearly approached it, and what then the typical Aryan system was.

This question is especially forced on the attention in studying the *Cité Antique,* which thrusts into extreme prominence precisely that religious and metaphysical side of Roman institutions which finds so strong analogies in Egypt. And it is a question peculiarly interesting to the race that claims a German descent, because the archaic German appears to have known little or nothing of the Roman refinements in law and philosophy. The Germans may perhaps have worshipped their ancestors, but they built upon this worship no such structure as the Romans did. The archaic German family, which must have shown traces of such an organization had it ever existed, was, on the contrary, a loose, flexible, almost indefinite association. The *paterfamilias* had no such absolute power as his Roman contemporary; his sons were subjected to no life-long despotism, and were at liberty to own all the property they could acquire; the wife had in her right of divorce an easy means of protecting herself from her husband's authority; she had ample and even excessive rights of dower and inheritance; the daughter was not excluded from her own family by marrying into another; her children looked upon their mother's sisters and brothers as equally near with their father's nearest relations; kinship was reckoned back equally through father and mother, and the blood-feud was shared by both sides of the family alike; the German did not fight *pro aris et focis*; he had no Lares or Penates; he was not shocked at the idea of committing his dead king or lord to a ship and sending it out to meet its destiny on the wide ocean; he does not appear to have offered incense or food at his ancestors' tomb; he did not regard the cobolds and goblins of his house as beings of peculiar sanctity, though they would seem to have been all that was left of the spirits of his ancestors; in short, hardly a trace is to be found in the German family of that elaborate religious and legal formalism which is so prominent in the Roman.

The usual and obvious explanation of these differences is offered by the easy assumption that the Germans, like the Romans, had possessed all the religious and legal characteristics of the extreme family system before they began their wanderings, and had subsequently lost them; therefore Roman society is the typical Aryan society. But another explanation is conceivable, and even probable. If it be true, as need not be denied, that the Germans during their wanderings lost much that was characteristic in their Aryan religion and law, it may still be equally true that the Romans, in contact with other races and a more developed religious creed in Italy, may have wrought out with their logical directness a social and religious system which in severity of legal sequence went far beyond their own original customs,—were perhaps, in one sense, depravations of those customs, especially in the inordinate elevation of paternal authority, and the corresponding degradation of the mother and children.

What, then, was in fact the original Aryan family system? This is a question which can only be answered by a comparison of widely separated forms of society and law, the materials for which have not yet been collected; but that the Aryan law was in some respects much nearer German than Roman law is indicated by a curious fact lately brought to light by Sir Henry Maine. In his lecture on the Early History of the Property of Married Women, Sir Henry has advanced an ingenious theory in regard to the origin of the practice of Suttee, or widow-burning. It appears that the oldest monuments of Hindoo law and religion gave no countenance to the rite. "These inquiries pushed much further have shown that the Hindoo laws, religious and civil, have for centuries been undergoing transmutation, development, and in some points depravation at the hands of successive Brahminical expositors, and that no rules have been so uniformly changed—as we should say, for the worse—as those which affect the legal position of women. It is extremely likely that what the Romans would call the *dos* was at one time a much more important institution among the Hindoos than it is now, and, indeed, that the married woman's authority over it was a great deal more extensive than was that of a Roman wife. . . . . There is much reason to believe that the text, which one of the most authoritative of the Hindoo legal treatises attributes to the mythical, semi-divine legislator Manu, describes a condition of the law very like that which in very ancient times prevailed in India. 'Stridhan,' says the rule, or woman's property, includes 'all the property which a woman may have acquired by inheritance, purchase, partition, seizure, or finding'; and this is a comprehensive description of all the forms of property as defined by the modes of acquisition. Nothing, however, in the existing Hindoo law gives this amplitude, or anything like it, to the Stridhan."

In this respect, however, the ancient Hindoo law agrees very well with the ancient German law, which was also very liberal to wives and widows, as well as to daughters. The assumption is inevitable that this was Aryan law. The Romans modified it by the religious autocracy which they conferred upon the *paterfamilias*. The Hindoos, as Sir Henry affirms, unable to change the law, restricted it wherever restriction was possible, and in order to escape its effects adopted the ingenious expedient of working upon the religious credulity of the widow, and so making a law of Suttee. In both cases the same influences and the same tendency are evident.

But if this is an example of the character of pure Aryan law, that law would appear to have had a far more liberal character than the early Roman. Such power in the hands of the wife is incompatible with the Roman conception of *patria potestas*. It implies a family tie much more closely resembling the German. In other words, it points to the inevitable conclusion that the Roman family and the law derived from it were not universal to the archaic society; that they were peculiar to Rome; that they were in their peculiarities essentially perversions of the Indo-European customs, and that these perversions mark the whole history of Roman jurisprudence. It points also to the necessity of creating something that can claim the name of scientific legal history; and perhaps to the student of English law it points especially to the conclusion that no really thorough historical acquaintance with his subject is possible without tracing the stream of legal institutions back through the German hundred, as well as through the Roman city, to its Aryan source.

10

SATURDAY REVIEW 'SKETCHES AND ESSAYS'

The great shift in Adams's experience began with the death of his sister Louisa, while he was with her, in Italy in mid-July 1870. His friend Gaskell at the same moment published an unsigned article in the *Saturday Review*, a British periodical much read in America; and the following winter, while Adams was struggling to bring out his first issue of the *North American Review*, Gaskell contributed an unsigned article to the *Saturday Review* on country houses, reported to Adams that more articles were in the making, and intimated that the articles would figure in a larger publication of unspecified design.

What Gaskell planned was a book reprinting a selection of his articles. The book's appearance was delayed at the insistence of the magazine. During the delay, Adams, now married, returned to England, bent for the Continent and Egypt. The friends met and parted; Gaskell arranged the book's publication; and something rather striking occurred. "Sketches"—a word which Gaskell had not himself used about his articles—became the first word on the title page.

The book was ready in October 1873; and, at Gaskell's direction, a copy was sent to Adams in Boston. Soon thereafter, Adams wrote to his friend, "I mean myself to notice your book in April."

The sketch below is Adams's sketch about his friend's book of sketches. It also is part of a pattern which may warrant delineation. Adams was (1) a man whose closest American friend (Clarence King) openly authored a book of sketches in 1871–1872, (2) a man whose closest English friend (Charles Milnes Gaskell) authored unsigned sketches in an English magazine and had a selection anonymously reprinted as a book in 1873, (3) a man who reviewed his friends' books in anonymous sketches of his own, and (4) a man who would not reprint his own sketches as a book, either signed or unsigned. It remains uncertain whether Adams was (5) a man who had had a long-standing agreement with Gaskell that they both would write personal, informal pieces—be they "articles" or "sketches." It further remains uncertain whether Adams thought his own sketches comparative successes or failures.

Adams's copy of Gaskell's *Sketches and Essays* is preserved in the Henry Adams Library at the Massachusetts Historical Society. It contains marginal scorings and clearly was used by Adams while writing his notice. Read with an eye to his scorings, the copy is evidence that Adams thought Gaskell an accomplished comic writer—at his funniest perhaps as funny as any.

As a writer, Gaskell today is unknown. His book is rare but unvalued. If attention is ever given it, the cause might be the extended quotations that appear in Adams's pages about it.

—*North American Review* (April 1874); unsigned—

Sketches and Essays. Reprinted by permission from the Saturday Review. William Blackwood and Sons: Edinburgh and London. 1873.

THE Saturday Review does not appeal to one's sympathies. It is arrogant, carping, ill-tempered, and frequently ill-informed. Its criticism and its wit, like its sentences, are too much in one mould, monotonous even when most clever. It suggests fearful possibilities of a literary future in which an average excellence of execution may satisfy the demands of respectable society, without creating or advocating a single idea, except the abstract one of negation. Nevertheless, when all has been said against the Saturday Review, and all its faults have been abundantly exposed, the fact will still remain that it has done a world of good. It has been a terror to literary impostors. It has elevated the standard of literary work. It has done much to break down the insular prejudice of English society and its belief in its own superiority. It has heartlessly ridiculed all the most deeply rooted convictions, all the most firmly established customs, of the British matron and of the county member. For this, the public owes it a debt of gratitude which may be all the more readily acknowledged by Americans, since, of late years, the tone it has adopted towards America has been quite as civil as it has held towards any other country, including its own, and a great contrast to that which English periodicals were used to adopt. Add to this the significant fact that English dicta are no longer regarded by Americans with the same respect or fear as of old, and it is reasonable to suppose that even a Saturday-Reviewer may count upon a very friendly reception among Americans.

Among the sketches reprinted in this little volume, whose author still persists in his incognito, are some which have already gone the rounds of the American press. That on "Weddings and Wedding-Presents" is one of these, and, although human memory is utterly inadequate to the task of recalling the contents of old newspapers, there is here and there an expression or a paragraph in several of the other sketches which has surely had a certain degree of vogue in American journals. But the four essays on London schools, with which the volume begins, are not familiar. The author appears to have been one of the sixty or seventy inspectors appointed by the Education Department in the spring of 1871 to visit and report upon the efficiency of the London elementary schools, some three thousand in number. His first sketch is an account of what he calls "adventure schools," where the teacher gained a livelihood by his or her vocation. A large proportion of these are "dames' schools," and his account of them is very suggestive and highly amusing:

There is no want of schools in the neighborhood, such as they are. In proportion to the poverty of the district is the number of day-schools. When a certain stage of pauperism has been reached, recourse is had either to keeping a mangle or a preparatory school, though which of the two is less productive we will not venture to say. The stock in trade required for the latter is very slight. The hire of a little room, or outhouse, or shed, at 3 *s.* 6 *d.* a week, two chairs, three low benches, four or five fragments of slate, and two torn spelling-books, constitute all that is necessary. The education of others is a last recourse when all other means of livelihood have failed. The consequence is that the dames inveigh loudly against one another, and complain of the seduction of infants to their neighbors' back-kitchens. It is a generally received opinion that any place is good enough for children, and the opinion is one which is acted upon. The schools, however, of the poorer class perform a certain service in keeping their tenants out of the streets for five hours during the day. Many are baby-refuges, where there is hardly any question of instruction, and the old lady in charge very truly says that she is no 'scholard, and just teaches the alphabet.' Sometimes the whole of the front and back parlor is devoted to the purposes of teaching, and forty children may be seen propped up against one another, whilst in the middle, rolling about the floor, admirably fenced in by the barrier of elder children, are a dozen babies between one and three years of age, with their hands well fixed in each other's hair. Sometimes the room is a cellar, so dark that a little time must elapse before the eye gets accustomed to the want of light, and through the dirt and *débris* and bedding which encumber the entrance, a passage can be made to the school, which turns out to be the fender, upon which three miserable-looking children are sitting, unconscious of instruction, and playing with the cat.

The English are modest enough about their educational system, or want of system, and it is not for Americans to throw stones at them so long as their own glass house in the Southern States remains in its present shape. These sketches of the deplorable condition of primary education in London are, therefore, only curious as showing what a task the British government has undertaken in its attempt to construct a satisfactory mechanism for educating the children of the poor in its great cities. According to the new standard, all these dames' schools, with few exceptions, are to disappear. One would think that this would be an unmitigated blessing, yet it falls with crushing weight upon some two thousand teachers in London who at least deserve pity. "No small amount of interest," says the writer, "attaches itself to the dame who keeps thirty children out of the streets, and herself from pauperism, by her exertions, and who says without complaint that she supposes she shall go to the workhouse when her school is taken away from her." No wonder that their temper was sometimes ruffled. One is inclined to sympathize with the "infuriated woman with dishevelled curls who runs into the middle of the road and says that 'it is worse than the Inquisition, that it is outrageous, most outrageous, and that she well knows the tricks of government, whose desire it is to shut up all other schools in order to fill its own.'"

Of the other eight or nine sketches, all of which deal with national customs or fashions in the usual tone of the Saturday Review, that on country-houses is to be cordially recommended to the American public. Addison and Irving have much to answer for in having spread a certain halo of sentiment over the intolerable dulness of an English country-house.* The English themselves in their struggles to over-

---

*As printed in the *North American Review,* "answer" incorrectly appears as "answert" (E. C.).

come this dulness have developed the style of festivity which is described by the reviewer, and which many Americans believe to be the ideal perfection of human society. But there are accents of truth in the description here given which, with all the acknowledged cynicism of the Saturday, must certainly come from the heart:

Nothing, perhaps, is more trying to the nerves than the arrival [at the country-house], and the entry into a half-lit drawing-room, where through the fog can be seen dimly teacups and bonneted women. You search for your hostess in vain, and eventually discuss the dangers of your journey with your host, whom it is needless to say you have never spoken to before. After seeing four relays of women drink tea, the unhappy guest is conducted through innumerable catacombs, up countless stairs, down corridors like the galleries of a coal-pit, to what proves to be somebody else's bedroom. The search continues and is at last rewarded by success. More troubles may, however, attend him. A neighboring grandee has been waited for, and dinner does not take place till half past eight o'clock. . . . . The ball takes place on the following evening. Hostesses declare that they must hold out some attraction and offer some excuse for the formation of a party. It is cruel to drag a man away from his business or his pleasures in order that he may take part in rational conversation, live with agreeable people, or see a beautiful country. He must either shoot away three hundred cartridges each morning, and thus retire to bed with a consciousness of a well-spent day, or he must be taken to a ball. . . . . To shoot all day, to dance all night, and wear curiously colored stockings, will thus have been the occupation of the typical guest. Even should he share Mr. Freeman's views, self-defence will probably drive him into the shooting-party. The alternative is fearful to contemplate. Driven from his bedroom by the housemaids, from the library by the children of the house, the victim loses all presence of mind, and, after luncheon, is ultimately induced to accept, with apparent cordiality, the proposition that he should take a walk. Four girls and one chaperon, attended by the victim, whose trembling hands open successive iron gates, pace three times round the pond, or twice up and down the avenue, till, cold and muddy, he returns to find the same assemblage of women and teacups.

And yet, "without a periodical influx of guests, an Englishman's house would not only be his castle, but also his lunatic asylum." The ponderous English social system, now almost the only complete system of aristocratic society left in Europe, continues to *fonctionner* under these trying conditions, and Americans, even of the shoddy class, yearn for no social position more ardently than for that of an inside spectator of the ducal or noble mansion. And they are quite right if they look at it as they look at the party-colored legs of the *guardia nobile* at Rome, as a curious and somewhat grotesque relic of a historical past, which deserves to be seen. Even in this case, however, they must always bear in mind a remark of Horace Walpole's which contained a profound social truth: "The most remarkable thing I have observed since I came abroad is that there are no people so obviously mad as the English. . . . . If one could avoid contracting this queerness, it must certainly be most entertaining to live in England." The Saturday Reviewer, considering him as a type, has been struck like Walpole with the first of these facts, and if he succeeded in following Walpole's advice, and "avoided contracting that queerness," he would be less amusing than he now is.

11

SOHM'S 'PROCÉDURE DE LA LEX SALICA'

President John Adams started his rise as a lawyer. His son John Quincy Adams trained as a lawyer and similarly rose to be president. One of his sons, Charles Francis Adams, trained as a lawyer and in the 1870s was expected by many to be president; and three of his sons, John, Charles, and Brooks, trained as lawyers. Henry, the other son, meant to be a lawyer but, in 1858, when his turn came to study law, asked first to go to Europe and learn languages. One postponement led to many. Secession, a Civil War, and threatened huge embroilments with England and France required his serving in Washington and abroad. He neither clerked in a Boston office nor enrolled at the Harvard Law School. When freed at thirty, he was not a lawyer.

Yet Henry did study law. As a son in a political family, he absorbed law from infancy as freely as he ate his meals. In the winter of 1859–1860, alone in Dresden, he studied Roman law in German books. During his long service in Washington and London, he was required to deal with large amounts of American, English, and international law. On returning to America as a freelance politician, he passed for a lawyer of the first ability and took part in great legal struggles, invariably as a winner. When he was conscripted to edit the *North American* and added to the Harvard faculty, half of his teaching assignment, the half relating to "medieval institutions," was a legal assignment. He was wished to be, if not a professor of law, a professor of the history of law.

Seven years of professoring (six of teaching and one of study while on his wedding journey) confirmed him in a belief he to some extent had from the start: law and history were profoundly opposed. One could be a lawyer *or* a historian. He, though an Adams, could not be a lawyer. He could gladly be a historian.

This sketch—at first sight unattractive, in fact unreadable—reflects the joy of an ambitious historian on learning belatedly, in his early thirties, that, adjacent to Roman law, there was barbarian law; that records of barbarian law survived; and that, for him, their implications for history were wildly exciting.

Much of the sketch paraphrases in English a French translation of a book in German by Sohm which Adams considered a turning point in the history of history. The sketch grows readable and attractive if taken personally. For instance, it can tell a reader what he or she can legitimately do, under old German law, if owed money by a neighbor who fails to pay it.

The sketch, too, has larger uses. It can tell a reader that the German neighbors of the ancient Romans were organized as free individuals, met at regular intervals, and governed themselves. It can quicken hope that democracy is not something new and fragile, created, possibly, in eighteenth-century France or America, but instead is something as old and strong as the human race.

—*North American Review* (April 1874); unsigned—

La Procédure de la Lex Salica. Par R. SOHM, Professeur à l'Université de Strasbourg. Traduit et annoté par Marcel Thévenin, Répétiteur à l'École des Hautes Études. Paris. Librairie A. Franck. 1873.

PROFESSOR SOHM's little work on the Procedure of the Salic Law appeared in 1867, when its author was still *privat docent* at Göttingen. Its workmanship was so masterly as to attract immediate attention in Germany. Its author became professor at Freiburg in Breisgau, where he published the larger work on the Frankish Political and Judicial Constitution, which has placed him fairly at the head of his profession. Neither work appears yet to have excited attention from English writers,—except from Professor Stubbs, who uses the *Gerichtsverfassung* in his new Constitutional History,—although no class of persons are likely to profit more by an acquaintance with them than English historians. The task of spreading the influence of Sohm's investigations beyond Germany has therefore been assumed by M. Thévenin, who, with M. Gabriel Monod, M. Auguste Longnon, and a small body of scholars centring in the École des Hautes Études at Paris, is offering great promise for the future of honest scholarship in France, which, in the field of history, has of late been low enough. M. Thévenin has had to struggle with no small difficulties in rendering the terrible periods and German archaisms of Professor Sohm into intelligible French, but he has succeeded so well as to enable the student to dispense with further labor on the German original in perfect confidence that the idea is clearer in the clearer medium.

The Lex Salica was the law of the Salian Franks when they dwelt on the banks of the Meuse and Scheldt, in the fifth century, before Clovis had yet risen to place them at the head of a new empire, and to bring them within the influence of Christianity. It is written in barbarous Latin, with an old German gloss now only partially intelligible. It was first reduced to writing about the year 470 or 480, and at that time had a strongly marked archaic character, which vanished so rapidly under the sudden stress of political development that within fifty years afterwards its most archaic features had already become obsolete. As it stands, it is the most perfect type that has been preserved of that German system of archaic law which not only prevailed in Germany itself until the fourteenth century, but held sway in Scandinavia, in England, Iceland, France, Italy,—in short, wherever the German race, throughout the Dark Ages, set its conquering foot. It was this system under which law was administered in England for seven centuries until the Plantagenets succeeded in substituting a better in its place. The earlier law was, however, the common law of England during a longer period than has elapsed since the change, and the law and procedure substituted by the Plantagenets was, in its origin, not law, but pure equity, administered by royal courts of equity, though it is still strongly marked by characteristics of the old common law which it overthrew. English historians have done little to clear away the darkness which rests on this portion of their history. Perhaps in time they will wake to the necessity of at least translating the commonest German books which bear on the subject; not the flighty and diffuse essays of Von Maurer, but the "recherches patientes qui témoignent hautement de cette continuité d'efforts et de cette discipline qu'on sait être les conditions indispensables à l'établissement et au progrès de toute science," as M. Thévenin says in his Preface; the books of Sohm and Brunner, Thudichum, Heusler, and so many other German scholars. Meanwhile, for such students as wish to get a general idea of the nature of Sohm's book on Salic Procedure, the following abstract may be of use. But it must be fairly understood at the outset that Sohm deals here strictly with the procedure alone, and sets an example against loose theorizing which it would be rash not to imitate.

Three forms of procedure appear specially prominent in the Lex Salica. Two of these are simple forms; one is double, or composite, combining the characteristics of both the others. The first of these is called by Sohm the (1) Executive Procedure. It is directed to the summary satisfaction of a private right. It is an *ex parte* proceeding, and does not require the intervention of a judgment by a court. It is, in fact, private redress subjected to legal forms, but still betraying its origin. Sohm, following and improving upon many previous investigators, has reconstructed this procedure from more or less fragmentary allusions under three separate heads of the Lex Salica; first, the Cap. 50, *De fides factas,* which appears to regard the enforcement of simple, unilateral, formal contracts; second, the Cap. 52, *De rem prestitam,* which concerns loans; third, the Cap. 45, *De migrantibus,* which recounts the legal steps by which any member of a village community may prevent any new-comer from acquiring a legal residence within that community. No other actions are mentioned as coming under the Executive Procedure.

The composite or intermediate form is called by Sohm the (2) Procedure for the Vindication of Movables, or, in other words, for the recovery of property lost, when found in strange hands; in effect it is equivalent to a civil suit for the recovery of stolen goods, combined with a criminal action against the thief or receiver.

Finally the (3) Judicial Procedure is the criminal procedure of the Lex Salica. Unlike the executive, which is mainly extra-judicial, this procedure aims at first and throughout at establishing judicial proceedings before the court.

There is also in the Salic Law the summary process of punishing the thief caught in the act; but it is to be observed that the *Lex Salica* knows no real action. Land was not yet recognized as property subject to legal process. This recognition only took place in the latter part of the next century.

1. *The Executive Procedure.*   For the sake of clearness it may be as-

sumed that this is a suit for the recovery of a debt formally contracted, and is to be followed out under the provisions of *Lex Salica* 50, *De fides factas*. It begins then with:

a. *The Testatio.* The suitor, accompanied by three witnesses, goes to the house of his debtor and demands payment. This summons (*testatio*) is a formal act; it must include a specification of the debt; as a formal act it entails a penalty for its misuse, or for disobedience. The defendant has no alternative but to obey it, and pay the debt; or to refuse to obey, in which case he incurs a fine for the disobedience.

b. *The Mannitio.* On a refusal of payment, the suitor summons his opponent before the hundred-court (*mallus*) and its presiding officer, the hundred-man (*tunginus*). The mannitio is here used as a formal act, not to originate judicial proceedings in the hundred-court, which is its purpose in the judicial procedure, but to arrive at the next formal step:

c. *The Nexti Canthichio.* In other words the procedure seems to assume that the defendant will not appear in response to the mannitio, and that the next formal step will follow as a matter of course. This is, however, one of the obscure parts of the subject. Sohm is clearly of the opinion that the defendant might appear and plead, in response to the mannitio.* He might object either to the form or to the substance of the claim. Bethmann-Hollweg, who has since gone over the same ground, is of opinion that the defendant might here deny the debt with the usual oath. He also calls attention to the fact which Sohm had overlooked, that in the case of the *homo migrans* the defendant has the right to produce here the royal re-

*Sohm is less satisfactory than usual when he touches upon this question of the rights of defendants. The following sentence is an example of a fault rarely found in his writings: "Die unterliegenden Verhältnisse, welche von den positiven Voraussetzungen für die Wirksamkeit des Formalacts ausgeschlossen sind, sollen durch das Vorgehen der Gegenparthei ihre negative, zerstörende Macht zu üben im Stande sein." M. Thévenin has struggled with this sentence with the following result: "Tandisque l'élément positif des rapports juridiques servant de base au procès n'exerce aucune influence sur la vertu de l'acte formel, l'élément négatif, par la comparution de la partie adverse est mis en demeure d'annuler les suites de l'acte formel." The private execution or distress which Sohm characterizes as one of the most archaic institutions of the Salic law continues to exist down to this day, in the common law of England, in a form more archaic than that of the Salians,—a form which requires no preliminary notice, summons, or authority from a court of law. The English lawyer would be tempted to maintain that the mannitio of the Salians, with its resulting privileges conferred on the defendant, was only a Frankish innovation upon the more archaic form of distress.

script, which bars the suit. Sohm has since, in his *Gerichtsverfassung* (p. 62, n. 14), noticed this oversight, though M. Thévenin in his notes has not referred to the point. It may therefore be assumed that the mannitio does here, as well as in the judicial procedure, establish a regular judicial process in court, that is, "allows the underlying circumstances to exercise their negative, destructive power," although the normal, usual result may be merely executive, and not attended with contradictory proof, nor specially directed to obtaining a judgment of the court. If, therefore, the defendant fails to appear, or can offer no objection, the complainant proceeds to make oath with his witnesses as to the formal correctness of the preliminaries, and then addresses the *tunginus*: "I call on you, tunginus, that you strictly oblige (*nexti canthichius*) my adversary" to satisfy the claim set forth. The rigor of the formal act compels the tunginus then to declare his bann against the debtor: "I strictly oblige (*nexti canthichio*)" him to what the law commands. The next formal act follows:

d. *The Solem collocare.*   After the complainant has given public notice (*testatio*) in the mallus that his opponent be restrained from disposing of any property before he has satisfied this immediate claim, he instantly proceeds with his witnesses to the debtor's house, and calls (*rogat*) upon him to pay. If the demand is not met, the complainant waits with his witnesses till sunset (*solem collocat*), which adds three soldi to the debt. He then waits a week, and repeats the same formal demand, with its accompanying delay till sunset. Another week must then elapse, followed by a third solemn collocare. The debt is thus increased by nine soldi.

e. *The Pignoratio.*   Only after careful observance of all these forms can the suitor proceed to distrain. This is not a judicial, but a private act. The complainant proceeds with his witnesses to his debtor's house, and there seizes (*pignorat*) a sufficient amount of his personal property to satisfy the debt. If not enough property can be found for this purpose, it would appear that the debt remains unsatisfied. The creditor cannot proceed against the person of his debtor. It is probable that the debtor might at the last moment, by a formal display of resistance, stop the distress. In this case a new term must be fixed, and a judicial process inaugurated. It is also probable that even after the distress the defendant might take advantage of any illegality or oversight on the part of the complainant, to bring a judicial action against him *quia male pignoraverit.*

2. The Procedure for the Vindication of Movables is more complicated, because it combines both civil and criminal procedure in one. It is a curious phenomenon in legal history, and offers a striking example of the effort of archaic law to adapt its procedure to the nature of the complaint, instead of including the greatest possible variety of complaints within one procedure. It stands, relatively to the others, as the connecting link between the executive procedure, which still bears the stamp of a society that has no courts of law, and the judicial procedure, which is to furnish the type of the next development in legal history. Its forms begin with,

a. *The Vestigium minare.*   As no special police system existed among the Franks, neighbors were by law obliged to assist in the search for lost or stolen property. When, therefore, any man discovered that his slaves, or cattle, or other property were missing, he summoned his neighbors to follow the trail (*vestigium minare*). They had a general right of search wherever the trail led. Any one who impeded or molested them was liable to a heavy fine. Any one who refused to allow their right of search within his house was, by law, regarded as the thief.

b. *The Anefang.*   The owner is assumed to discover his property. He at once lays his hand upon it (*mittat manum super eum*). This is the anefang, the first step in every vindication. The formal force of the anefang obliges the possessor either to surrender the property on the spot, or to become party to proceedings before his hundred-court. Moreover, the refusal to surrender entails a fine.

At this point the procedure is regulated according as the anefang has taken place either before or after the lapse of three days from the time of the loss. If three days have not yet elapsed, the claimant has the right to take the conduct of the case by proceeding to the next formal act:

c. *The Agramire.*   This is an obscure and difficult part of the procedure. *Per tertiam manum agramire* is rendered as "a promise to perform the acts which the rules of the third-hand procedure impose." The "third-hand procedure," according to Siegel and Sohm, is the procedure which allows the defendant to vouch his auctor into court; that is, the third hand, from whom he obtained the property by lawful transfer. The agramire in this instance, however, where discovery has been made within three days, is considered by Sohm as having the object of excluding precisely this third-hand procedure. The defendant, where the right to agramire is given to his opponent, cannot vouch in his auctor. The agramire in this instance, therefore, means "a promise which compels both parties to perform the acts which the law prescribes."

d. Both parties are then obliged to appear in court; but the claimant, having in this case the presumption in his favor, has in the agramire the advantage of position. According to Sohm, he is not obliged to offer any proof whatever. Bethmann-Hollweg, however, maintains that the agramire of the complainant was a promise to make oath with three witnesses that the lost property was in his possession within three days before the anefang.* Both Sohm and Bethmann-Hollweg seem, however, to agree that in the face of this procedure the defendant is powerless. He has no means of arresting execution. He cannot, if Sohm is rightly understood, plead even an irregularity of form. He must either surrender the property on the spot, and pay a fine for disobedience to the anefang, which included the fine for theft; or he must refuse to surrender, in which case the procedure terminates with the nexti canthichio and private execution, as before.

The process ends summarily in this case, without judgment or proof. But if the proprietor fails to lay hand on his lost property within three days after the loss, the legal presumption is in favor of the possibility that the defendant has acquired the property by lawful transfer, and therefore the law confers on him the right to agramire, and with it the right to conduct the case. He may now vouch his auctor into court. Or, if he cannot find his auctor, or has no proof of his title, he may still, by giving up the property, purge himself of the theft,

---

*Compare the Year Books, 21 & 22 Edward I. A. D. 1294 (pp. 466–468): "Note that where a thing belonging to a man is lost he may count that he (the finder) tortiously detains it, &c., and tortiously for this, that whereas he lost the said thing on such a day, &c., he (the loser) on such a day, &c., and found it in the house of such an one, and told him, &c., and prayed him to restore the thing, but that he would not restore it, &c., to his damage, &c., and if he will, &c. In this case the demandant must prove by his law (his own hand the twelfth) that he lost the thing."

with the proper oath, and so escape the fine. If he is able to resist both claims, he proceeds thus:

e. *The Contravindicatio.*　As already said, the defendant pronounces the agramire. Both parties appear in court together with the disputed property. In response to the claim of the plaintiff, the defendant may now advance one of three pleas:

1. He may assert original title by virtue of his own manufacture or production. Three witnesses are required as formal proof of original production.

2. He may produce his auctor; the person from whom he received the property, either by sale or gift, as loan or pledge. The auctor then stands in his place and is bound to produce his own auctor, or other proof. The law grants the bona fide purchaser redress against his auctor, or his auctor's heir; but it is not stated whether the plaintiff in this action could recover more than his capital.

3. He may prove inheritance. In this case he must produce three witnesses to prove that the disputed property was a part of the inheritance (*in alode patris*), and three other witnesses to prove that it was rightfully there. This is analogous to vouching in the auctor, with the difference that the party from whom the inheritance comes is to be represented by the heir.

3. The Judicial Procedure, exemplified in criminal cases, aimed throughout at obtaining a judgment from the court. It began with:

a. *The Mannitio.*　The complainant goes with his witnesses to the defendant's house and summons (*mannit*) him to appear "this day fortnight," or at some like term, before the hundred-court to answer such and such a complaint. In the absence of the party, the summons may be addressed to a member of his family. It is to be observed that this judicial mannitio differs from the executive mannitio. The latter aims at forwarding the next executive formal act, though without excluding the defendant from proof if he has it to offer. The former aims principally at bringing the defendant before the court in order that he may plead to the claim or accept the judgment. The judicial procedure does not act *in contumaciam*. Failure to obey the mannitio and to appear on the appointed day entails a heavy fine upon either party unless he pleads an essoin (*sunnis*). Lawful essoins are: the king's service; sickness; the death of a near relation; or fire which has left the party homeless.

b. *The Tangano.* Both parties having appeared in court, the complainant states his complaint with the utmost exactness. He then calls (*hic ego te tangano*) upon the defendant to repeat the charge, word for word, thus compelling either absolute denial or absolute confession. Sohm is of the opinion that with the confession a plea (e.g. of payment) might be united. Apparently, too, the defendant may here object to any irregularity of form. The statement and answer being completed, the plaintiff turns to the bench of rachimburgi (*schöffen, échevins*). These are, according to a probable suggestion of Bethmann-Hollweg, twelve in number, of whom seven, the majority, are necessary for a judgment. The complainant calls upon them to propose a judgment, using the formal tangano if necessary.

c. *Lex dicere.* The judgment thus proposed by the rachimburgi in no way expresses their convictions on the merits of the case, but adheres with the utmost exactness to the superficial forms. If the defendant has confessed, the judgment fixes the amount of his fine. If he denies, the judgment determines how the question of proof is to be decided. (Aut componat, aut juret, aut ad ineo ambulet.)

d. *The Contradictio.* The party who may think the proposed judgment contrary to the law must immediately challenge it (*contradicere quod legem non judicant*). This originates a suit against the rachimburgi, pending which the original suit remains in abeyance.

e. *Fidem facere.* If neither party challenges the proposed judgment, and it is now formally accepted by the assembled freemen who constitute the court, and has thus become the judgment of the court, the defendant must proceed to make oath or give surety (*fidem facere*) that he will perform the judgment on the appointed day.

f. *The Proof.* (Jurare. Ad ineo ambulare.) If the judgment is a judgment to proof, it prescribes the kind of proof. There are two kinds: oath, and ordeal of boiling water. Ordeal of battle is nowhere suggested. The law fails to say what rules regulated the judgment in requiring ordeal rather than oath. A man condemned to the ordeal may, however, "redeem his hand," and, by paying a certain sum, obtain the privilege of offering proof by oath. On the appointed day the defendant appears; if his proof is successful, whether oath or ordeal, he is acquitted, unless the oath is challenged, in which case another action is originated. The ordeal cannot be challenged; it is the only final and indisputable proof. If the proof breaks down, the fine to be paid is already indicated in the judgment.

The course of this procedure depends upon the voluntary acceptance by the defendant of the jurisdiction of the court. But it is conceivable that the defendant may refuse to appear in court at all; or having appeared, may refuse to give the pledge (*fidem facere*) to perform the judgment; or having given the pledge, may refuse to carry it out.

In the last case, where the defendant by his formal act (*fidem facere*) has voluntarily contracted the obligation to fulfil the judgment, and then fails to appear at the fixed term, the claimant may proceed against him to a judicial execution. This is a different form from the executive execution or distress, inasmuch as it requires the co-operation of the sheriff (*graff*). On the non-appearance of the defendant to fulfil judgment, the claimant waits till sunset with his witnesses (*solem collocat*). The defendant is by this formal act put in contumacy (*jactivus*), and his prosecutor next goes to the sheriff. After the usual declarations to the formal correctness of the past proceedings, the complainant calls upon the sheriff for execution. The sheriff must now go with seven assessors to the delinquent's house, and seize enough of his property to satisfy the law; two parts of the amount seized go to discharge the private claim; one part goes to the king. If the personalty is not sufficient to meet the demand, the claimant remains unsatisfied. Land, though perhaps already recognized as property in fact, is not property in view of the law, and not liable to execution. The person of the debtor is liable to seizure only in the action resulting from manslaughter, for recovery of the blood-money or *wergeld*.

But the accused may refuse to submit himself to judgment at all. He will then decline to take the preliminary obligation (*fidem facere*). This offers another curious illustration of archaic principles. The claimant has against this refusal no redress at law. The law is only for those who voluntarily accept its jurisdiction. The complainant cannot proceed to private execution or distress; he cannot oblige the sheriff to a judicial execution. He must resort to equity, or at least to such rudimentary equity as the age knows. He must go to the king himself, sitting as a judge in equity; and if he does this with the proper forms, at no little trouble and expense, the king will at last declare the delinquent an outlaw, the effect of outlawry being to give all the outlaw's property to the king and his person price to his enemies. But the outlawry punishes the contumacy, not the original offence. The complainant remains without satisfaction at law, unless the outlaw may choose to submit. In other words, archaic law aims first at bringing the individual into submission to its process; the satisfaction of a private wrong was only a secondary result.

Space is wanting for any further examination of Professor Sohm's work. A mere reference is all that can be made here to the two forms of procedure which alone restrict the personal freedom or endanger the life of the freeman: the one, against thieves caught in the act; the other, against the criminal condemned to pay the *wergeld,* or blood-fine, and unable to raise the money. The law itself never condemns to imprisonment or death; its action is limited to surrendering the criminal into his enemies' hands.

The book closes with a rapid sketch of the steps by which the more archaic, private procedure fell into disuse, and all actions, civil as well as criminal, were brought within the more elastic judicial process. To the original volume M. Thévenin has added, by way of appendix, monographs extracted from Sohm's larger book on the Gerichtsverfassung, illustrating certain important points of Salian law.

It need hardly be said that Sohm's books are not intended for amusement. They are undeniably hard reading, even for specialists. They aim at establishing the exact basis of history. It is the business of the future historian to popularize their results. But the future historian of early English society and law who undertakes to write without having first mastered the works of Sohm and his German critics will throw his labor away.

12

STUBBS'S 'CONSTITUTIONAL HISTORY OF ENGLAND'

Adams did not withhold his ideas about the history of England. He published them unsigned as soon as he could get them formed and intelligibly worded. The statement below calls itself a "notice." In part it is a notice of a great work by William Stubbs. Yet it literally is a sketch. Its main business is to outline the history of England as understood by Henry Adams.

Somewhat incidentally, the sketch raises the question whether history is, or should be, a science, an art, or both. Adams's answer is plain: he believes that history is history, in the true sense of the word, only when it is both; and he believes that the art of history is inescapably a narrative art.

It followed that he would be a historian if two conditions were met: if he acquired an understanding of some portion of the past grounded in all the known, relevant, surviving evidence; and if he imparted his understanding to others by writing a successful narrative. Since the sketch is hardly a narrative, and the essay he was preparing to write on the history of England would not be a narrative, it also followed that, in his own mind, Adams would not fully be a historian until some years later, when he would at last write a book he had long known he would have to write, a narrative history of his own country.

In short, on Adams's terms, both the sketches in this book and his difficult essay "The Anglo-Saxon Courts of Law" are mere preliminaries, and the work that constitutes his claim to being a historian is his *History of the United States of America during the Administrations of Thomas Jefferson and James Madison,* published in 1889–1891.

—*North American Review* (July 1874); unsigned—

The Constitutional History of England in its Origin and Development. By WILLIAM STUBBS, M. A., Regius Professor of Modern History. Vol. I. Oxford: At the Clarendon Press. 1874.

THE authority of Professor Stubbs deservedly stands so high, that a critic who undertakes to deal with his works must always feel the task to be one of no little difficulty and danger. His name has often been mentioned in the pages of this Review, and always with respect and praise. He is not only learned and accurate, but, unlike some of his rivals in the same field, his judgment is admirable, and his caution almost excessive. As Regius Professor at Oxford, he gives dignity to the study of history. Even yet this study stands at that University in comparatively slight esteem, overshadowed as it still is by the prescriptive authority of the classics; and the present work is doubly valuable if it is an evidence that Oxford intends at last to interest herself seriously in the history of England, and to tolerate no longer that indifference which has thus far left the national annals in the hands of Scotchmen or amateurs. A scientific training is as necessary to the historian as to the mathematician, and it is the misfortune of England that she has never yet had a scientific historical school.

Mr. Stubbs's first volume deals with the constitutional history of England during the long period of seven centuries between the first establishment of the Germans and the adoption of Magna Charta. There is no use in disguising the fact that, to the mass of readers, early English history is dull reading, and early English constitutional history is peculiarly dull reading. Yet its scientific interest is very great. The constitutional changes which marked these seven centuries were more radical than any which have occurred since their close. They include the entire conversion of an archaic, pagan community into a nation which was only waiting for the masterly touch of Edward I. to become a model in history. The various stages of this preliminary progress; the obscure forms of society and law, with their irritating and pedantic details; the experiments in government which succeeded, or, still worse, those that failed; the incessant and always intricate struggle between the old that was passing away and the new that was at hand;—all these changes and varieties of the story require a profound treatment and consume infinite time. That Professor Stubbs should have succeeded in compressing this part of his subject into only six hundred pages is to be explained by his careful exclusion of all extended argument, and his moderation in the display of learning. He has produced a work which for compactness and solidity can be compared with nothing but a dictionary. A different arrangement or a careful index might easily convert it into a sort of English Ducange. And although Mr. Stubbs's History is far in advance of any previous work of the kind, and will probably long retain its superiority over all rivals, still the critic may be allowed to express a regret that the author, instead of writing a history, did not rather compile a glossary like that of Ducange or Spelman. Experience has proved that such immortality as the antiquarian can ever expect is best to be earned in this manner. Even the best histories are soon superseded and cease to be read; but Ducange, Spelman, Grimm, must always be consulted and re-edited. Professor Stubbs could propose for himself no task so brilliant or so useful as that of furnishing the world with a complete index and glossary to all the records of early English history. How valuable such a work may be has been shown by Dr. Schmid, who has done it for the laws alone. There are no books so essential to the student and so little accessible in English history as this sort of cyclopædia. There are none which bar so effectually the influence of dangerous or feeble theorizing, or which tend so directly to shorten the labor of good historians.

There is another reason why this method of proceeding would have been especially suitable in the present case. Without the slightest disrespect to Professor Stubbs, who stands above the range of captious criticism, even his strongest friends must concede that his mind is better adapted to the work of compilation than to the art of story-telling. The historian must be an artist. He must know how to develop the leading ideas of the subject he has chosen, how to keep the thread of his narrative always in hand, how to subordinate details, and how to accentuate principles. But of such an art Mr. Stubbs is altogether innocent. He would perhaps regard it as slightly contemptible, and, indeed, in England it has really become so, although, strange to say, in Germany it has been of late superbly developed. Mr. Stubbs has no theories to advance, no principle to demonstrate. His History aims at the correct appreciation of facts, so far as they are at hand, rather than at the development of an idea. He is a perfect editor; he would be an admirable lexicographer; but as an historian he will infallibly be voted dull.

This is the more to be regretted because there is no reason nor excuse for it in the subject itself. The mass of mankind, of course, will always think constitutional history dull, but Mr. Stubbs does not write for the mass of mankind. He writes for a small class of lawyers or students who are peculiarly interested in the subject, and fully alive to its extreme importance. To them the constitutional history of England is perhaps the most interesting history that ever was written. England offers to them the spectacle of a nation which has passed through all the stages of change both in public and private law, from pure archaism down to the latest germs of future institutions now struggling into life, either in her own soil or that of her offshoots, and in all this mass of public and private law it can hardly be said that there is a single serious interruption of legal continuity. She is therefore a curiosity among nations, unique in her development. Rome can alone claim a rivalry with her, but at least on the political side England has an indisputable advantage over Rome.

So far as private law is concerned, the early history of this great system is still almost a blank. Neither Mr. Stubbs nor any other writer has seriously attempted it, and it is destined to remain untouched until Germany has forced England into scholarship. All that is known of early English private law must as yet be read in German books. Until the appearance of Mr. Stubbs's work, this was also very much the case in regard to constitutional law; the excellent books of Kemble and Palgrave were becoming antiquated. Mr. Stubbs, however, is a German scholar, and is not ashamed of acknowledging his indebtedness to Germany. Yet it is safe to say that even Mr. Stubbs might have gone with advantage still more deeply into the study of German historians in the more technical branches of private law. Nevertheless, a great point has been gained by the general concession that English constitutional history begins with the coming of the Germans in the latter half of the fifth century, and Mr. Stubbs has done much to clear men's minds by rejecting at the outset every suggestion of Roman influence, and resting his whole structure upon the simple foundation of German archaic society.

The outlines of this society, thanks to German investigators, are now sufficiently clear. The Angles and Saxons who drove out the old

British population brought to England a constitution of their own. In Germany they had adopted, before the earliest historical period, an organization which bore the name of *hundred*; and although the term itself does not appear in their laws till a much later period, Mr. Stubbs admits that the earliest Anglo-Saxon society was probably founded upon this division or its equivalent. They lived in small settlements where the land was, perhaps, held in common, or where, at all events, there were extensive rights of common, but their constitutional activity centred in the hundred, of which the village or community was but a fraction. The hundred was their unit of organization. At the hundred court, the mallus, methel, or thing, which met every month, each freeman was probably bound to appear. The legal procedure peculiar to this court was certainly in essentials the same as that described in the Lex Salica as existing among the Franks at the same period, and has already been sketched at considerable length in this Review. Perhaps at the beginning, when the German settlements were very small, the hundred court was parliament and law-court in one, and all questions of every kind may have been settled there under the presidency of the ealdorman. But as larger districts were occupied, the hundreds appear to have been grouped together in shires, and twice a year the freemen met together at a fixed spot and transacted business both legal and political in the shire-court, which had an appellate jurisdiction in all suits, and was probably presided over by the ealdorman.

Thus the early constitution was simple enough. It was purely democratic. The ealdorman was a president whose powers were no greater than the freemen chose to concede. The free citizens administered their own law and their own political system in their own courts. They went out to war as they went to their hundred-court; law-court, parliament, and army were the same. If any reliance is to be placed in the general characteristics of German society, these or similar institutions must have existed in all the numerous shires which are called kingdoms in the early history.

In regard to this period, however, the records are very vague, and results are not easily fixed beyond dispute. Nearly four centuries elapsed after the Germans first settled in England before any clear notion of their government can be obtained from their literature. During that time a whole civilization had spread over Europe under the Frankish empire, and had introduced a characteristic constitutional system. England was strongly influenced by it. Of that system the elevation of royal authority, and the administration of the hundreds by royal officials, were marked incidents. It is, therefore, natural enough that a law of Edward the Elder, of about the year 920, should direct his reeves to hold their court every four weeks. The royal sheriff presided therefore in the hundred-court. To this extent administration had been centralized. England was now united under one king, and a great council assisted in the political government. Later times have given to this body the name of Witenagemot, or court of the elders; in Anglo-Saxon days it seems to have been known as merely the Witan or the Gemot.

Here, then, begins the division of English constitutional history into its two main branches, the political and the judicial. Omitting all else in order to keep these great objects clearly in view, the single point of special interest in regard to the first must be to ascertain how far the Witan is to be considered as identical with the later Parliament. On this subject the English historians are rarely to be trusted. They are apt to be led, by a sentiment of patriotism, into the assertion as an article of faith of what is not only incapable of proof, but inconsistent with facts. Even Mr. Stubbs, cautious as he is, allows himself to dwell rather on the points of resemblance than on the differences between the two assemblies. The great German historian, Sohm, has described more clearly than Professor Stubbs has done the peculiarities of the Anglo-Saxon political system. These peculiarities rest mainly on the fact that in England the ealdormen represent the old tribal independence, the petty kings who preceded the national union. Their authority was not created by the throne, but was older than the throne. What the crown won, it won from the ealdorman. He was a viceking, with an authority not derived from, but independent of, the king. No law of the king's, but a principle of the constitution, defined the plenitude of his power. Not the will of the king alone, but a judicial sentence, could deprive him of his office. The ealdorman excluded the king from the immediate government of his province. Local government was therefore the rule, not of the king, but of the ealdorman. The king, in appointing him, appointed not a servant of his will, but a prince and lord of the province.

In the Witan the king and the Church alone represented the principle of national unity and the tendency to centralization. The ealdormen represented an antagonistic force, the ancient constitutional rights of local independence. How strong this principle was, can best be seen in the lives of Aelfric and Eadric Streona. It made the kingdom a prey to internal treachery and foreign conquest. It was the natural forerunner of a feudal chaos; and when Harold, imitating the Capetians, raised himself to the throne, the natural consequence would seem to have been that England should share the fate of France.

To have prevented this was the one great service which William the Norman rendered to mankind. His crown depended upon success in trampling the last spark of life out of that local aristocracy, descended from the heptarchy, which found its expression in the Witan. Nor is there any other single point in William's policy which stands out in equal prominence with this. Here is the justification of his course in making Northumbria a desert, and in cutting off Waltheof's head. To guard against any possible revival of the old system, he scattered his grants to the Norman nobles over all England, nowhere allowing the revival of a local aristocracy. His policy was wise and successful, however rough it may have been. Never again after William's reign does one hear of Wessex, of Mercia, or of a Northumbrian Witan.

As a necessary consequence of this policy, the old Anglo-Saxon Witena-gemot perished with the class it represented, nor is this result in the least affected by the fact that the conqueror maintained for a time a certain hollow form which still bore its name. It is even made more conspicuous by the fact, pointed out by Mr. Stubbs, that the judicial powers of the Witan were henceforward wielded by the Curia Regis, which thus acquired a prominence hitherto denied it. Neither Mr. Stubbs nor even Mr. Freeman would probably maintain that there is any evidence whatever to establish the existence of a legislative assembly under Rufus, Henry I., Stephen, Henry II., Richard or John. The utmost that can be demonstrated is the occasional indication of a consultative body, which, to say the least, has no stronger affiliations with the Witan than it has with the Curia Regis or the Norman court of the barons. Two whole centuries elapsed between the last genuine meeting of the Witan and the first meeting of Parliament. When at length the practical wisdom of the English mind and the administrative genius of Edward I. organized parliamentary government, the constitution of that body was essentially the opposite to that of the Witan. It was national, it was representative, it was popular. The Witan had been sectional, self-constituted, aristocratic. The Witan represented the heptarchy, Parliament the consolidated nation. The Witan perpetuated all that was worst in the old system: Parliament offered all that was best in the new. The Witan, as an experiment in constitutional government, had never worked easily or thoroughly; it was a failure. Parliament was from the first a success. There is little in common between them, except that both were legislative and judicial assemblies.

If Mr. Stubbs's caution has prevented him from advancing any very strong or very peculiar views in regard to the logical sequence of English political institutions, the same cause is possibly accountable for his failure to mark sharply what he would consider the essential elements in the judicial constitution. His description is confused by details. He begins, too, by a statement which is hardly tenable: "The unit of the constitutional machinery [in early Anglo-Saxon times] is the township, the *villata* or *vicus*." If he had said that the unit was the shire, the statement would have had grounds of support. If he had said it was the hundred, he would have agreed with the highest modern authorities. If he had called it the tithing, or the family, an argument might have been made in his favor. But one is at a loss to understand in what single particular the *villata* or township was a unit of constitutional machinery. It had not a single constitutional function of any kind, sort, or description. It had, if Mr. Stubbs pleases to insist upon it, some small police functions; and it is possible that it may have had some sort of police-court, although even the existence of this court can hardly be proved. Mr. Stubbs cites one charter of Richard I. to show that the word "townshipmot" occurs at all. Mr. Stubbs further says that the township appears in its ecclesiastical form as the parish. But, on the other hand, the laws, the records, the constitution itself, and the whole literature of Germanic society leave no possible doubt as to what the English people considered their unit of constitutional machinery. It was the hundred, of which the township was a mere fraction or subdivision, with no separate activity of its own. The hundred-court, consisting of at least a certain number of freemen from every *vill*, and meeting every four weeks, was the foundation of everything in Anglo-Saxon history: of king, ealdorman, shire-court, army; of all except the Church. The hundred-court was the lowest court of civil and criminal jurisdiction; no complaint could be taken to the shire-court or to the king that had not been first heard in the hundred. It was the lowest organization used by the king for judicial or administrative purposes. Even so late an authority as Henry I. shows that the hundred at that day was still the unit of constitutional machinery as it was in the time of the Saxon kings: "Henricus rex . . . . omnibus baronibus suis.—— Sciatis quod concedo et præcipio ut amodo comitatus mei *et hundreda* in illis locis et eisdem terminis sedeant, sicut sederunt in tempore regis Eadwardi et non aliter. Ego enim quando voluero, faciam ea satis summonere propter mea dominica necessaria ad voluntatem meam. . . . . Et volo et præcipio ut omnes de comitatu eant ad comitatus et hundreda, sicut fecerunt in tempore regis Eadwardi." Mr. Stubbs himself cites ample evidence to the same effect. The entire fabric of civic society, as described by Mr. Stubbs, testifies to the same fact. The very construction of Domesday Book and the Rotuli Hundredorum proclaims it.

If this were a point of secondary consequence, there would be no occasion to comment upon it. But if the clew offered by the hundred is once lost, or even if it is loosely held, the entire history of the English judicial constitution becomes a confused jumble of words. The one permanent Germanic institution was the hundred. The one code of Germanic law was hundred-law, much of which is now the common law of England. The hundred and its law survived all the storms which wrecked dynasties and Witan. It was the foundation of the judicial constitution under the Conqueror as it had been under Cnut and Alfred. Nor is this principle contradicted by the fact that the Conqueror, like Charlemagne, and perhaps too like Alfred, Cnut, and Edward the Confessor, occasionally sent special judges to hear special cases in these courts, and to decide them by the royal, equitable procedure, which substituted the *inquisitio per testes* for the oath and ordeal. Excepting the royal equitable jurisdiction, hundred-law was the sole law of England. The Conqueror, however, in an unlucky moment, allowed the archbishops and archdeacons to withdraw from the hundred-court all cases involving the Church, and to decide them in ecclesiastical courts, *non secundum hundret sed secundum canones,* not by hundred but by canon law. But neither William I. nor his sons, nor Stephen, nor even Henry II., made any essential change in the judicial constitution. The Assize of Clarendon merely shows the more regular and developed use of a power which seems to have been exercised by

Alfred nearly three centuries before. The introduction into the judicial procedure of those new forms of proof which were to exclude the oath and the ordeal proceeded, as Glanvil says, from the highest equity, but was hardly in itself a revolution in the old constitution. The real change came when the king's judges, who had hitherto been chiefly bishops and sheriffs, and had sat in the county or hundred courts, began to form a professional class, and by means of their equitable powers drew suits before a court of their own. Thus their jurisdiction gradually overlay the old hundred-jurisdiction and sucked the blood from it; but even then the hundred died slowly, inch by inch, peacefully, and without a moment of cessation in the continuity of English law. One of the best paragraphs in Mr. Stubbs's book describes the result:

The fixing of the Common Pleas at Westminster broke up the unity of the Curia, but it was not until the end of the reign of Henry III. that the general staff was divided into three distinct and permanent bodies of judges, each under its own chief. But the court or courts thus organized must no longer be regarded as the last resource of suitors. The reservation of knotty cases to be decided by the king with the council of his wise men, continues the ancient personal jurisdiction of the sovereign. The very act that seems to give stability and consistency to the ordinary jurisdiction of the Curia, reduces it to a lower rank. The judicial supremacy of the king is not limited or fettered by the new rule; it has thrown off an offshoot, or, as the astronomical theorists would say, a nebulous envelope, which has rolled up into a compact body, but the old nucleus of light remains unimpaired. The royal justice, diffused through the close personal council, or tempered and adapted by royal grace and equity under the pen of the chancellor, or exercised in the national assembly as in the ancient witenagemots, or concentrated in the hands of an irresponsible executive in the Star Chamber, has for many generations and in many various forms to assert its vitality, unimpaired by its successive emanations.

Yet, notwithstanding this great development of royal justice, the old hundred-jurisdiction long retained vitality, and especially in the form of manorial courts has retained it down to our own time. The manorial jurisdiction has given rise to much confusion of ideas. It is perhaps popularly supposed that, under Norman influence, the manor court created a new and peculiar kind of law in England; that it wrung sovereignty from the Crown and their liberties from the people, and set up a legal system of its own. On this point again Mr. Stubbs is not so clear as one would wish. He neither states the nature and extent of manorial jurisdiction in England with all the preciseness possible, nor compares it with that in France and Germany, nor does he even declare any very decided opinion as to its historical origin. Indeed, on this point he returns to what has been above criticised as a very hazardous opinion in regard to the township. Starting apparently from the former assumption that the township was the unit of constitutional machinery, he quotes Ordericus to the effect that the manor was merely the ancient township now held by a feudal lord, and then adds: "The manorial constitution is the lowest form of judicial organization. . . . . Every manor had a court-baron, the ancient gemot of the township, ... and a court customary." Possibly Mr. Stubbs may be right, but it would be extremely interesting to know on what evidence he rests his assertion that the court-baron was the ancient gemot of the township. Surely the charter of Richard I., already referred to, is not all the evidence he has to offer on this point, though it is all that is furnished. On the other hand, Mr. Stubbs knows better than any one else, and intimates in various places that the jurisdiction of the court-baron, which is certainly the true object of interest, was not the jurisdiction of the township-gemot, but of the hundred. Almost in the next line to that above quoted, he goes on to say that certain manors "had also a court-leet or criminal jurisdiction cut out, as it were, from the criminal jurisdiction of the hundred." If the criminal jurisdiction of the manorial court came from the hundred, Mr. Stubbs ought at least to have said where the civil jurisdiction came from. Certainly not from the township. Undoubtedly both civil and criminal jurisdiction came from the hundred, for the simple reason that there was no other source from which it could have come. Every legal authority has always assumed it to be hundred-jurisdiction. Scroggs and Scriven, Gneist, even Mr. Stubbs himself, are in accord on this point. At least Mr. Stubbs, on the following page, says in a note that the jurisdiction of the hundreds fell more especially into the hands of the territorial proprietors, whose courts "were in fact, as they had been earlier, public jurisdictions vested in private hands."

The manorial court, as known in the later law, was a private hundred; its jurisdiction was the same, its constitution the same, its procedure the same, as those of the hundred. The continuity of history requires that this point should be strongly asserted. By confusing manorial jurisdiction with the jurisdiction of some unknown village police-court, the logical development of the judicial constitution is seriously disturbed. No one would for an instant suppose that Mr. Stubbs is ignorant of the facts, but there is a certain vagueness in his modes of expression which sometimes leaves the reader in the dark as to his actual opinion, and on a capital point like this no historian can afford to be vague. Too much stress cannot be laid on the fact that manorial jurisdiction was in its origin and essence hundred jurisdiction; unless, indeed, the author believes that it was not hundred jurisdiction, and in that case too much stress cannot be laid on the negative. The mere fact that the popular court was at one period presided over by an elected officer, at another by a royal official, and at a third by a lord of the manor, makes no difference in the legal character of the institution. Whatever happened in France, it would be hard to prove that any baron ever wrung one attribute of sovereignty from the grasp of the Norman kings. The manorial courts after, as before, the conquest, were but private hundred-courts, in which, not the lord, but the freemen declared the law, and such they have ever remained. The chain which unites our modern judicial constitution with that of Alfred the Great is perfect in its more archaic as in its more royal sequence.

This notice has already exceeded its proper limits, and there is no space left for examining Professor Stubbs's treatment of the great ecclesiastical questions in which he is peculiarly at home. But perhaps a critic may be allowed to express regret that he is not to have the assistance of Professor Stubbs's great knowledge and judgment in regard to one point which is of some interest to specialists. An active controversy has for years occupied much attention in Germany on the relative merits of the two characteristically Germanic or modern systems of judicial machinery,—that of the jury, and that of the Echevins, Schöffen, or Scabini. English historians have hitherto been so exclusively interested in their own jury system as to show little interest in that other procedure which was once its rival. Yet there are indications which suggest that even in England the older institution may have been for a long period in active existence. Mr. Stubbs does indeed call attention to the fact that in the twelfth century justice appears to have been administered in the shire-court by a distinct class of freemen who were bound by oath to the honest performance of their duties. He points out that there was a very numerous body of men, distinct from the ordinary members of the court, upon whom the duty fell of acting as *judices* or *juratores,* and whose fines for neglect of that duty fill the Pipe Roll of Henry I. "The judges and jurors of Yorkshire owe a hundred pounds that they may no more be judges or jurors"; and so in a number of other cases. Mr. Stubbs is, however, very cautious in expressing an opinion as to the precise functions of these judges and jurors. That at so early a time they could have had little in common with modern jurors, is obvious. But the same class of men seems to be meant by the paragraph in the so-called Laws of Henry I.: "Regis judices sunt barones comitatus qui liberas in eis terras habent, per quos debent causæ singulorum alterna prosecutione tractari." And their existence would seem to go back into Anglo-Saxon times, if any inference can be drawn from entries in Domesday like that in the Customs of Chester: "Tunc (tempore regis Edwardi) erant XII judices civitatis, et hi erant de hominibus regis et episcopi et comitis: horum si quis de hundred remanebat die quo sedebat, sine excusatione manifesta, X solidis emendabat inter regem et comitem." To the same institution may possibly be traced the reference in the Consultum de Monticolis Walliæ, a document which is commonly ascribed to the age of Ethelred, but which Schmid inclines to refer to that of Athelstan or even earlier: "XII lahmen, i.e. legis homines debent rectum discernere Walis et Englis, VI Walisei et VI Anglici; et perdant omne quod suum est si injuste judicent, vel se adlegient quod rectius nescierunt." There may not be sufficient evidence to prove the adoption into the English constitution of the Frankish Schöffen system, but there is certainly enough to make it desirable that the point should be more thoroughly investigated, and its constitutional interest explained.

13

KITCHIN'S 'HISTORY OF FRANCE'

Adams did not believe that any and every part of history could become a subject for a successful historical narrative. He instead believed that a story can succeed only if it has a "central interest" and that the presence or lack of such an interest inheres in the particular occurrences the historian studies.

In the rather miscellaneous sketch below, Adams directs attention to a subject, French feudalism, which he may have thought could lend a "central interest" to a historical narrative; but the subject is one he strongly disliked, as being aristocratic and thus, in his eyes, representative of "a disorganized state of society." Along the way in the sketch, he directs attention also to the career of an early French king, Henry I. Indeed he stops and tells the king's story.

His doing so deserves notice because, in the future, while attempting to write a great historical narrative, Adams would write many other things, several of which would be ambitious biographies. It also deserves notice for a subtler reason. He says about the French king, "He followed paths of tortuous and secret intrigue, which at this day can only be divined from their results." The line is memorable, relates to an eleventh-century Frenchman, yet also applies to a nineteenth-century American—at least in some portions of his career. And, considering that both were named Henry, the line appears to show that Adams knowingly would write at times about someone else partly as a means of writing also, and very pointedly, about himself.

—*North American Review* (October 1874); unsigned—

A History of France down to the Year 1453. By G. W. KITCHIN, M. A., formerly Censor of Christ Church, Oxford. At the Clarendon Press. 1873.

THIS book is a considerable improvement on the ordinary school-history of English production. Mr. Kitchin is, it is true, a little infected with the pedantry which Mr. Freeman has made fashionable, and appears to imagine that he recommends a text-book by writing it, as he says, "from original sources," instead of following the results gained by far deeper students than himself. But this is a mild species of affectation which has the excuse of thoroughly good intention, and is only mentioned here because it seems to have really injured the usefulness of the book, as will be seen hereafter; a result not wholly encouraging to such students as hoped to see better fruit from the new English school. In other respects, however, the result is more satisfactory. The author has taken some trouble with his maps and tables, which are the most useful parts of his work, and may perhaps be exact and extensive enough for ordinary scholars. Yet more thorough students, especially in the universities, will regret that the author could not overcome his apparent terror of tediousness so far as to make the tables and maps even more complete than they are, especially in regard to genealogies. In mediæval French history, countries like Flanders, Normandy, Burgundy, Anjou, Champagne, Acquitaine, are quite as important as the duchy of France. The succession in their ruling families, the dates of accession, the marriages and the deaths, are essential to any tolerably informed reader. Mr. Kitchin could not do better than to amplify his Tables VI. and VII., as well as his royal genealogies, until they contain all that can be desired in regard to the great feudal families of France. So too with the useful Table IX. of successive additions to the French monarchy, a less rigid conciseness would be an advantage. For example, we are told that Provence was annexed in 1487, on the death of the last count. Some risk of confusion would be avoided by explaining the fate of the marquisate as well as of the county. Among the innumerable perplexities of French history the relations of Navarre to France are one special source of exasperation to ordinary students; an explanation of this difficulty in the tables would be very welcome. Yet of course no one can require that Mr. Kitchin should reprint the huge tomes of the *Art de vérifier les Dates,* and it cannot be expected that he should satisfy every kind of reader.

Of the author's skill as a story-teller the less scholarlike part of the public will perhaps think more highly than of his efforts to produce accurate maps and tables. His difficulty lies, however, deep in the nature of the subject. France has no early history of which one can make a central interest. As a Roman province, her affairs can be made important only by connecting them with the fate of the Empire. Gaul had no separate political life. With the disappearance of Rome's authority arose new divisions,—Acquitaine, Burgundy, Neustria,— whose activity forms properly a part of the larger movement of German civilization, and ends in the glories of Charlemagne's empire. Even after the separation of France and Germany, and the election of the first national king, the history of the new kingdom remains almost absolutely subordinate to that of Germany and the Church, and can be understood only by studying the larger subject. This is so much the case that French historians, even M. Guizot himself, turn their backs with contempt on this early portion of their national records, and refuse to tell even what is known, little as this is. Not until near the year 1200 does France assume an authority in European affairs. Such a story is of course broken, desultory, and dreary, and the attempt to tell it as though there were any consecutive interest in it must always fail.

More than this, Mr. Kitchin is so deeply impressed with the necessity of amusing and of calling attention to the "original authorities," that he sometimes fails to cover the whole field of vision. The petty squabbles of small feudal lords are of little consequence, except so far as they connect themselves with the great movement of Church and Empire. When they do so their importance is obvious. The French kings before Philip Augustus left no marks on history that are worth recalling, except where they interfered with or were used by the popes and emperors. But they were incessantly interfering in this manner. One of the early Capetians, Robert I., who is treated with contempt and pity by Mr. Kitchin and the French historians, began his career by an ambitious marriage with Bertha of Arles, who brought her husband a claim to the throne of Burgundy. The German Emperor and the German Pope Gregory V. at once compelled Robert to give

up this match on the nominal ground of too close relationship, and
Robert at once chose the next most ambitious match in his power, that
with the house of Acquitaine, to which Germany appears to have offered no objection. Mr. Kitchin seems to be quite unaware of this
political intrigue, and wastes, like most historians, some needless sympathy on Robert's blighted affections.

So again in regard to Robert's son, King Henry I., it might have
been well to qualify the expressions of contempt with which, on the
authority of an Angevin chronicle, Mr. Kitchin and every other English and French historian mention him. The German records are by
no means so dogmatic on the subject, and if Mr. Kitchin had been
contented to quote even very second-hand German books, he might
have shown reasons for doubting the truth of the Angevin account.
In some respects the reign of Henry I. was dramatically interesting.
That king reigned contemporaneously with one of the most able and
powerful of the German emperors, Henry III. He was, too, a contemporary of some very extraordinary characters,—Leo IX., Victor II.,
Hildebrand, afterwards Gregory VII., William the Conqueror, Ma-
tilda of Tuscany, the Guiscards, Godfrey of Lorraine, and many of
less note but of marked ability. From Mr. Kitchin's account one would
suppose that the French king was utterly incapable of holding his own
among these great powers, but the facts hardly bear out this theory.
It so happens that the French throne was at that time an object of the
Emperor's most elaborate attacks. The Emperor was absolute master
of the Papacy, he had married into the great and in fact royal house
of Acquitaine, and this alliance connected him closely with Anjou.
France was therefore hemmed in by his influence, and he intended to
reduce her Capetian king to the same condition of vassalage to which
his predecessor Otto the Great had a century earlier reduced the
Carolingian monarch. Against this result the Capetian, whose actual
power as compared with that of Henry III. was not much greater than
that of a good-sized German bishopric or margraviate, struggled for
years and struggled with success. The means he used were naturally
not those of armed force, since he had no army and no means to
create one. He followed paths of tortuous and secret intrigue, which
at this day can only be divined from their results. But then, as often
since, French intrigue was successful. The autocratic policy of the
Emperor caused resistance in Germany. Godfrey of Lorraine and

Baldwin of Flanders rose in arms. France encouraged and fomented the rebellion. It was crushed, but soon began again, more formidable than ever, and the Empire was in every direction undermined by conspiracy. How decisive a part the despised French King Henry I. played in this matter may be judged from the following extract from an "original source," which may be found cited in any German history of merit:

> 1056. Imperator regressus de Italia . . . . perrexit ad villam Civois, in confinio sitam regni Francorum ac Teutonicorum, colloquium ibi habiturus cum rege Francorum. A quo contumeliose atque hostiliter objurgatus, quod multa sæpe sibi mentitus fuisset, et quod partem maximam regni Francorum dolo a patribus ejus occupatam, reddere tam diu distulisset; cum imperator paratum se diceret singulariter cum eo conserta manu objecta refellere, ille proxima nocte fuga lapsus in suos se fines recepit.

In short, the Emperor had apparently tried to buy off the opposition of France by a secret offer of Lorraine, just as Bismarck is charged with having done to Napoleon. Finding that France was not to be quieted thus, the Emperor sought an interview with the king, which took place. As the price of neutrality the king demanded Lorraine, and met a sharp refusal, whereupon the two monarchs gave each other the lie, and the German challenged the Frenchman. If this does not prove that the Capetian was by no means insignificant, original sources are indeed useless. One can only add that the Emperor went home from this interview a broken-down man; that he immediately made peace with Godfrey and Baldwin on their own terms, and died, leaving Godfrey the most powerful man in Europe, to develop with Hildebrand's aid that influence hostile to the Empire which was to build up Norman and French power on the ruins of Germany. Had it not been for Henry I., who can say that Hildebrand would ever have seen a suppliant Emperor at the gates of Canossa?

Again: Mr. Kitchin says that Henry I. and Philip I. "suffered Norman William to win a new kingdom, unhelped, unhindered." The conquest took place in 1066. Henry I. died in 1060. Had Norman William attempted to win his new kingdom while Henry was alive, the statement would be more accurate. Further: as Philip I. was then a child of about twelve years, it is hardly to be wondered at that "the foolish young king," as Mr. Kitchin says, should have "listened to his counsellors," even though they gave him the excellent advice not to aid William. "The poor creature's tastes" would have been very mar-vellous if, at that age, he had refused to listen to his counsellors.

On page 205 Mr. Kitchin gives a sketch of the accession of Leo IX. to the Papacy. He assumes that Leo first obtained his notions of ec-clesiastical polity from Hildebrand while passing a night at Cluny on his way to Rome as elected Pope. Hildebrand was, no doubt, "one of the world's giants," as the author says, but there is no use in overstating his influence. There is no sufficient reason to suppose that Leo IX., a man of very unusual strength of will and character, was ever greatly under Hildebrand's influence. At that time Hildebrand played indeed a very subordinate part in the Church.

If a student going into examination for his degree were asked what was the legal ground upon which Philip Augustus adjudged John of England to be forfeit of his fief of Normandy, he would probably reply, if he relied upon Mr. Kitchin, that this ground was the charge that John had murdered Prince Arthur. Yet such a reply ought to cost an English student his degree, since there are few subjects in English mediæval history which ought to be taught more exactly and in which accuracy ought to be more urgently required than that of the loss of Normandy. Almost any second-hand authority states the case more clearly than it is stated here.

These, however, are only small instances of what must be called slovenly work. The chapter on Feudalism and Chivalry can only be qualified as downright rubbish. "We know," begins the author, "that conquering races, settling in a new land, possess themselves of the soil, while the former owners fall away into dependence and slavery. We know that when the Germans seized on Gaul this was the case." We know just the contrary. That the Roman land-owners retained their land, and that feudal dependence was not the subjection of one race to the other, is a part of the alphabet of feudal history. "The lord had full power, in cases even of life and death, over the original inhabitants of the land who became villains or serfs." Mr. Kitchin should have quoted his authority for these facts, which to the vulgar ear seem to echo the statements of no original source, but only of a modern and highly imaginative French historian.

If feudalism, which as it appeared in France was but a disorganized state of society, can be called a political institution, the honor of in-venting it belongs to France, and every history of that country is all

the more bound to give the most accurate account of feudalism, because it may almost be characterized as the only very important political institution which France ever has originated down to the present
day. Yet there is not in the whole range of literature, English, French,
or German, a sketch of French feudalism which is even approximately
complete or can be used for instruction. Mr. Kitchin settles the difficulty by giving no account at all. Without attempting to define the
institution, which he says originated in "confusions and anomalies,"
he flies off at once to the "clean-cut theory," exhibited in the *assises* of
Jerusalem, which had about as much to do with France as the United
States Constitution with that of England; that is, the study of feudalism there is positively misleading to the student of French history. Mr.
Kitchin, however, again escapes the difficulty. After telling us that "the
feudal towers of Jerusalem stand up in strong relief, bright under the
western sun, against the thunder-cloud of the Moslem power, ever
ready to enwrap them in its angry storm," and that there were three
courts of justice in the kingdom, he makes no attempt at further
explanation or analysis, but again hops away to another branch of his
subject, and chirrups about the "page in my lady's bower," and the
other commonplaces of chivalry. In comparison with such fine writing,
the French series of historical text-books which bear the name of
M. Duruy rise to the dignity of historical monuments. Mr. Kitchin
could not do better in a new edition than to omit the whole chapter
on Feudalism, and substitute for it a simple translation of that in the
Moyen Age of M. Duruy.

14

PARKMAN'S 'OLD RÉGIME IN CANADA'

Adams's admiration of Parkman as a historian remained an admiration but became a limited one, as this sketch subtly shows. The trouble, it seems, was that Adams, who sometimes subordinated his love of art to his zeal in science, suspected his older friend of being his opposite—of permitting art to subordinate knowledge.

The older man did two things which for Adams were greatly restorative of admiration. The better to understand the experiences of the French and the English in America, Parkman plundered the archives of Europe. Using new materials found abroad, he wrote a thought-provoking book, to which this sketch is an appreciative annex.

Parkman's book was thought-provoking for Adams in part because Adams saw two phenomena forever opposed in history: conservatism and innovation. Himself inclined to study innovation, he was the more delighted that his friend should have taken it upon himself to study and write about an act of conservatism.

The innovation Adams wished to write about was the creation of the United States. The subject of Parkman's book was the creation of Canada. The two subjects seemed to recommend and require each other.

—*North American Review* (January 1875); unsigned—

The Old Régime in Canada. By FRANCIS PARKMAN. Boston: Little, Brown, & Co. 1874.

IN the series of works which have placed Mr. Parkman among the first of American historical writers, this volume deserves to rank high-

est. This is to be understood, however, as the estimate of a literary
critic only, not as that of the public. That book will of course have the
most readers which interests or amuses the largest number, and it is
very possible that more than one of Mr. Parkman's previous volumes
have a more absorbing and more consecutive interest than this. By
natural inclination and cast of mind Mr. Parkman has an objective
way of dealing with history. He prefers to follow action rather than to
meditate upon it, to relate rather than to analyze, to describe the
adventures of individuals rather than the slow and complicated move-
ments of society. This lends to his books a freshness and a simplicity
of structure which are very agreeable, and which in turn suit well the
general subject he has chosen. In following out this subject, he has
now, however, entered a wider field of thought. The present volume
deals with matters which, if not themselves of the highest philosophical
interest, are still on one side at least illustrative of great and permanent principles in political science. The story he tells is curious and
unusual. The annals of America are rich in illustrations of the various
methods by which new states may be created. Virginia, Maryland,
Pennsylvania, New York, Massachusetts, have each furnished striking
examples of experiments in colonization and of the results which different processes may attain. But in each of these cases, even where,
as in New York, the interests of the Colony were most subordinate to
the interests of European governments or corporations, a wide range
of independent action was still allotted to the colonists themselves, who
were left to work out their own destinies so far as their aims did not
clash with more powerful political or commercial interests at home.
To complete the series in these experiments on human nature, and
to fill up one great void in the subject, an example was needed of
what could be done by the faithful effort of a truly paternal government to found and support a new state on principles of protection.
Such a government, at least with reference to Canada, was that of
Louis XIV. The principles on which he acted and the motives by which
he was influenced appear to have been as elevated and as honest as
human nature can ever hope to attain. His ambition, in this instance
at all events, was laudable and to a certain extent justifies his claim to
the title of Great. Holding as he did strong opinions as to the nature
of government, the necessity of a union between Church and State,
the importance of religion as part of a well-ordered society, and to

the unconditional but if possible voluntary submission of the people to the will of their king and their church, he undertook to realize these theories in a practical form in the New World, far away from the possibility of interference. Mr. Parkman describes the colony as he ruled it. A line of dwellings ranged along the river-shores, with the dense wilderness behind them, and at Quebec a cluster of some seventy houses, contained the population which was to form the future state. A population so situated, exposed on every side to the temptations of savage life, and pushed by many motives to the wildest sort of liberty, was considered and treated by Louis as though it were a model farm within the park of Versailles. The theories of paternal government and the facts of natural liberty never came into sharper contrast. Mr. Parkman has drawn these contrasts with great skill; his work is that of an artist. On the one side he collects all the curious details which an elaborate search through the French archives and elsewhere has brought to light, in regard to the king's care for the colony; his lavish expenditure; his minute instructions to the royal officials; and his religious zeal for the eternal welfare of those who were so peculiarly dependent on his bounty. On the other side are described in strong colors the natural forces which were unceasingly in action to neutralize the king's efforts and to undo his work. Of these the two most potent appear to have been the beaver-trade and the Indian women, although a natural antipathy to the dull and penurious life of the *habitant* lay at the foundation of the uncontrollable restlessness. How serious the defection was, and how deeply the morals of this carefully guarded community were affected, is told by Mr. Parkman in the words of the original documents. "The intendant Duchesneau reported that eight hundred men out of a population of less than ten thousand souls had vanished from sight in the immensity of a boundless wilderness. Whereupon the king ordered that any person going into the woods without a license should be whipped and branded for the first offence, and sent for life to the galleys for the second." The penalty of death was added, but equally without avail. "You are aware, Monseigneur" (writes Denonville), "that the *coureurs de bois* are a great evil, but you are not aware how great this evil is. It deprives the country of its effective men; makes them indocile, debauched, and incapable of discipline, and turns them into pretended nobles, wearing the sword and decked out with lace, both they and their relations, who all affect to be gentlemen and ladies. As for cultivating the soil, they will not hear of it. This, along with the scattered condition of the settlements, causes their children to be as unruly as Indians, being brought up in the same manner." Of the morals of this class of men, some idea may be formed from the curious letter of the Père Carheil dated at "Michilimakina, le 30 d'Aoust, 1702," and given in the original by Mr. Parkman, Appendix H. The particulars given by the holy father were too strong for Mr. Parkman to translate into his text, and the curious had best look them up for themselves. The sum is that "tous les villages de nos Sauvages ne sont plus que des cabarets pour l'ivrognerie et des Sodomes pour l'impureté." "It was a curious scene when a party of *coureurs de bois* returned from their rovings. Montreal was their harboring-place, and they conducted themselves much like the crew of a man-of-war paid off after a long voyage. As long as their beaver-skins lasted they set no bounds to their riot. Every house in the place, we are told, was turned into a drinking-shop. The new-comers were bedizened with a strange mixture of French and Indian finery; while some of them, with instincts more thoroughly savage, stalked about the streets as naked as a Pottawattamie or a Sioux. The clamor of tongues was prodigious, and gambling and drinking filled the day and the night. When at last they were sober again, they sought absolution for their sins, nor could the priests venture to bear too hard on their unruly penitents, lest they should break wholly with the Church and dispense thenceforth with her sacraments."

"One cannot but remember," says Mr. Parkman in commenting upon the unruliness of the Canadians whom twenty-eight companies of regular troops could not keep in order even in 1736, "that in a neighboring colony, far more populous, perfect order prevailed, with no other guardians than a few constables chosen by the people themselves." But while admitting the force of this curious and dramatic contrast, one must also remember that the "order" of New England was in the eyes of Louis XIV. and ninety-nine Europeans in every hundred, the height and license of disorder, anarchy, and wickedness. Even in England few persons indeed could have been found to defend and justify the institutions or the order of Massachusetts Bay. One must judge a creation to some extent by the objects of its authors. The first object of the French monarch appears to have been to found a French society in the New World, which should reflect and support his ideas of obedience and docility in politics and religion. Commercial and military success belonged more peculiarly to the government at home. In spite of the difficulties he encountered, in spite of *coureurs de bois,* drunkenness, the climate, the English, and all economical laws, it cannot be said that the experiment failed. On the contrary, its remarkable and permanent success is the very point which makes it worth studying at all. One cannot deny that the character stamped by Louis upon this favorite political creation has been on the whole the most permanent of all the achievements of that once great monarch. The exciting adventures which Mr. Parkman loves to relate, and which gain so much under his touch, the daring exploits of Jesuits and *gentilshommes,* the vices and lawlessness of the *coureurs de bois,* were but the more or less inevitable consequences, the appendages, and one might almost say the dramatic *mise en scène,* which introduced the new society to existence. The real subject of interest, which survived Jesuits, Indians, and all the external forms of its original foundation, which survived conquest itself, and has proved the solidity of its foundation by preserving the stamp of Louis XIV. through all the vicissitudes of a century of alien rule, the true core of Canadian history is of necessity the quiet and industrious part of the colony, whose manners and mode of life are admirably described in this volume. It is true that this people has added nothing to the sum of political knowledge, and has neither originated nor followed new paths of philosophy or science. The interest that connects itself with them, such as it is, arises from the fact that this negative career was the very object for which they were created. Had they, like their English neighbors, led in the march of progress, and begun by discarding their old gods and their old creed, the scientific interest in them would be of a very different kind. As it is, they have completely realized the ideas of their founder. They are one of the few examples of a conservative triumph. The political and religious conceptions of the *Ancien Régime* were successfully propagated here, and even to-day the spirit of Louis XIV. might look down upon them with satisfaction and challenge mankind to show a more perfect community, according to those ideas of perfection which the Church and Legitimacy maintain.

As the colony itself is the centre of interest, so the public life of the colony is the principal object of study, as showing how the desired results were obtained. And here the industry of Mr. Parkman has left little to be asked. Every detail is presented that can throw light on the actions and motives of the actors. Necessarily one great factor of interest is wanting, since the people neither had nor claimed any share in the management of their affairs. The colony was an experiment destined to prove that the Crown and the Church were more capable of conducting a good government than the people could be. It must be allowed that both the Crown and the Church did their duty faithfully and on the whole successfully. It is true that in the investigation Mr. Parkman has brought to light some facts in regard to the first Bishop of Quebec, Laval Montmorency, which will perhaps sound rather harshly to Canadians whose reverence for Laval is hardly less than that they feel for the most sacred names in Church history. Mr. Parkman incidentally shows that he was arbitrary and not always just; that he put incompetent men into office, and "made men charged with gross public offences the prosecutors and judges in their own cause." On the other hand, it must be allowed that in doing what he did he seems only to have acted according to his own ideas of public good, and quite within the accepted principles of the Church. Mr. Parkman's account of Laval is rather calculated to raise than to lower his reputation for worldly ability, whatever effect it may have upon his reputation as a Saint. But whatever may have been his shortcomings, he toiled devotedly for his people, and if he occasionally set the Church above the State, or uttered the sentiment so annoying to the governor d'Argenson, that "a bishop can do what he likes," he was still the most effective servant the king ever had in Canada; and Louis showed great wisdom in ignoring the faults he committed, and in sustaining him against the civil and military officials. If Canada owed much to Louis XIV., her principal debt was that he gave her Laval.

Of the episodes of adventure with which the volume abounds, less need be said. The public is familiar with Mr. Parkman's skill as a *raconteur*. But the reader's interest can only increase as Mr. Parkman goes on to give the public, as he alone can do, an account from the Canadian standpoint of those bloody wars with the English colonies, which, carried on as they were under great disadvantages of numbers and resources, can hardly fail to excite wonder and deep interest at Canadian energy and enterprise.

15

VON HOLST'S 'ADMINISTRATION OF ANDREW JACKSON'

Histories of the United States had been appearing from the time the Constitution was ratified. An instance especially relevant to Henry Adams was a three-volume work by John Adams, *A Defense of the Constitution,* published in 1787–1788 and continued in a one-volume work, *Discourses on Davila,* written in 1790. A copy of the four volumes owned by John Quincy Adams was uniformly bound in calf and lettered on the spines *Adams's History of the Republic.*[1]

That Henry Adams when a child saw his grandfather's copy of his great-grandfather's *History* seems a fair assumption. It also seems a fair assumption that growing Henry began by supposing that politics and history were congenial and he could be a politician and historian quite without harm to himself in either capacity. But how much he remained a politician when he wrote these sketches may be a hard question to answer on the basis of the sketches themselves. In the sketch that follows, he may seem purely the historian, who as a service to history translates for American readers portions of an emerging German account of democracy and constitutionality in the United States. Yet, restudied, the sketch can acquire a quite opposite appearance. It might be urged that Adams puts on his cloak of historian and translates things said by another historian merely in order to strike two hard blows as a politician. The blows are directed at generals who became presidents. One blow, perfectly open, falls on Andrew Jackson, an enemy of Adams's grandfather. The other, implied, can only be aimed at an opponent of his own, Ulysses S. Grant.

[1] Goodspeed's Catalogue 492.

Restudied again, this time as politics and history fused, the sketch can be valued for suggesting that Americans have been led in some years by their best, in other years by their most typical, representatives. The idea has obvious very wide application. Advanced by Hermann von Holst, it seems to have elicited Adams's positive interest and complete agreement.

—*North American Review* (January 1875); unsigned—

Die Administration Andrew Jackson's in ihrer Bedeutung für die Entwickelung der Demokratie in den Vereinigten Staaten von Amerika. Von Dr. H. v. HOLST, o. ö. Professor an der Universität Freiburg. Düsseldorf: Julius Buddeus. 1874.

THAT a German professor should think it worth while to establish a course of lectures on American History is a significant event to Americans. Not merely that it indicates the political importance of the country, for political importance alone would not necessarily produce such a result; nor that it implies admiration, for it may just as well imply the contrary. What it does signify is that our country at last is considered as having a history at all, as offering material for scientific treatment. Whether that history is a matter for pride or not, whether it is one which will establish new political ideas in the world, whether it will, even at this early day, bear the test of careful scientific analysis, is the point to be ascertained. All that Americans can appreciate is the fact that their country has had a career which is studied in Germany with the same care and thoroughness that German scholars devote to every branch of knowledge.

At some future time, when Professor von Holst has completed his work on *Verfassung und Demokratie der Vereinigten Staaten,* this Review will devote to it the careful criticism its merits demand. The pamphlet whose title is cited above is but a lecture delivered on entering into the duties of the Freiburg professorship, and is published as a fragment. No doubt it will soon be, if it has not already been, translated. But in order that the public may be able to form an opinion of the temper and knowledge of the author, as well as of his capacities as critic, a few roughly rendered extracts may be given here.

The present lecture begins with an account of the Presidential election of 1824, and, after narrating its result, proceeds to criticise the position assumed by Jackson and his friends:

Jackson had a not inconsiderable plurality of the electoral as well as of the popular vote, and in several States which had voted for Crawford or Clay he was the favorite candidate of the minority. On this ground he maintained that the House of Representatives had presumed to trample upon the will of the people. This was his honest conviction, and this, even more than the personal disappointment, was the source of the bitterness which he displayed at every opportunity in the most unseasonable manner.

The reproach was loudly re-echoed by the people. Naturally the constitutionality of Adams's election was not denied, but its "moral" authority was questioned.

Moral authority, as it was viewed in this conception of the "democratic principle," was not, under all circumstances, covered by the Constitution, and a majority of the people set up with Jackson the demand that the latter should be unconditionally subordinated to the former. This demand not only stood in direct contradiction with the letter and the spirit of the Constitution, but it struck at the principle of the majesty of law; in its ultimate consequences it raised the will of the majority (or on occasion the plurality) of voting citizens to the sole law of the land; it was not a postulate of democracy, but the abrogation of the constitutional state. In a democratic constitutional state the binding rule that regulates the expression of the will of the majority is, legally and "morally," not the expression in any way that may happen, but *only* in the way appointed by the Constitution. Unquestionably, the people's will in such a state is the will of the state; but the highest, the unconditionally controlling expression of the people's will is the Constitution. Beyond its limits lies revolution. The Jackson Democrats demanded the subordination of the well-considered popular will, which had been fixed as a permanent fundamental law, to the momentary wish of the people, which in part could only be ascertained by means of unsafe conjectures.

The constitutional provisions in regard to the election of President rested on two ideas: the election should be indirect, and, in case no candidate received a majority of electoral votes, a more restricted choice should be undertaken by another elective body. Thus the people had been pleased, without admitting an exception of any kind, to forego the direct choice of President, and to intrust that choice to men of their own selection. If there was here any reprehensible infraction of the "democratic principle," the people alone were responsible therefor; if the cause of such infraction of the democratic principle was a want of confidence in "the capacity of the Demos to choose a safe President for themselves," the undemocratic doubt was chargeable only to themselves; if, four years later, the election of Jackson was a victory of the true democratic principle, it was a victory of the people over their own self-appointed provisions, and that too while retaining them in the fundamental law. The people slapped themselves in the face and played pranks with their own Constitution. If the electoral college had without resistance let slip the power intrusted to them and contented themselves with an empty form, their course laid no obligation on the House of Representatives to imitate the example, if the choice fell into its hands. The Constitution required that the House should actually *choose*. A plurality of electoral votes was not to be a sufficient expression of the popular will, for the framers of the Constitution cannot be supposed to have adopted any provision which was intended to be a completely unmeaning and objectless ceremony.

The author then proceeds to the election of 1828 and to the character of Jackson's administration. He gives an elaborate sketch of the democratic policy of rotation in office, for which he holds Jackson only partially responsible, and he gives an estimate of Jackson's character, as follows:

Since Louis XIV., the maxim *l'état c'est moi* has hardly found a second time so naïvely complete expression as in Andrew Jackson, only it was translated from the monarchical to the republican. That such an apparition was possible in the Republic, and that at the same time the political and social-political development should proceed undisturbed and in logical sequence, just as though the extraordinary man had never sat in the President's chair, is easily explained. As Washington was the incorporation of the best traits of the popular American character, Jackson was the incorporation of *all* its typical traits. Unquestionably his was a personality of marked importance, but with all this he was still wholly incapable of raising himself from any point of view to the elevation of a great man, because the misfortune of circumstances in the time of life when he was capable of education kept him in the simple crudity of a child of nature. In spite of the literally fearful influence which he exercised during his eight-year Presidency, he yet showed no controlling genius in pointing out and opening new paths for his nation, but only by the demonic force of his will dragged it faster along the path upon which it long since had moved. The supports of his policy were the instincts of the masses, and its object was the contentment of those instincts; the force of his will brought them into unconditional acceptance.

The author then turns to the controversy in regard to the United States Bank, and follows its course down to the Veto Message, which he thus criticises:

Whatever Jackson's opinion as a private individual may have been, as President he was bound to see in the Bank charter, not only a legally valid, but a constitutional law. If a law has been enacted in a constitutional manner, the Constitution recognizes only one authority, the judicial, which can declare it unconstitutional. Jackson, however, claimed the right,—as President whose

highest duty under the Constitution is the faithful execution of the laws,—
not merely to deny the constitutionality and consequently the validity of a law,
in the absence of any such judicial decision, and to avow this conviction of his
as the motive of his official acts, but he did it in the face of an express decision
of the Supreme Court. It is true he would not admit the judgment in Mc-
Culloch *vs*. The State of Maryland to cover the whole ground, because the
court had declared only the creation of a bank, and not all the provisions of
this particular charter to be constitutional. But the court had also declared
that it was only competent to decide upon the first question, because in regard
to the second the Constitution left full discretion to the legislative authority;
and the legislative authority is Congress, not Congress *and* President.

But Jackson actually went a step further. He flatly denied the competence
of the court to decide the interpretation of the Constitution in similar questions. In the Veto Message it stands: "Every public official who takes an oath
to support the Constitution swears to support it as he understands it, not as
others understand it." This was doubtless true as regarded open questions,
but it was as certainly false in regard to questions which were no longer open,
because that authority which the Constitution vested with the right of final
decision had already given judgment. If the Constitution does not mean to
oblige the executive and the legislature to accept the decision of the Supreme
Court as conclusive in constitutional questions, then there is no such thing as
a constitutional law of the Union; the fundamental idea on which this constitutional state rests is, then, that law shall not rule it; the law negatives itself.
The Supreme Court has then *its* constitutional law; each President his own;
every new majority of Congress theirs; the public law of the Union is in
principle the chaos of law; the decision of a legal question lies beyond the
limits of possibility.

The summing up of Jackson's political career follows the account
of the removal of the deposits:

> The curse of Jackson's administration may be summed up in one word: it
> systematically undermined the public sense of law, and lowered the respect of
> the people for their government. . . . .
> And yet he who was the inventor of this new method claimed to be *par
> excellence* the defender of the Constitution by duty as well as in purpose. This
> quite peculiar position was said to "result from the nature of the office," but
> it was also averred that the founders of the Republic, by means of the oath
> which the President took on entering office, had given to this position "a
> particular solemnity and force."
> The views which, at the close of the last century, were commonly held, not
> only in the United States, but in the rest of the western civilized world, in
> regard to the attitude of the "executive power" towards the free development
> of the people, leave scarcely room for a doubt that the guiding idea in the
> prescription of this oath was not so much to give the Constitution into the

special charge of the President against domestic enemies, as rather to secure the people, so far as this could be done by an oath, against the President's own attacks upon the Constitution. In the Convention at Philadelphia, as in the ratification conventions, much stress was laid on the transference of the executive power to a college, because the history of all times and of all people teaches to what dangers freedom is exposed if too much power is placed in the hands of one man. Whatever the United States may since have learned from bitter experience as to the tendency of the legislature to overstep its legitimate authority, at that time the principle of mistrust of government, on which the continuance of free institutions was supposed to depend, applied primarily to the executive power. Only the most far-sighted recognized that the danger was equally or more seriously threatening from the other side; and only by pointing to the experiences of the War of Independence did they succeed in effecting the co-ordination of the executive with the judicial and especially with the legislative power. But even to their minds it never occurred to make the President the defender of the Constitution as against Congress. That was the domain of the judicial power. The competence of the President in this respect was limited to his qualitative veto. Jackson, however, claimed the right to resist the assumed violations of the Constitution by the Senate, but placed himself altogether above the Senate and between the people and both the other factors of the government. "The President," he declares, is "the *direct* representative of the American people," "chosen by the people and responsible to them"; the Senate, on the other hand, is "a body which is not *directly* accountable to the people." As representative of the people, he owes it therefore also to their representatives to resist the violation of their constitutional prerogatives by the Senate, and his "fixed determination" is "to return unharmed to the people the sacred pledge which they have intrusted to me,— to heal the wounds of the Constitution and to preserve it from further injuries."

The Constitution knows a President only as bearer of the executive power; of a "direct representative of the American people" it knows nothing. Hence, too, it knows nothing of a choice of President "by the people." According to its intention, the electors were to be, not mere figures, but the only actual choosers of the President. And more than this, it does not even cause the electors to be chosen directly by the people, but by the people as divided into States and as represented in the popular house of Congress, giving two additional electors to each State for its representation in the Senate. Finally, the Constitution knew nothing of the President's responsibility to the "people." If Jackson meant only a general political responsibility, certainly no one could object. But such responsibility he shared with every other political personality, and least of all could any rights be derived herefrom. Further, such a general political responsibility could not be called *direct*. In this expression the thought was held out that the people were the legal forum which was to decide in the last resort upon the political acts and omissions of the President. Of such a right of the people, too, the Constitution knows nothing. The only forum before which it summons the President to answer for his political acts and omissions, if the House of Representatives impeaches him, is the Senate. The Constitution nowhere recognizes the "people" in the sense of the word as used by Jackson. It creates legal relations, but it does not overturn the law by raising any haphazard majority of voters over the law, on the ground that their will is the law. It is true that in the United States the "people" are the one original source of law, but it is the people in their strictly defined, collective-political, that is to say, constitutional organization. Every other "people" as an independent source of law, as a lawful political forum, is not only unknown to the Constitution, but is its abolition; for the Constitution aims at creating a state founded on law, and such a people is the negation of such a state. To the "people" in this unconstitutional sense Jackson in his legal controversies always appealed; in other words, the executive magistrate made the subordination of the state to society the guiding principle of the Republic, which was meant to have been, in the most eminent sense of the word, a government of law.

One more extract to show Professor v. Holst's opinion of the tendency of American politics, and this, with the reservation that it is followed in the original by expressions so strong that, however true they may be, they are best read in the original; especially as similar opinions are only too familiar to readers of this Review:

No one expected to see Jackson set up as a candidate for the third time. But with his retirement came also the end of the 'reign of a single man.' Possibly his influence went far enough to make his candidate the party nominee for the succession. But whoever might be his follower, Jackson could not bequeath his influence to him. . . . . The heir to Jackson's authority was not one man, but, on the contrary, the great masses. But in great political commonwealths, and especially in one so peculiarly constituted as the United States, these can practically maintain the rule only for moments. The deception which the permanent heirs of Jackson's power have succeeded in imposing upon the great masses of the American people, for the most part down to the present day, is equally gross and mischievous, namely, that since Jackson's time the rule has been in their (the masses') hands. The undeniable fact, which indeed finds harsh expression, is that since his time the people have begun to exchange the *leadership* of a small number of statesmen and politicians of the higher class for the *rule* of an ever more colossally growing swarm of politicians of all classes down to the political bar-keeper and the common thief in the protecting garb of the demagogue. At first it appeared to be the result of local evils, when people standing on the border between society and the house of correction won a decisive influence in politics. And so long as business developed itself satisfactorily, no one would recognize it as a misfortune that politics became a profession in which mediocrity in an ever-descending scale held sway, and moral laxity was the rule if not the requisite. Live and let live! became to such an extent the universal motto, that politicians were actually astonished at the uprising with which the people broke from the long-accustomed reins when they saw themselves about to be ridden into the abyss, nearer and nearer to which, since the foundation of the Republic, they had partly slipped and had in part been dragged.

16

THE QUINCY MEMOIRS AND SPEECHES

As editor, Adams allotted far more space in his magazine to materials by members of two Massachusetts families, the Adamses and the Quincys, than might seem justified. In the issues he edited, he published six articles and four notices by his brother Charles; an article and two notices by his brother Brooks; two notices by his father (both about books of which the father was editor); three notices by Edmund Quincy (two of them about books by Adamses); and twenty-odd sketches of his own devising, including this one about the two families.

Subscribers and chance readers could not tell how heavily the issues were freighted with Adams and Quincy materials. Of the eighteen contributions by the editor's brothers, father, and Quincy, a mere five were signed—four by Charles, one by Brooks.

Henry had good reason to publish the Adams and Quincy contributions. What could seem a case of concealed favoritism was mostly a case of abject economy. The magazine was desperately short of money, and the editor needed contributors he would not have to pay. It is known that he did not pay his brothers. It can be assumed that he did not pay his father—nor Edmund Quincy, who, in an earlier epoch, had been his father's groomsman. And the money saved permitted better payment by Henry for articles and notices by other contributors.

—*North American Review* (January 1875); unsigned—

1. *Memoir of the Life of Josiah Quincy, Junior, of Massachusetts:* 1744–1775. By his Son, JOSIAH QUINCY. Second edition. Boston: Press of John Wilson and Son. 1874.

2. *Life of Josiah Quincy of Massachusetts.* By his Son, EDMUND QUINCY. Sixth edition. Boston: Little, Brown, & Co. 1874.

3. *Speeches delivered in the Congress of the United States.* by JOSIAH QUINCY. 1805–1813. Edited by his Son, EDMUND QUINCY. Boston: Little, Brown, & Co. 1874.

IN these books the public has at last the advantage of possessing a uniform and excellent edition of the memoirs and personal remains of the two Quincys. There is, it is true, nothing in these three volumes which is new, except the title-pages. There is nothing, therefore, to justify an extended criticism, or to call for renewed examination, so far at least as the separate volumes are concerned. Yet taking them together, as a series, their appearance in this new form may be said to create almost a new work.

The "Saturday Review," or some such English periodical, in noticing, not long since, the new Memoirs of Mr. J. Q. Adams, informed its readers, with its usual depth of study and zeal for sound information, that the Adams family was the only one in all America which could be considered as a family at all, in the English sense of the term. Never was there a grosser misconception of the society which the reviewer attempted to describe. From a Massachusetts point of view, the Adamses are hardly a family at all; they are a creation of yesterday, barely a century old. The Quincys are, strictly speaking, an old family. They belonged to the colonial aristocracy. The first Edmund Quincy came to Boston with John Cotton in 1633. From that day to this, the family has always been a prominent one in the colonial and State annals. In a community which, with a pure democracy, is still second to none in the tenacity with which it maintains family traditions and pride of descent, and where hardly a distinguished family name of the colonial time is without its living and pugnacious representative to-day, the Quincys are an interesting and an important historical study.

Few readers need to be told how attractive the two Memoirs of father and son are to all persons who rise above the level of novels. Mr. Edmund Quincy's Life of his father is a model, as all the world knows; that father's Life of his own father is less known to this generation, but not less worth reading. The Life of the elder Quincy is, however, only a fragment; he died at thirty-one. The younger Quincy lived to be ninety-two, but, with the true instinct of the old colonial families, cut short his own most brilliant national career at forty-one, and retired to the more congenial pursuits of his native city and Province. To complete the record of his Congressional life, his speeches are now published in a separate volume. The merits or defects of these are matters for more serious consideration than can now be given them; but if any despondent patriot of the present day, inclined to despair at the condition of public affairs, wishes to obtain comfort and encouragement, he can easily do so by reading Mr. Josiah Quincy's speeches and the comments of Mr. Edmund Quincy upon them. If John Adams could console Josiah Quincy in 1811 by writing that "we were no better than you," the generation of 1875 may obtain similar comfort at the same source.

17

BANCROFT'S 'HISTORY OF THE UNITED STATES'

Adams was interested in both peace and war; but, as he said of Jefferson, peace was his passion. Certain chapters of American history accordingly had particular meaning for him. They were the *Trent* Affair in 1861, when a third war between America and England was barely avoided, in some measure through his own exertions; the negotiation at Ghent in 1815, by John Quincy Adams, among others, which ended the second war between America and England; an action in 1799 by John Adams as president which averted an incipient war between America and France; and the negotiation in Paris in 1782, mainly by Benjamin Franklin, which ended the first war between America and England.

The paragraphs below may not be greatly important as a review of Bancroft's *History*. They are important for being Adams's "sketch" of the diplomacy of Franklin—hence of a chapter of history which, as Adams saw things, made all American chapters possible.[1]

—*North American Review* (April 1875); unsigned—

History of the United States from the Discovery of the American Continent. By GEORGE BANCROFT. Vol. X. Boston: Little, Brown, & Co. 1874.

THE first impression created by Mr. Bancroft's tenth volume is that he is hastening his steps. There is no sign of weariness, but there are

[1]In a letter to Bancroft dated 10 January [1885], Adams said that "the diplomatic part of that notice was alone mine." But the notice is almost all "diplomatic"; its parts are in one style and share one vocabulary; and it can be held that Adams alone wrote the notice in its entirety.

unmistakable marks of haste, and these are sometimes annoying, as, for example, the omission of all maps and plans of battles, and also of an index. The reason is not far to seek. Mr. Bancroft is no longer young. The first volume of this work appeared forty years ago, and at the same rate of progress its conclusion was impossible. One can hardly find fault with the author whose haste springs from the earnestness of his wish to complete his task.

Undoubtedly, too, Mr. Bancroft's work improves as it goes on. This last volume is an immense advance upon the first two or three of the series. No doubt Mr. Bancroft entertains as ardent a faith now as forty years ago in the abstract virtues of democracy and "the gentle feelings of humanity," but time and experience have tempered this faith with a more searching spirit of criticism than was fashionable in the days of President Jackson. Not that Mr. Bancroft has or ever will have a strictly judicial mind, to whatever age he may live, but that his idiosyncrasies are now less prominent in his pages; and an acquaintance with the details of his subject, far more extensive than that of any other individual, living or dead, now gives those pages a practical value which the critic must begin by acknowledging in the fullest and frankest terms. In order to criticise at all, one must use the materials which Mr. Bancroft himself has supplied.

The present volume covers a very important period both in military and civil affairs. The military history embraces the campaigns of 1778, 1779, 1780, and 1781; and thus includes the retreat of the British from Philadelphia to New York, the campaigns of Gates and Greene in the South, and of Washington in Virginia. The history of the army under the immediate command of Washington is always satisfactory reading and loses nothing in Mr. Bancroft's hands. The account of its proceedings in this volume is clear, concise, and straightforward. Every reperusal of this familiar story brings to notice only fresh causes for admiring the combination of prudence with daring, patience with energy, and military skill with political foresight, which distinguishes Washington from all other generals of whatever time or nation, and which appears in strong contrast to the mistakes and faults of his rivals and subordinates. Of these, the most dangerous, if not the most capable, was General Gates, whose short and disastrous Southern campaign in 1780 forms a part of this volume. Mr. Bancroft's treatment of this subject, severe as it is upon the conduct of Gates, appears to be just and in accordance with sound criticism. General Gates was superseded and General Greene put in command. The campaign of 1781 began in the month of January by Tarleton's attack on General Morgan at the Cowpens. Mr. Bancroft's account of this battle, though correct in its facts, gives to Morgan more credit for this victory than military critics will readily allow. The estimate of Morgan's abilities is a very high one indeed, while his mistakes are very gently dealt with. Yet at the Cowpens General Morgan deliberately chose a position on open ground where his troops, mostly infantry, could be advantageously attacked by the British cavalry, with a river in his rear which precluded escape in case of defeat, and he drew up his little army in order of battle with the raw volunteers in advance, where they were exposed to the whole brunt of the enemy's attack. In fact Morgan did almost everything which he should not have done, and yet by his own bravery and the heroic behavior of his troops he utterly defeated the flower of the British army and gained a very undeserved reputation as a general.

General Greene's campaign is related with much fairness by Mr. Bancroft. Greene's measures seem to have been conceived with judgment and carried out with energy and courage, although his singular system of disposing his forces for battle was undoubtedly the cause of several defeats. There seems to be no occasion for objecting to Mr. Bancroft's treatment of this very important part of the military history of the war; and the same remark may be also made of his account of the campaign at Yorktown. All is here simple, clear, not disfigured by the author's radical fault of excursiveness, and, with the single exception of maps and plans, nothing essential seems to have been omitted.

As between the Americans and the English, it cannot be denied that Mr. Bancroft betrays a strong inclination to favor his countrymen. This leads him occasionally to state facts in language that is liable to a charge of misstatement, as, for instance, in the account of the engagement at Hanging Rock (p. 314), where his language is certainly calculated to convey the idea that the post was captured by Sumpter, whereas in fact the Americans were repulsed and obliged to retreat. So too in regard to the execution by Cornwallis in 1780 of those among his prisoners who had formerly given their parole and were again taken in arms, Mr. Bancroft asserts that their paroles were cancelled by Clinton's proclamation of June 3, 1780, and asserts that "to bring these men to the gibbet was an act of military murder." But it is to be observed that the proclamation in question refers only to those persons who were paroled prior to the capture of Charleston, and does not affect those captured at that place and in subsequent engagements, and it does not appear from Mr. Bancroft's account that those who were executed belonged to the former class, while, on the contrary, the English accounts state that they belonged to the latter. These executions, therefore, as well as the so-called murder of Mr. Isaac Hayne, in July, 1781, although doubtless cruel and unnecessary, must be regarded as strictly in accordance with military law. Mr. Bancroft's further assertion (p. 492) that the loss by the British of the power to protect Mr. Hayne released him from his parole, is a new and strange interpretation of military law and custom, and one which, if generally accepted, would tend to increase the rigors of war by greatly limiting the use of paroles.

But it is in the diplomatic history of this period that Mr. Bancroft's success is most striking, and here no candid critic can deny that he has rendered in this volume an immense service to his countrymen. For the first time the whole field of European diplomacy is laid open. Mr. Bancroft has ransacked the archives of Europe and drawn from them a vast amount of new and valuable material; he has worked with all the advantages of diplomatic experience and with the broadest plan. It is true that he falls here at times into his old excursive ways and runs into digressions that interrupt the development of his story, as, for instance, when he devotes an entire chapter of thirty-three pages to a review of German history from prehistoric times,—a review which has no special value, except as a personal compliment to the nation in whose capital it was written. Nor does the actual influence of Germany on American affairs seem to justify the relative prominence which is given to Frederick the Great, although the subject is new and interesting as well as valuable within its own range. On the other hand, there is nothing better in the volume than the manner in which the hitherto neglected story of Spanish influence in American affairs is worked out. For this the public is under a real obligation to Mr. Bancroft of a very decided kind, for his story puts at rest forever the old charge of ingratitude to France, which has been so often and so strongly pressed against the American negotiators of the peace.

Mr. Bancroft's weak point, however, seems to be a certain vivacity or restlessness of mind which is apt to mislead his readers as to the relative importance of events. He himself understands perfectly well what these relative values are, but a new idea or a new fact stands out in more prominence in his pages than it does in his own mind. Hence he devotes great care and excessive space to the subordinate but novel story of German and Russian diplomacy, including more than thirty pages of pure German history, while the story of the negotiation for peace, the most important and the most brilliant effort of American diplomacy, occupies little more than forty pages. Possibly, indeed, the sudden compression may here be due to a rapidly increasing conviction that the historian must delay no longer to complete his task; but if so, the result is unfortunate, since another opportunity for writing the history of that negotiation as it should be written is now lost. Yet even in Mr. Bancroft's story, short as it is, there are some opinions expressed which are open to question. His treatment of the negotiation as a matter of English politics, for example, seriously affects his entire view of the subject, and leads to results which diminish the natural effect of the drama.

Lord Shelburne is a favorite with Mr. Bancroft, from which it naturally follows that Mr. Fox is, at least as opposed to Shelburne, his antipathy. This is perhaps a natural feeling enough, since Fox certainly showed himself in a very indifferent light in his coalition with Lord North which overthrew the Shelburne Ministry in 1783. But Mr. Bancroft is here dealing with a previous affair; and as between Fox and Shelburne, the two great and equal forces of the short-lived Rockingham administration of 1782, there is more to be said for Fox and against Shelburne than Mr. Bancroft, or even Sir G. C. Lewis, has found room to say. That Shelburne was supported by the king is alone a very suspicious fact, for the king hated Fox, and Shelburne knew it and fell a sacrifice far more to his compliance with the king's prejudices than to Fox's ambition. A short sketch of the whole affair will show how it affects the character of Mr. Bancroft's history of the negotiation.

The news of Cornwallis's surrender reached England on the 25th of November, 1781, and shook the authority of Lord North to its foundation. On the 20th of March, 1782, North announced in the House of Commons that his administration was at an end. The king sent for the Earl of Shelburne, who insisted upon bringing the Rockingham party, of which Fox was the real chief, into the Cabinet, "cost what it would, more or less." At this time it is clear that Shelburne perfectly understood that union with Fox at any cost was his true policy. "Necessity made me yield," said the king, who would have taken Rockingham readily enough, but who could not endure Fox. The Cabinet was then formed by a fairly equal division of power between Shelburne and Rockingham. Rockingham took the Treasury; Fox became Secretary of State for Foreign Affairs, which gave him the negotiation with France, Spain, and Holland; while Shelburne became Home Secretary, which gave him the control of colonial business, and therefore the negotiation with the revolted Colonies, since Great Britain had not yet recognized their independence.

From the first Fox distrusted Shelburne, whom Junius fifteen years before had nicknamed Malagrida, that is, a Jesuit of a peculiarly rabid kind. Mr. Bancroft affirms that Shelburne was straightforward. His contemporaries were not of that opinion. But honest or not, Lord Shelburne was imperious, jealous, and suspicious. Fox very soon got the idea that he was betraying the liberal party into the king's hands, and this idea was correct to the extent that Shelburne drew further and further away from Fox and leaned more and more upon the king. The divergence was due, according to Mr. Bancroft, to Fox's desire of power; he wanted to get the negotiations for peace wholly into his own hands, and therefore urged the immediate recognition of American independence as a preliminary to negotiation, because this act of recognition would have made the colonies a foreign state and transferred their affairs from the Home to the Foreign Office. And why not? From every point of view this was sound policy, and Shelburne ought to have conceded the point. By doing so, he would have saved his administration and acted a wise, straightforward, and vigorous part. And in fact he did appear to do so. On the 10th of June Fox was directed by a cabinet order to instruct Mr. Grenville, the British envoy at Paris, that he was "no longer to mention the independence of America as a cession to France or as a conditional article of a general treaty; but he was at the same time instructed to observe to the French ministry that the independence of America was proposed to be acknowledged; and to remark that this, which they had emphatically called the object of the war, being done spontaneously, little difficulty ought to remain in regard to other points," etc. Mr. Grenville accordingly, on the 15th June, went to Vergennes and Franklin, and told them that "he was now authorized to declare the independence of America previous to the treaty." Instructions were also sent in the same words to Sir Guy Carleton at New York. The sequel may be best told in Mr. Fox's own words: "What then must be his (Fox's) astonishment and torture, when in the illness and apprehended decease of the noble Marquis (of Rockingham), another language was heard in the cabinet, and some even of his own friends began to consider these letters only as offers of a conditional nature,—to be recalled if they did not purchase peace. I considered myself as ensnared and betrayed. I therefore determined to take the measure by which alone I could act with consistency and honor. I called for precise declarations. I demanded explicit language; and when I saw that the persons in whom I had originally had no great confidence, were so eager to delude and so determined to change the ground on which they had set out, I relinquished my seat in the Cabinet." Fox's retirement immediately preceded the death of Lord Rockingham, which occurred on the 1st July.

Whether the ground taken by Fox will justify his action is a question that need not be discussed. Shelburne apparently thought the issue a decisive one, for he allowed Fox to go out upon it. Indeed, a month earlier Shelburne's agent, Oswald, had betrayed his chief's opinion by a stupid remark to Grenville in Paris, "that the Rockingham party were too ready to give up everything"; a remark which indicates that the difficulty was not merely one of power, as Mr. Bancroft asserts, but of policy. And as a point of policy there can be no question that Fox was right and Shelburne wrong.

But right or wrong, Fox went out, and Shelburne allowed him to do so, having apparently forgotten his conviction of four months ago that the assistance of Fox was necessary, "cost what it would, more or less." Is it unreasonable to assume, as Fox, Burke, and Sheridan assumed, that, in following this course, Shelburne was acting merely as a tool of the king? At all events the ministry were now in an extremely weak position. Without a majority in Parliament, without the support of any strong popular sympathy, Shelburne's only chance of saving, not his office, but his reputation for ordinary common-sense, depended on his meeting Parliament with a peace of some kind in his hand. The terms of this peace, so far at least as America was concerned, were a matter of secondary importance. In other words, Shelburne had no choice but to throw himself into Franklin's hands. He allowed Franklin to select even the negotiator, and the excellent Oswald proved wax to the touch of his astute opponent. The interests of England were flung to the winds, and Franklin for the time became the most powerful as he was the ablest diplomate in Europe.

Franklin was ready to negotiate, but Jay now intervened. Jay insisted upon what Fox had required,—a preliminary recognition of independence. Shelburne thereupon yielded so far as to issue a new commission to Oswald, authorizing him to conclude a peace or truce with commissioners of the thirteen *United States of America*. This satisfied Jay, and on receiving intelligence of the fact from him in a letter dated September 28, John Adams hastened to Paris.

Franklin, having now overcome this last difficulty, had only to guide his impetuous colleagues and prevent discord from doing harm. How dexterously he profited and caused his country to profit by the very idiosyncrasies of those colleagues with which he had least sympathy; how skilfully he took advantage of accidents and smoothed difficulties away; how subtle and keen his instincts were; how delicate and yet how sure his touch;—all this is a story to which Mr. Bancroft has done only partial justice. Sure of England, Franklin calmly ignored Spain, gently threw on his colleagues the responsibility for dispensing with the aid of France, boldly violated his instructions from Congress, and negotiated a triumphant peace.

But in all this, what can be said in praise of Lord Shelburne, unless it be that he was inspired by a philanthropic wish to reconcile the new nation and prevent future wars? If he had been in a stronger position at home, however, this philanthropy, born of Franklin's cajolery and Oswald's incompetence, would hardly have prevented him from insisting upon the line of the Penobscot as the Canadian frontier; and had he insisted, he would certainly have carried his point, in spite of New England. That Canada has no winter seaport, wanting which she is condemned to a maimed existence, is Lord Shelburne's doing and America's good fortune. Nor was this all. Nothing was really refused to the American commissioners. Whatever they claimed was conceded. For this America may indeed be grateful to Shelburne; but the world can hardly be expected to admire his abilities as a statesman.

And finally, as an example of Lord Shelburne's straightforwardness, one more incident is to be mentioned. When the provisional treaty was brought before Parliament, Fox asked Ministers whether the recognition of independence which it contained was final, or depended on the success of the general negotiations. Townshend, Pitt, and Conway in the Commons replied that it was final, and only so far provisional as it was dependent upon the ultimate conclusion of peace with France; that is, that a rupture of the present negotiation would not make the recognition void, but only postpone its effect. In the House of Lords, Shelburne asserted just the contrary. And when in the next debate he was pressed by the astonished Lords for a categorical reply to the same question in a written form, Shelburne positively refused to answer, though the question was the same he had answered before, and gave for his reason of refusal the statement that "declaring war and making peace were the undoubted prerogative of the crown, and ought to be guarded from all encroachment with the most particular care." If this is an example of straightforwardness, it must be acknowledged that Fox was wrong in doubting Shelburne's honesty.

One is somewhat at a loss to understand why Mr. Bancroft has chosen the conclusion of the provisional treaty with America as his stopping-point. No doubt he has sufficient reasons for doing so, but it would have been perhaps advantageous to the unity of his story if he had added another chapter to complete the history of the negotiations within the present volume. In this case he would have given his view of the interesting collision between Vergennes and Franklin, and the serious charges of duplicity and discourtesy which Vergennes brought against the commissioners. Fortunately, however, the earlier chapters of the volume leave little doubt upon the point. From the extremely valuable material which Mr. Bancroft has brought to light, the motives of Franklin's action are made perfectly clear. The key to the whole situation is found in Franklin's letter to Jay of April 22, summoning Jay to Paris: "Spain has taken four years to consider whether she should treat with us or not. Give her forty, and *let us in the mean time mind our own business.*" From the first, therefore, Franklin pursued the policy of avoiding entanglements with Spain, but to do so it was absolutely necessary to keep the negotiations in his own hands, since the pressure of Spain upon Vergennes was such that France could not, even if she would, have avoided subordinating American to Spanish interests. This was effectually prevented by

Franklin and his colleagues, though at the cost of acting in the teeth of their instructions. In the light of Mr. Bancroft's investigations, the wisdom and good faith of this course are established beyond further dispute. If Vergennes was irritated by it, the irritation was due to the fact that it debarred him from using the Americans for the advantage of Spain. So far as French interests were concerned, the American commissioners acted in perfect good faith, and Vergennes had no ground of complaint.

Passages in the present volume will no doubt rouse more grandsons to opposition, but on the whole Mr. Bancroft seems inclined to evade strife of this kind. He is perhaps somewhat harsh towards Jay, and surprisingly gentle towards Adams, who was yet in close sympathy with Jay, and whom Franklin at this time officially declared to be "sometimes and in some things absolutely out of his senses." On the other hand, Mr. Bancroft's treatment of this most brilliant part of Franklin's brilliant career is, as has already been intimated, more subdued and simple in tone than might have been expected. Yet after making all fair allowances for these merely personal matters and for the inevitable peculiarities of Mr. Bancroft's literary style, there remains to this volume a degree of merit and solid value which will compare most favorably with that of any preceding volume, and which will inevitably and permanently affect the ultimate judgment of mankind on the great period here described.

18

MAINE'S 'EARLY HISTORY OF INSTITUTIONS'

Occasionally in his sketches, Adams turns to contemporary affairs. In sketch 13, he mentions Bismarck. In this one, he regrets the continued depression that is holding millions of Americans in its grip. But far more often, the sketches show Adams traveling into the past, searching in other ages, and commonly finding that what the past was alleged to be by historians and what it proved to be in surviving evidence were very widely at variance.

While writing his sketches, Adams obtained and studied large collections of medieval data mostly relating to northern Europe, especially England. Where existing histories assured him that he would find tribes, say, or primogeniture, he—and the students who studied with him—found a remarkable absence of tribes, and no primogeniture. Where he and his students were assured that they would not find individuals who owned land, or voted, or were organized into states, they found such persons in abundance.

For Adams, one result was a kind of solitude, not so much of opinion as exposure to evidence. He here reports himself as being at odds even with Sir Henry Maine, a great investigator, but one not familiar with forests of data which an American teacher and some students had traversed and found to be strange.

—*North American Review* (April 1875); unsigned—

Lectures on the Early History of Institutions. By Sir Henry Sumner Maine, K. C. S. I., LL. D., F. R. S. New York: Holt & Co. 1875.

The American public owe a debt of gratitude to Mr. Holt for the taste and judgment which have led him to produce this American edition of Sir Henry Maine's works. Its form leaves nothing to be desired. It is creditable at once to the publisher and to the public that in these days of universal distress such an undertaking should be attempted.

A new work by Sir Henry Maine is one of those pleasures to which a certain portion of the most highly educated class of English and American readers look forward with hardly less interest than to a new work of Darwin or Spencer. Few men of this generation have had a more distinct and active influence on the minds of the younger and future lawyers and historians than Sir Henry has exercised. Few men have done more than he to stimulate thought and enlarge its range. In the field he has chosen there is no English writer who approaches him.

The new volume is a chapter on the old subject. Sir Henry's first book on Ancient Law treated the dark history of law chiefly from a Roman stand-point. The author then went to India and drew fresh illustrations of his favorite topic from native Indian custom, publishing these on his return under the title of "Village Communities." He has now launched into another investigation at the opposite extremity of his hemisphere, and utilized the ancient customary laws of Ireland for the same purpose. Science has not been idle since he began to write. He finds a considerable change in the conditions of the subject. Opinions which he freely hazarded in his first book might now be greatly modified or entirely suppressed. But all the essentials of the purely historical investigation are unchanged and unchangeable. As to the speculative portions of his books, both of the present volume and its predecessors, the author himself would certainly be first to recognize their provisional character. He is too brilliant to be dogmatic. He is too genial a writer to deny himself or others the fullest liberty of changing or questioning an opinion.

The study of Celtic law is one great branch of a subject which embraces already the study of Roman, German, and Scandinavian archaic systems in Europe, and Indian in Asia. Perhaps in time, when all that remains of these codes has been carefully published and the principles common to two or more of them have been extracted, as has been done in philology, it will be possible to reconstruct the archaic Indo-European jurisprudence, as the archaic Indo-European language has been reconstructed in its successive stages. At present science is far from this point. It is still seeking painfully for the most essential facts. It avoids hazardous guesses, and it looks not altogether favorably on Sir Henry's brilliant hypotheses. The field of investigation is more promising than any that has been opened since Niebuhr's time; it is indeed merely an extension of his labors and a readaptation of his method; but promising as the field is, many an over-eager pioneer is likely to come to grief in it before it is fairly cleared.

As regards the branch of this great subject which Sir Henry has now chosen, there are one or two preliminary points, a settlement of which is essential to a fair understanding of the subject. Of these, the most important regards the relative stage of development which is to be attributed to the Brehon law. Is it to be considered as pure or as debased law? Developed for the better it can hardly be. It would rather seem to be debased as compared with any other known Aryan type. If so, however, there is great danger of its misleading investigation. And here, at the outset, it might be wished that Sir Henry had employed a more rigid series of tests than he has thought necessary. Before using the tribal system of Brehon law as an illustration of an archaic principle, it is necessary to ascertain whether it is itself archaic.

The late investigations into the earliest known forms of Teutonic law seem to have rendered one conclusion probable which was hardly to have been expected. They show that German society, when it first emerged into the view of the civilized world, was not founded on a tribal system. The state, not the tribe, was already supreme. The political, the judicial, the military, and the religious systems were none of them tribal. In all, the individual full-grown man, associated with other men in artificial groups, constituted the state. If often the individuals whose union made the village community were united by ties of relationship, this may have been the result of propinquity quite as well as of the fiction or reality of a common origin. As a matter of fact the entire free male population met in assembly in each geographical district, and this assembly was, as occasion required, parliament, law-court, or army. To the obligations thus imposed all persons were equally subject. The tribe was unknown, and the family, however powerful it might be, was in law wholly subordinate to the state. The German *magenschaft,* or kindred, was a loose organization, without a patriarchal head and without a common property. It included the mother's as well as the father's relations. In it, the duties and privileges of its members were confined to a sphere of reciprocal assistance in case of trouble, and to inheritance, as in our own law, in case of failure of direct heirs. In the family itself, the *patria potestas* was, in the Roman sense, utterly unknown. The son came of age at a fixed time of life, and became at once *sui juris,* with all the rights of our own law.

More than this, it is not necessary to assume and it would be difficult to prove that the Teutonic race ever had known any other condition of society. There is just as much reason in supposing that they adopted this system without passing through any stage of tribal organization, as in assuming the contrary. There is just as much ground for assuming that many small families associated together from the first as equals, as there is for supposing that one large family developed into a tribe with a patriarchal head. One hypothesis is as good as the other until its falsity is demonstrated.

Naturally, therefore, the first question that arises in regard to the Celtic law is, whether its tribal organization is genuinely archaic or only the result of disorganization? and on the answer to this question the whole treatment of the Brehon law depends. If really archaic, it represents a typical system, older than the Teutonic, and therefore forms a most important link in the chain of human development. If not, it sinks to the level of a kind of savage feudalism in which only a hint here and there can be turned to the uses of comparative jurisprudence. And even a hint from such a source would be apt to mislead.

Unfortunately this preliminary investigation is precisely that part of the subject which Sir Henry has least developed. Possibly it is the part which is least capable of development. The essential point to be ascertained is, whether the Irish ever had a political, military, or judicial organization corresponding to the Teutonic. From Sir Henry's language (pp. 286–291) it appears that there are traces at least of a legislative and judicial organization at some doubtful period,—traces which subsequently disappeared in practice. This evidence as well as the general character of the private law would seem to indicate that the Celtic society may have originally had the same organization as the Teutonic, in which case the whole paraphernalia of Irish septs and tribal law would have to be considered merely as debased Teutonic law, and be treated as Irish feudalism. Its value would on this assumption be very trifling. But without a most thorough and searching criticism, no assumption is admissible.

This difficulty does not, however, affect the value of Sir Henry's speculations upon points of law which in any case may be supposed to have remained essentially unchanged, whether the theory of pure or debased archaism is adopted. Such a point is the law of distress, and generally what Sir Henry calls the primitive forms of legal remedies, to which he has devoted two chapters. These are very suggestive and interesting. So is also the chapter on the early history of the settled property of married women, with its remarkable explanation of the Hindoo practice of suttee. Perhaps the most striking idea contained in the entire volume is the identification of the Irish practice of "fasting upon" a debtor with the Indian custom of "sitting dharna." It appears that the Hindoo who wished to enforce payment of a demand sat down at his debtor's door and fasted; if he were suffered to die of hunger, the sin lay forever on the debtor's head, and therefore, "as he seldom makes the attempt without the resolution to persevere," in practice this method of compelling payment rarely failed of success. The religious sanction was more effective than the strictly legal remedy. In Irish law it is written, "He who does not give a pledge to fasting is an evader of all; he who disregards all things shall not be paid by God or man." By some strange process of survival, this remedy, which is strictly speaking an extra-legal form of distress, seems to have maintained its hold on the Indian and Irish branches of the Indo-European stock, while among all the intervening European races it would seem to have been unknown. Possibly, however, traces of the custom may yet be discovered elsewhere. In any case it makes an interesting point of comparison between the most distant systems both of law and religious doctrine.

Occasionally, however, Sir Henry advances a theory which, however probable in itself, ought by no means to be assumed as a foundation for reasoning without at least some attempt at demonstration. He repeats, for instance, a previously expressed opinion, "that our modern English conception of absolute property in land is really descended from the special proprietorship enjoyed by the lord, and more anciently by the tribal chief, in his own domain." Here he assumes a number of points on which one would much like to hear argument.

As, for instance, was there ever a time when the English people were without the idea of absolute property in land? Is there any conclusive evidence to prove that the English people ever saw a tribal chief? Or that the Saxons, Jutes, or Angles ever recognized such a chief? Or can it be proved that the idea of absolute individual ownership in land is different in kind from the idea of joint ownership by village communities? Or can Sir Henry demonstrate that at any period whatever the Teutons of the village communities were not absolute owners of the houses in which they lived and the close about those houses? And if English ownership is descended from the ownership of the tribal chief, why were the grants of land in such absolute ownership always acts of the political government, of the king and the people in a legislative capacity?

Again: "It is quite certain," says Sir Henry, "that the appearance of primogeniture in the West and its rapid diffusion must be connected with the irruption of the barbarians and with the tribal ideas reintroduced by them into the Roman world." Why is this quite certain? What were these tribal ideas which the barbarians reintroduced? Clovis established his empire by going over to Christianity in the year 496. Presumably, therefore, it was then or soon afterwards that the barbarians introduced their ideas. And accordingly it is found that they did in fact introduce ideas, though by no means tribal ideas, over the whole of Gaul, Spain, Italy, England, and Iceland. Primogeniture was not among them, nor was it a result of such introduction. The dynasty of Clovis flourished for centuries and then declined. The Pepins rose in their place, two hundred and fifty years after the barbarians had introduced their ideas into the Roman world. Charlemagne carried the power of the new dynasty to Rome, and ruled with the name and power of the Cæsars. And still there was no primogeniture. Charlemagne passed away and his empire after him; society fell to pieces; the dark tenth century came on, when there was no literature, little law, less peace; in short, the lowest point of modern history; and then at last primogeniture makes its appearance. Full four centuries were then required, according to Sir Henry, to give effect to the tribal ideas of the German invaders by creating primogeniture. Surely such an assertion requires cogent proof.

"Primogeniture, therefore," Sir Henry continues, "considered as a rule of succession to property, appears to me to be a product of tribal leadership in its decay." This question of the origin of primogeniture has always been a very favorite one with Sir Henry. He has developed extremely clever theories in regard to it. But where is the need for this ingenuity? Primogeniture, historically speaking, appears to be a simple creation enough, just as feudalism is, of which primogeniture is a part. It flourished where feudalism flourished. It took an endless variety of forms. It may be explained in strict agreement with facts, by considering it as the natural result of the military and economical exigencies of the time. There is nothing to connect it with the tribal ideas of the conquering Frankish race, for the simple reason that the Franks had no tribal ideas. They had strong family ideas, but no sign of a tribal organization, of which the distinctive mark must be a tribal, patriarchal chief enjoying despotic power in practice if not in law, and extensive rights over the tribal lands (pp. 115–118).

In other words, without denying the beauty or ingenuity or even the probable truth of Sir Henry's theories, it may be safely said that there is hardly a theory advanced by him which does not require that two or three volumes should be written by way of a preliminary clearing of the ground before it will be possible to arrive at an approximate decision of the point in question. With this precautionary understanding, however, his books have very great interest and value. It is true that the science of comparative jurisprudence is far less advanced than may be supposed by readers of the "Ancient Law" and the "Village Communities." What is called Aryan or Indo-European law is likely, however, one day or another to become a tolerably complete science and one of no little value to mankind. As for still more ancient systems, however, the temptation to speculate becomes strong in proportion to the mystery of the subject. The mania for producing philosophical systems of social development, like that of Auguste Comte; the temptation to make such a system symmetrical and to pass every individual human being through every phase which has left a trace of its existence behind it; the fervor with which each new investigator presses his own historical novelty;—all this is merely the symptom of advancing knowledge, but has little intrinsic value. The man who will give to the world the texts of the oldest Indo-European codes, in the most accurate readings and with the most precise translations; who will arrange these laws in the order of subjects, and make for them a perfect index, so that the resemblances and differences may be seen at a glance;—such a man will do the most that can be done for a science of comparative archaic jurisprudence. To have conceived the idea of such a science; to have sketched its outlines; to have described or divined some portions of its vast domain; and to have done this in a temper so admirable, a style so delightful, with so wide a range of knowledge, and with an imagination so fascinating as these volumes display, is a great service, for which the public can hardly feel so strong an obligation as it ought; and this is the service which Sir Henry Maine has rendered in English literature.

The twelfth and thirteenth lectures, which close the volume, will to many readers appear the most interesting of all. They are a criticism of Austin and Bentham's views on sovereignty,—a criticism which appears to be just and is certainly very agreeable reading. If for nothing else, all students of law should read this volume to enjoy the charm of an intelligible discussion of Austin's doctrines.

19

PALGRAVE'S 'POEMS'

That Adams became a great writer can be attributed in part to his having first become a great reader, especially of poetry. Of his own accord, he read all the American poets, all the English, and any number of poets in other languages, modern, medieval, and ancient. In the process, he carried patience to a fault, looking for gold where another reader might expect only barren sand.

Privately, Adams thought his English friend Francis Palgrave not a poet but a superb critic who tried to write poems and sometimes succeeded as a writer of hymns. Publicly, in this sketch, the American makes the best case he can for his friend as a poet and, while so doing, illustrates his own care and watchfulness as a reader.

The love Adams felt for Palgrave was augmented by a cause relating to history. His friend was one of the sons of a historian, Sir Francis Palgrave. Late in life, thinking back to the time when he had studied the subject with a view to writing about it, Adams said in his *Education* that the elder Palgrave was "much the greatest of all the historians of early England." The compliment was resounding. One must believe it was meant.

—*North American Review* (April 1875); unsigned—

1. *Lyrical Poems.* By FRANCIS TURNER PALGRAVE. Macmillan & Co. London and New York. 1871.

2. *Hymns.* By FRANCIS TURNER PALGRAVE, late Scholar of Balliol and Fellow of Exeter College, Oxford. Third Edition. Macmillan & Co. London. 1870.

3. *A Lyme Garland, etc.* By FRANCIS TURNER PALGRAVE. Printed for
the School Fund. Lyme Regis. 1874.

AMONG the minor poets of our own day and generation, there have
been three in England who seem to fall easily and naturally into a
single group. These are Clough, Matthew Arnold, and Palgrave.
Clough is long since dead, leaving behind him some fragments of
poetry that promise to retain their gentle hold on the popular mind
long after some noisier music of the time has ceased to rouse even an
echo. Mr. Arnold seems to have abandoned the mistress whom he
pursued with much success in early life, and to have transferred his
affection to an object which in the long run will have little to give him
that can make up for the loss of his first love. Mr. Palgrave alone
remains, and still finds time to write.

The fate of the poet is hard at best, if his work is conscientious and
his sense of poetry keen. All the three writers just mentioned are in
fact as much critics as poets. Mr. Palgrave especially shows this tendency to criticism not less in regard to himself than in regard to
others; he trains and curbs his own Pegasus with as much anxiety or
more than he shows in selecting perfect gems for his Golden Treasury,
or in applying rules of art in his Essays. His highest ambition would
be to offer the classical beauty of Greek form to an age and generation
which has hardly a notion of form at all; which loves roughness and
extravagance for its own sake rather than for what it is pleased to
think these exteriors conceal; or which loves only such beauty of form
as the time has to offer, and is far too ignorant of the higher types of
beauty even to sympathize with the modern Hellenist. Such a poet
can expect no large audience and few warm admirers. He must consider himself sufficiently rewarded if by any chance some verse or
stanza of his shall linger long enough on the ear of the public to
vindicate his claim to a place, as Mr. Palgrave has elsewhere said, above
the vast and pathetic array of singers now silent, who have been hon-
ored with the name of poet, and among the smaller and more for-
tunate body of those who for some one moment at least have attained
excellence.

Will Mr. Palgrave have this good fortune? The question is not one
for the critic to answer. Many a poem which has been admitted by Mr.
Palgrave into his Golden Treasury would have been certainly excluded

by the critics who lived when these poems were written. Many a poem which they would have surely admitted has been rightly excluded by Mr. Palgrave. It becomes the critic, therefore, to be very cautious in his judgments, especially in dealing with a poet who is himself so sure a critic as Mr. Palgrave. What he calls "the vague general verdict of popular fame" must be waited for to decide the rank which the fashion of a day is apt to settle only by tests made for its own creations.

The poem of "Alcestis" is one of the best examples of Mr. Palgrave's classical taste. Let us quote, for example, two of the stanzas in which Alcestis bids farewell to her husband and children:

> Going with downcast eyes and captive tread
> Through the dim garden of the happy dead,
>   Where summer never comes, nor voice of spring,
>
> Nor frost nor sun; but the dim rose-red glow
>   Of autumn dyes the insuperable hill:
> Nor past nor future are, nor wish nor vow;
> But the white silence of the eternal Now
>   Wipes out the thought of joy, and fear of ill.

Of course it is unfair to take a few lines from their context and quote them as specimens of a poem which is intended to be taken as a whole, and the merits of which consist largely in the harmony of all its parts. Yet these lines illustrate at least the impression which the poem conveys,—an impression of subdued tone and careful finish; a subordination of passion to form; a self-restraint which is not timidity, but a result of the effort to realize a Greek ideal. The drawback is obviously in the too great sense of effort which such a task inevitably carries with it. Neither the English language nor the English mind is made for that sort of perfection which seems to have come without an effort to the Greeks. Neither Euripides nor Sophocles would have cared to throw their treatment of Alcestis into a mould which was difficult for their countrymen to appreciate, and if they had done so, the sense of effort would have taught them and their audience that they were following an unnatural process. And so with Mr. Palgrave and with all the other poets, great and small, who have imitated the Greeks; as studies, their work is no doubt not only valuable, but necessary to high excellence; as poems, one might almost say that the greater the success the greater is the failure; the closer the copy the more obvious is the *tour de force*.

Study of Greek art is therefore only the stepping-stone to success, and Mr. Palgrave, after showing, as in his "Alcestis," how careful his study had been, was yet to find his natural vein and to prove the quality of his genius. That this is refined is obvious enough. That it is generous in its sympathies, is evident. If the poetry were less good than it is, still Americans would owe Mr. Palgrave something for lines like these:

> As when one fair land
> Saw, North and South, her bright-armed myriads stand,
> Saw herself rent in twain by matricidal hand:
> Though both were gallant, though
> High deeds on either side were wrought,
> Yet one for self and one for mankind fought:
> And when war's lurid cloud
> From the clear skies had passed,
> The golden eye of life
> From heaven shone bold and free
> On white-robed Victory,
> And the Right won at last.

But the vein which Mr. Palgrave seems at last to have followed with especial sympathy is that on the debated line between science and religion. He has returned to this subject again and again of later years, as in his "Reign of Law," "The Voices of Nature," "'Αγνώτω θέω," and "To Fidele." The subject is one which offers no small obstacles to poetical treatment, and it is interesting to see how so critical an author as Mr. Palgrave has managed it. Let us quote, by way of example, the close of "The Voices of Nature":

> Voice of Nature in the Heart,
>   Narrow though our science, though
> Here we only know in part,
>   Give us faith in what we know!
> To a fuller life aspiring,
> Satisfy the heart's desiring;—
>
> Tell us of a force, behind
>   Nature's force, supreme, alone;
> Tell us of a larger mind
>   Than the partial power we own;
> Tell us of a Being wholly
> Wise and great and just and holy;—

Toning down the pride of mind
    To a wiser humbleness,
Teach the limits of mankind,
    Weak to know and prompt to guess,
On the mighty shores that bound us,
Childlike gathering trifles round us;—

Teach how, yet, what here we know
    To the unknown leads the way,
As the light that, faint and low,
    Prophesies consummate day;
How the little arc before us
Proves the perfect circle o'er us.

Or, again, in the "Reign of Law":

We may not hope to read
    Nor comprehend the whole,
Or of the law of things
    Or of the law of soul;
Among the eternal stars
    Dim perturbations rise;
And all the searchers' search
    Does not exhaust the skies;
He who has framed and brought us hither
Holds in his hands the whence and whither.

Then, though the sun go up
    His beaten azure way,
God may fulfil his thought
    And bless his world to-day;
Beside the law of things
    The law of mind enthrone,
And, for the hope of all,
    Reveal Himself in One;
Himself the way that leads us thither,
The All-in-all, the Whence and Whither.

Perhaps the reader, like the critic, will feel an uncomfortable doubt
whether this is, as poetry or as logic, quite satisfactory. He unconsciously feels that his argumentative powers are challenged, and he
follows the train of reasoning at the cost of the poetic sentiment. As
a matter of poetic instinct, one can join in the lament that "Great Pan
is dead," or can rejoice in the promise that "The world's great age
begins anew"; but one cannot cast the balance between materialism

and religion, with a demonstration of orthodox faith as the result, except at the cost of poetic fervor. For this reason, perhaps, the larger number of readers have seemed to prefer Mr. Palgrave's hymns to his philosophic poetry, and critics will probably acquiesce in the popular decision. Let us cite, for example, "The City of God":

> O thou not made with hands,
> Not throned above the skies,
> Nor wall'd with shining walls,
> Nor framed with stones of price,
>   More bright than gold or gem,
>   God's own Jerusalem!
>
> Where'er the gentle heart
> Finds courage from above;
> Where'er the heart forsook
> Warms with the breath of love;
>   Where faith bids fear depart,
>   City of God, thou art.
>
> Where in life's common ways
> With cheerful feet we go;
> When in his steps we tread
> Who trod the way of woe;
>   Where He is in the heart,
>   City of God, thou art.

Or, again, "The King's Messenger":

> He goes in silence through the crowd:
>   A veil is o'er his face;
> Yet where but once his eyes are turned
>   There is an empty space.
> The whispering throngs divide and stir;—
> 'T is he! 't is the King's Messenger!
>
> We may perforce buy off the thought,
>   Or stifle or ignore;
> The day at last will come on us
>   When day will come no more:
> When on the spaces of the sky
> We hardly lift a wearied eye;
>
> When Science folds her hands and sighs,
>   And cannot bridge the abyss;
> And That, which once seem'd life, seems naught
>   Before the enormous This;

> All days, all deeds, all passions past
> Shrunk to a pin's point in the vast;—
>
> Then face to face to meet the King
>   Behind his messenger!

Or, if doubt must be expressed and faith stimulated, the lines on "Faith and Light" are full of delicate feeling:

> Thou sayst, "Take up the cross,
>   O Man, and follow me":
> The night is black, the feet are slack,
>   Yet we would follow thee.
>
> Dim tracts of time divide
>   Those golden days from me;
> Thy voice comes strange o'er years of change;
>   How can I follow thee?
>
> Unchanging law binds all,
>   And Nature all we see;
> Thou art a star, far off, too far
>   Too far to follow thee!
>
> Ah, sense-bound heart and blind!
>   Is naught but what we see? etc., etc.

We can quote no more. Some of Mr. Palgrave's smaller pieces, like the "Reine d'Amour," have already gone the rounds of the American press, and are sufficiently familiar to the public. But wherever his volumes are opened, the reader will find the same subdued, self-restrained style, the same harmony of parts, the same care in execution, the same refinement and tenderness of feeling, always accompanied by a certain masculine strength which has its own peculiar modes of expression. We will not venture to fix Mr. Palgrave's precise place in the splendid array of British singers, but at least he belongs to a school which can hardly produce anything but what we must all be grateful to have.

20

GREEN'S 'SHORT HISTORY OF THE ENGLISH PEOPLE'

An argument could be made that Adams, as one of America's national historians, began by thinking he should write a history of the United States during the administrations of five presidents, Washington through John Quincy Adams, from 1789 to 1825. By what steps he arrived at a plan to write a history limited to the administrations of Jefferson and Madison, from 1801 to 1817, is unknown. What is known is that he was affected by efforts made by two contemporaries he admired.

Clarence King, as head of the United States Geological Survey of the Fortieth Parallel, planned a study, not of the Rocky Mountains in general, but of an east-west strip across the mountains one hundred miles wide and one thousand miles long. By concentrating attention on a sample area, King improved the chances of observational accuracy and thus the likelihood that general principles adduced from his survey's work would gain credence in the scientific community. John Richard Green, though not yet a friend, was a historian whom Adams had met, respected very highly, and wanted to know. In his *Short History of the English People,* Green attempted to tell the story of the English during their entire possession of the British Isles, from 449 to 1873.

When Adams wrote the sketch below, the conclusions of King's survey were still in the process of being written and published; but their comparative validity—and hence their importance—was for Adams already assured. Green's *History,* in contrast, was finished. Adams studied it with such feelings that the sketch below has claims to being the best of his sketches; also the most heavily tinged with regret.

175

When he wrote the sketch, Adams's decision to limit his own *History* to sixteen years, as opposed to Green's fourteen centuries, possibly was made, even made very firmly. It is easy to imagine, however, that the decision was not wholly settled until Adams suffered the excruciation of seeing glaring inaccuracies in Green's pages—and took them to be the inescapable penalties of a wrong plan of work, which, instead of concentrating attention, dispersed it.

—*North American Review* (July 1875); unsigned—

A Short History of the English People. By J. R. GREEN, M. A., Examiner in the School of Modern History, Oxford. With Maps and Tables. London: Macmillan & Co. 1875.

IT is difficult to speak of this book in any other terms than those of unqualified praise. Its learning, its style, its imagination, and, almost above all, its sound common-sense, are most remarkable. Readers of this Review will readily acquit its criticisms of any tendency towards indiscriminate laudation, and may therefore be less disposed to scepticism if the critic for once frankly begins by asserting that Mr. Green cannot be ranked among contemporary English historians second to any one but Macaulay himself.

Never has the popular style of historical writing been raised to so high a standard as in Mr. Green's work. He has hit a curiously happy vein of picturesque, yet unaffected narration. As an example, one among hundreds, here is a description of the mental state of England at the time of Wat Tyler's rebellion, about the year 1380:

> The cry of the poor found a terrible utterance in the words of "a mad priest of Kent," as the courtly Froissart calls him, who had for twenty years been preaching a Lollardry of coarser and more popular type than that of Wyclif, and who found audience for his sermons, in defiance of interdict and imprisonment, in the stout yeomen who gathered in the Kentish churchyards. "Mad," as the land-owners called him, it was in the preaching of John Ball that England first listened to the knell of feudalism, and the declaration of the rights of man. "Good people," cried the preacher, "things will never go well in England so long as goods be not in common, and so long as there be villains and gentlemen. By what right are they whom we call lords greater folk than we? On what grounds have they deserved it? Why do they hold us in serfage? If they all came of the same father and mother, of Adam and Eve, how can

they say or prove that they are better than we, if it be not that they make us gain for them by our toil what they spend in their pride? They are clothed in velvet, and warm in their furs and their ermines, while we are covered with rags. They have wine and spices and fair bread; and we eat oat-cake and straw, and water to drink. They have leisure and fine houses; we have pain and labor, the rain and wind in the fields. And yet it is of us and of our toil that these men hold their estate." It was the tyranny of property that then as ever roused the defiance of socialism. A spirit fatal to the whole system of the Middle Ages breathed in the popular rhyme which condensed the levelling doctrine of John Ball, "When Adam delved and Eve span, who was then the gentleman?"

The rhyme was running from lip to lip when a fresh instance of public oppression fanned the smouldering discontent into a flame. . . . . Quaint rhymes passed through the country, and served as summons to the revolt, which soon extended from the eastern and midland counties over all England south of the Thames. "John Ball," ran one, "greeteth you all, and doth for to understand he hath rung your bell. Now right and might, will and skill, God speed every dele." "Help truth," ran another, "and truth shall help you! Now reigneth pride in price, and covetise is counted wise, and lechery withouten shame, and gluttony withouten blame. Envy reigneth with treason, and sloth is take in great season. God do bote, for now is tyme!" We recognize Ball's hand in the yet more stirring missives of "Jack the Miller" and "Jack the Carter." "Jack Miller asketh help to turn his mill aright. He hath grounden small, small: the King's Son of Heaven he shall pay for all. Look thy mill go aright with the four sailes, and the post stand with steadfastness. With right and with might, with skill and with will; let might help right, and skill go before will, and right before might, so goeth our mill aright." "Jack Carter," ran the companion missive, "prays you all that ye make a good end of that ye have begun, and do well, and aye better and better: for at the even men heareth the day." "Falseness and guile," sang Jack Trewman, "have reigned too long, and truth hath been set under a lock, and falseness and guile reigneth in every stock. No man may come truth to, but if he sing 'si dedero.' True love is away that was so good, and clerks for wealth work them woe. God do bote, for now is time." In the rude jingle of these lines began for England the literature of political controversy; they are the first predecessors of the pamphlets of Milton and of Burke. Rough as they are, they express clearly enough the mingled passions which met in the revolt of the peasants; their longing for a right rule, for plain and simple justice; their scorn of the immorality of the nobles, and the infamy of the court; their resentment at the perversion of the law to the cause of oppression.

If this extract is an example of the skilful weaving of picturesque details into the web of history, the following is an example of constitutional theory of the best kind. Perhaps, however, this Review is no fair judge of the merit of Mr. Green's idea, which is one that supports opinions as to the origin of Parliament which have been heretofore pressed with some earnestness in these pages:

Amidst the many judicial reforms of Henry or Edward the Shire Court remained unchanged. The haunted mound or the immemorial oak round which the assembly gathered, were the relics of a time before the free kingdom had shrunk into a shire, and its Meetings of the Wise into a county court. But save that the King's Reeve had taken the place of the king, and that the Norman legislation had displaced the bishop and set four coroners by the sheriff's side, the gathering of the freeholders remained much as of old. The local knighthood, the yeomanry, the husbandmen of the county, were all represented in the crowd that gathered round the sheriff, as, guarded by his liveried followers, he published the king's writs, announced his demand of aids, received the presentment of criminals and the inquests of the local jurors, assessed the taxation of each district, or listened solemnly to appeals for justice, civil and criminal, from all who held themselves oppressed in the lesser courts of the hundred or the soke. It was in the county court alone that the sheriff could legally summon the lesser baronage to attend the Great Council, and it was in the actual constitution of this assembly that the crown found a solution of the difficulty which we have already stated. For the principle of representation by which it was finally solved was coeval with the shire court itself. In all cases of civil or criminal justice the twelve sworn assessors of the sheriff represented the judicial opinion of the country at large. From every hundred came groups of twelve sworn deputies, the 'jurors' through whom the presentments of the district were made to the royal officer, and with whom the assessment of its share in the general taxation was arranged. The husbandmen on the outskirts of the crowd, clad in the brown smock-frock which still lingers in the garb of our carters and ploughmen, were broken up into little knots of five, a reeve, and four assistants, who formed the representatives of the rural townships. If, in fact, we regard the shire courts as lineally the descendants of our earliest English Parliaments, we may justly claim the principle of Parliamentary representation as among the oldest of our institutions. . . . . The court was composed of the whole body of freeholders, and no sheriff could distinguish the "aye, aye" of the yeoman from the "aye, aye" of the squire. From the first moment, therefore, of their attendance, we find the knights regarded, not as mere representatives of the baronage, but knights of the shire, and by this silent revolution the whole body of the rural freeholders were admitted to a share in the government of the realm.

The one great constitutional machine which characterized all Teutonic society in its earliest historic phase was, therefore, the Hundred or shire court, from which was developed all the public and private law of the Anglo-Saxon time, army, king, witan, and the whole administration of justice, even to the point of absorbing much church law; and this same primeval institution, surviving the shock of conquest, civil war, and social decay, even after the steady drain of centuries which carried its powers one by one into other hands, still retained force enough in the thirteenth century to become the foundation of Parliament. This historical principle is on the whole the most valuable of all those which modern investigation has discovered, since it stamps the whole theory of monarchy as understood in the high-prerogative period, as a mere historical blunder, and establishes beyond further question the historical truth of the principle that, at least in the Teutonic race, the people always have been the rightful source of political power.

The interest of Mr. Green's work culminates, however, in the period of the Renaissance, which he has seen proper to call the "Renascence." There is something petty and captious in finding fault with the words or the spelling an author chooses to employ, and the critic who does this by choice can have little else to say. But human patience has its limits. Alfred the Great could and did sign himself "Alfredus"; the English language has for ages known only this form of the word; but we are now obliged to call him by the pedantic form of Alefred, and Mr. Green joins with our persecutors. To this the reading public must perforce submit, because, like other antiquarian pedantry, the reform has a good side. But why should Englishmen insist on anglicizing foreign names and words; and if this must absolutely be done, cannot Mr. Green obtain some result less absurd than *Lewis Doutremer*, for instance, and less—nasty, shall we say,—than *Renascence*? Is there one living Englishman who thinks so ugly a Latinism as *Renascence* better English than so well-established a Gallicism as Renaissance? Not that the translation is a thing in itself objectionable, least of all in a popular work; but if anything so thoroughly understood is to be translated, at least the translation should be better and more intelligible English than the original.

At all events the period of the "New Monarchy" and the "New Learning" is that on which the interest of Mr. Green's history touches its highest point. The reigns of Henry the Eighth and Elizabeth are admirably told. To make extracts here is not easy, for the chapters are made to be read as a whole, not in fragments, but any one who wishes to form a judgment of this part of the work can turn to the delineation of Elizabeth as on the whole a very fair specimen of Mr. Green's quality as a writer and a critic.

Excellent as the political part of the work is, its excellence is almost thrown into the shade by the literary part. All ages have agreed in considering the public acts of men and states as forming the ground-work of history. Upon this foundation moderns have built two upper stories, so to speak; they have made it almost essential that every history nowadays should contain an account of the modes of life, and another of the modes of thought, which characterized the period described. Mr. Green has entirely omitted the first of these two duties. He has attempted no description of the changes in habits and manners. On the other hand, he has thrown his whole energy into the other and the far more important subject of the development of modern thought. His accounts of Chaucer, of Wyclif, of More, of Shakespeare, form as delightful reading as it has been men's lot to meet in these recent years. A page in regard to the close of the Elizabethan age is worth quoting, not because it is very much better than the rest, but because it contains the gist of this whole portion of the history:

The "obstinate questionings of invisible things" which had given their philosophical cast to the wonderful group of dramas which had at last raised Shakespeare to his post among the greatest of the world's poets, still hung round him in the years of quiet retirement which preceded his death. . . . . His last dramas, "Othello," the "Tempest," "Cæsar," "Antony," "Coriolanus," were written in the midst of ease and competence, in the home where he lived as a country gentleman with his wife and daughters. His classical plays were the last assertion of an age which was passing away. The spirit of the Renascence was fading before the spirit of the Reformation. Puritanism was hardening and narrowing, while it was invigorating and ennobling life by its stern morality, its seriousness, its conviction of the omnipotence of God and of the weakness of man. The old daring which had turned England into a people of "adventurers," the sense of inexhaustible resources in the very nature of man, the buoyant freshness of youth, the intoxicating sense of beauty and joy, which had created Drake and Sidney and Marlowe, were dying with Shakespeare himself. The Bible was superseding Plutarch. The pedantry of Euphuism was giving way to the pedantry of scriptural phrases. The "obstinate questionings of invisible things," which haunted the finer minds of the Renascence, were being stereotyped into the theological formulas of the Predestinarian. A new political world, healthier, more fully national, but less picturesque, less wrapt in the mystery and splendor which poets love, was rising with the new moral world. Rifts, which were still little, were widening hour by hour, and threatening ruin to the great fabric of church and state, which Elizabeth had built up, and to which the men of the Renascence clung passionately. From all this new world of feeling and action Shakespeare stood utterly aloof. Of the popular tendencies of Puritanism—and great as were its faults, Puritanism may fairly claim to be the first political system which recognized the grandeur of the people as a whole—Shakespeare knew nothing. In his earlier dramas he had reflected the common faith of his age in the grandeur of kingship as the one national centre; in his later plays he represents the aristocratic view of social life which was shared by all the nobler spirits of the Elizabethan time. Coriolanus is the embodiment of a great noble; and the reiterated taunts which he hurls in play after play at the rabble only echo the general temper of the Renascence. Nor were the spiritual sympathies of the poet those of the coming time. While the world was turning more and more to the speculations of theology, man and man's nature remained to the last the one inexhaustible subject of interest with Shakespeare, as it had been with his favorite Montaigne. Caliban was his latest creation. It is impossible to discover whether his faith, if faith there were, was Catholic or Protestant. It is difficult, indeed, to say whether he had any religious belief or not. The religious phrases which are thinly scattered over his works are little more than expressions of a distant and imaginative reverence. And on the deeper grounds of religious faith his silence is significant. He is silent, and the doubt of Hamlet deepens his silence, about the after world. "To die," it may be, was to him as to Claudio, "to go we know not where." Often, at any rate, as his "questionings" turn to the riddle of life and death, he leaves it a riddle to the last, without heeding the common theological solutions around him: "We are such stuff as dreams are made of, and our little life is rounded by a sleep."

As Mr. Green advances into the eighteenth century, there are symptoms of declining interest, of haste, perhaps, of natural fatigue. It is true that the "Augustan Age" is no longer in fashion. Dryden and Pope, Addison and Gray, are comparatively little read; but they are history for all that, and Mr. Palgrave's remark is worth remembering, that "an intelligent reader will find the influence of Newton as markedly in the poems of Pope, as of Elizabeth in the plays of Shakespeare." Fielding and Smollett, and the creation of the modern novel, are ignored like Pope, Gray, and Horace Walpole. The name of Burns is not to be found in Mr. Green's book, which contains no mention of the great revival he represented, which found its prophet in Wordsworth. Of Hume and Gibbon, of Samuel Johnson, of the philosophy and the mental struggles of the eighteenth century, Mr. Green says not a word. Even the political narrative of this period becomes labored. The mind at last refuses to assimilate this condensed essence of history, and one's last sensation is one of fatigue.

This is not altogether Mr. Green's fault. Any single mind has its limits, and even in the greatest human intelligence those limits are really not hard to reach, though its range of knowledge may seem infinite. A history of England must inevitably overstrain the powers of any mind, even the most capacious that has ever yet o'erinformed its tenement of clay. The field is too large. Great as is Mr. Green's ability and wide as is his learning, he cannot carry his own individuality thoroughly into every part of it. He cannot be equally sure of his judgment in every portion of the work. His mind must yield to human weariness. He cannot always be accurate even in his facts. It is true that, in the broad sense of absolute accuracy, there never was, and there never will be, a history written, so long as man is neither omniscient nor omnipresent, which can be more than approximately exact. Absolute truth in history is a thing which cannot be, at least so long as to err is human. But the more the historian's task is limited, the better is his chance of mastering every detail; in a compendious history of England, absolute mastery of detail is simply impossible. Probably no educated American has read Mr. Green's history without feeling that the American chapters, though admirably done, show only superficial study. The only American book referred to is Mr. Bancroft's History, even in regard to the colonization of New England. Dr. Palfrey is apparently unknown in British libraries; and that most delightful of all pictures of the Puritan, the "Life and Letters of Governor Winthrop," by Robert C. Winthrop, has never made its way to London. The ideal Puritan statesman, John Winthrop, is converted into a minister. Nine readers out of ten would understand Mr. Green to say that the crown granted a charter to Massachusetts, including Plymouth, and so created one Puritan colony, of which Boston was the capital. So, in the time of the American Revolution, an American would hardly have said that Washington gained his experience of war in Braddock's expedition, seeing that it was his experience in war that recommended him to Braddock. Nor would a Virginian have been apt to attribute so absolute an influence to Washington in 1770 over Virginia, as Mr. Green indicates. Virginia had at that time many great men, whose local influence was equal or superior to that of Washington. Nor would Americans generally concede that "even America hardly recognized Washington's real grandeur" till after his death. Americans, too, would hardly consider that Mr. Green understood or appreciated one of Washington's most brilliant military exploits, as described in the words, "The spring of 1776 saw them (the British army) withdrawn from Boston to New York." It was rather Montgomery's campaign than Arnold's raid that "nearly drove the British troops from Canada." Spain did not make an "alliance" with the States. These are mere matters of detail, and, in the great current of English history, American affairs are themselves a mere detail and may fill eight pages out of eight hundred. Nor is it intended to suggest that Mr. Green's book is inaccurate. On the contrary, it is probably as accurate as such a work can be. But if the American, who is a specialist in regard to the American portion of the book, detects in an instant that Mr. Green is not a specialist there, the probability is strong that specialists elsewhere will reach the same conclusion in their own peculiar fields.

In short, the difficulties inherent in the task of writing a compendious history of England are such as to defy complete success, and to make it almost a matter of regret that the highest order of mind should attempt it. There is another reason for regret, which is still more to the point. The time has not yet come when English history is well enough known to allow of its being written as a whole. Every year new light is thrown upon it, and the text-books of one decade are antiquated in the next. Even in regard to the last three hundred years, the most thoroughly known period of English history, new information is incessantly modifying the views of historians. Yet the writer who undertakes to deal with this period has one immense advantage. Since the fifteenth century the conditions of life have been tolerably uniform, so that any one now living may be supposed capable of entering without great effort into the thought, language, and manners of these centuries. But the life of England from the fifth century to the fifteenth is almost purely an antiquarian study. The original conditions of it are as yet not thoroughly certain. In spite of the labors of Sir Francis Palgrave, Mr. Freeman, and Professor Stubbs, early English history has by no means said its last word, and the harvest is still rich to the gleaner. And if this is the case with Saxon England, which has been so thoroughly and carefully worked over by men of such high abilities, what can be said of Norman and Angevin England? what of Lancastrian and Yorkist England? There are long gaps of frightful ignorance, wide chasms that have never been sounded, across

which Mr. Green leaps as he best can. For a long time yet the antiquarian must here be of more value than the generalizing historian;
the editor must precede the narrator; the microscope will be a more
valuable instrument than the field-glass. Sheer antiquarian drudgery
of the least attractive kind can alone bring those ages to life, restore
their modes of thought, their manners, and the logical sequence of
their steps.

The more highly, therefore, the critic appreciates the ability, the
genius that has so suddenly raised Mr. Green to the highest rank of
English historians, the more keen must be the regret that so charming
a work must soon cease to be abreast of the knowledge of the time.
Yet there is one consolation which will weigh against this drawback.
The advance of historical knowledge and the steady application of
sound historical method may diminish the authority and value of Mr.
Green's work as a mere statement of fact or theory, but nothing can
ever take away its calmness of judgment, its elevation of tone, or its
beauty of style.

21

TENNYSON'S 'QUEEN MARY'

Intimacy with Charles Milnes Gaskell brought Adams into close association with his friend's elders, notably his father, James Milnes Gaskell, who admittedly was an indolent member of Parliament, yet also was "a voracious reader and admirable critic"—as the American would later say in his *Education*—and knew all the English writers of the time, beginning with Tennyson.

James Milnes Gaskell died in 1872, while Adams was in Egypt. This sketch about Tennyson's new work can be viewed as homage to the elder Gaskell, although he is never mentioned.

The sketch applies to Tennyson an idea which perhaps was applicable to the poet but can be turned back on Adams—the idea that a writer should try to expand his mind "until it should embrace all mankind." As these sketches insistently show, the phrase is descriptive of Adams's own efforts while the sketches were being written.

The phrase is descriptive, too, of his future. He was planning a *History of the United States* which would not confine itself to the doings of Americans at home but also would embrace their dealings with all the nations with whom they had contact in the years considered, from the Indians and Canadians to the Latin Americans, Europeans, Russians, and Arabs. He was hoping as well to travel to innumerable places and before 1892 would actually get to many, including Spain, Morocco, Japan, Hawaii, Tahiti, Australia, and Ceylon.

The sketch takes Tennyson seriously as a would-be successor of Shakespeare. It can do so the more easily because Adams took himself seriously as a person of talent and enterprise, and attempted greater and greater things whether or not they should prove successful.

—*North American Review* (October 1875); unsigned—

Queen Mary. A Drama. By ALFRED TENNYSON. [Author's Edition from advance Sheets.] Boston: James R. Osgood & Co. 1875.

THE appearance of this drama is the most interesting event that has occurred for years in English literature, and the interest is peculiar in being quite independent of the success or failure of the poem. Mr. Tennyson's early poetry was graceful, sometimes thoughtful, sometimes, though not often, vigorous, but always reflected a mind which the public soon believed itself to understand and to feel no great difficulty in measuring. The poet did not at first roughly grapple with conceptions of human character; did not tear himself from the study and expression of those ideas which came easiest to him in order to put life into new creations. The Ulysses of Mr. Tennyson was but Mr. Tennyson himself under a mild restlessness, and not essentially different from Mr. Tennyson drinking his pint of port at the Cock. Most critics might well doubt and did doubt whether a mind self-limited in this manner could go far beyond its beaten path. They recalled Shelley and Byron, both naturally more vigorous than Tennyson, yet both apparently unable to conceive characters that were not either a counterpart of themselves or no characters at all. There was little reason to suppose that the author of the "Skipping Rope" and much more stuff could ever rise so high as to conceive a thoroughly human being. Yet as time went on it became evident that Mr. Tennyson himself was visibly tending towards and aiming at precisely that highest point of artistic ambition, the expansion of his own mind until it should embrace all mankind. Year after year saw him making one effort after another in the same direction, but always with a certain gain in the force of his grasp. The Idylls were in this respect an advance beyond "Maud," as "Maud" was an advance upon "The Princess." The "Northern Farmer," really a strong delineation, is like rough-hewn granite beside the flabbiness of the "May Queen." There were few attentive readers whose curiosity was not excited to learn how far it was possible for a poet to develop himself in this manner, and there were not many who had confidence enough in Mr. Tennyson's genius to believe that any other result than more or less complete failure was within the range of possibility. Nevertheless, even the attempt was deeply interesting.

And now Mr. Tennyson has not only made the attempt, but has
made it with an emphasis which cannot be mistaken. He has not only
discarded at one stroke all his old peculiarities, all those beauties of
form which made him famous, all those delicacies of expression which
formed a distinct mark in our literature, all those vague questionings
of social and superhuman problems which gave whatever appearance
of original thought there was in his early works; he has not only thus
cut loose from his own past and struck out into absolutely new seas,
but he has chosen a new method not less calculated to excite curiosity
and enthusiasm. He has aimed at nothing less than the highest mark.
This drama of "Queen Mary" from beginning to end, in its subject,
in its treatment, its language, its form, offers only one reasonable
explanation. Its subject is a close and direct continuation of Shakespeare's historical plays, its treatment closely adheres to Shakespeare's
mode of treatment, its language and its form are often startlingly
suggestive of Shakespeare. The play itself has been hailed from the
first by Mr. Tennyson's warmer admirers as the greatest drama since
Shakespeare's time. It is impossible to doubt that Mr. Tennyson has
intentionally and emphatically asserted his claim to the highest rank
among poets. He has challenged a seat by the side of Shakespeare.

That this should be Mr. Tennyson's meaning is not very surprising,
nor, if the conditions of success are closely examined, does there seem
to be anything very extravagant in the attempt, at least provided that
the idea of rivalry to Shakespeare be not too strongly suggested. In
point of fact, what historical English drama has been written since
Shakespeare's time? Why may not Mr. Tennyson reasonably aspire to
excel "Cato," "Venice Preserved," or "Beatrice Cenci" and "Marino
Faliero," or "Strafford"? And must not success in such an undertaking
result *pro tanto* in placing the successful poet next to Shakespeare? If
there be anything unreasonable in the attempt, it is because as a matter of fact the idea of actual rivalry to Shakespeare has been somewhat
too obviously suggested. Queen Mary is too near Henry the Eighth.
Cranmer and Gardiner are too directly the successors of Wolsey and
Cromwell. Mary is but the daughter of Queen Katherine, and Elizabeth of Anne Bullen. The clowns and crones of Tennyson tread on
the heels of those whose immortality has hitherto been the triumph
of the Elizabethan age.

Yet to institute a comparison, as thus suggested, between Queen

Mary and Henry the Eighth is out of the question. Queen Mary will not for a moment bear such a test. Nor is it proper in this instance to compare Mr. Tennyson with himself. He has abandoned his old paths and sought new ones. It would be unfair to him to test the new poetry by the tests which were once used for the old. There is no way in such a case but to throw aside comparisons, and to judge of Mr. Tennyson's success by abstract rules. There are two points to be settled: first, the question what Mr. Tennyson has created; and, second, by what means he has effected his result; or, in other words, what thought is embodied in the drama, and how is that thought expressed?

And to begin with, Mr. Tennyson must be acquitted of the suspicion of having written a political pamphlet. He is too thorough an artist not to have chosen his subject and his treatment of it with a full consciousness of its poetical capacities. If Queen Mary is, as has been said, not a subject for high tragical interest, it was for Mr. Tennyson to overcome that difficulty or abandon the subject. It must be acknowledged that the difficulty is not overcome. The drama embodies no profoundly tragical human interest or passion. The Queen Mary of this play is the Queen Mary of history, essentially prosaic even in her most exalted or depressed moments. Mr. Tennyson has added nothing to the thought, such as it was, that history furnished to him. He has not elevated it, he has not intensified it, he has not even suppressed the pettinesses of it. The power of the play, therefore, is not in its central motive, which Mr. Tennyson has simply adopted from history.

The list of Mr. Tennyson's dramatic characters numbers more than forty; and if to each of these the same test be applied, very much the same result will be reached. Philip hardly reaches the dignity of a conception at all. Elizabeth is better, but still more like a carefully studied imitation than a true creature of poetic genius. Cardinal Pole is much better. Here Mr. Tennyson evidently felt his character. Cranmer is the mere historical wax figure, one of the most disappointing of all; he embodies no thought of Mr. Tennyson's and suggests no moral meaning. Gardiner is better again, and has real life. But with all these and indeed with all the characters of the drama, except Joan and Tib and Old Nokes, the admiration felt by the reader is rather for Mr. Tennyson's capacity as an historian than as a poet. His figures, the incarnation of his thoughts, are not poetical creations. From beginning to end they are, as conceptions, prosaic. It is impossible to doubt that whatever Mr. Tennyson's power over language may be, his power over thought is not of the first nor even of the second order. Many English dramatists are here his masters.

So far there seems to be a tolerable agreement among Mr. Tennyson's critics, who may indeed differ as to the exact relative rank of their author among creative poets, but who are commonly agreed that this rank is not the highest. The difficulties increase, however, when the question of form is reached. If Mr. Tennyson is not one of the first among inventive poets, he has been at least pre-eminent as a master of form and expression. And one cannot but admire his courage when one sees him challenging the highest rank among creative poets and voluntarily stripping himself, as he steps on the stage, of all those advantages which have hitherto been his chief instruments of success. Mr. Tennyson must indeed have both great courage and great confidence in himself, to choose such an ordeal. There can be few more interesting subjects of criticism than to determine how far that self-confidence has been justified by success.

Certainly in no mean degree. If depth of thought is wanting, there is yet much in the manner in which the drama is worked out, much in the detail, that must claim high praise. There is even an excess of delicate analysis and refined execution where there should be broad conceptions. Yet the poet has rigorously confined this delicacy of touch to his development of character; the mere language is even at times unnecessarily rough. Perhaps the best part of the whole drama is the debate in the Council on burning heretics (Act III. Scene 4), where Cardinal Pole's character is finely delineated, and which is admirably supplemented by Scene 2, Act V., where Pole and Mary unite for the last time in expression of their common feeling, now of despair as at first of triumph. If Mary's historical character had been as sympathetic to Mr. Tennyson as Pole's, this drama would have been a very fine, perhaps even a very great work. But Mary's character has evidently wanted the poet's thorough interest. He never wholly becomes identified with her. Even in Mary's last scene, where her mind wanders, broken by the weight of its disappointments, and she sees the figures of Latimer and Cranmer in her wanderings, the vision inspires no terror, not even a shudder, in the by-stander:

O God! I have been too slack, too slack;
There are Hot Gospellers even among our guards,—
Nobles we dared not touch. . . . . But by God's grace
We'll follow Philip's leading, and set up
The Holy Office here—garner the wheat
And burn the tares with unquenchable fire!
Burn!
Fie, what a savor! tell the cooks to close
The doors of all the offices below.
Latimer!
Sir, we are private with our women here—
Ever a rough, blunt, and uncourtly fellow—
Thou light a torch that never will go out!
'T is out,—mine flames. . . . . Ah, weak and meek old man
Seven-fold dishonored even in the sight
Of thine own sectaries. No, no. No pardon!—
Why, that was false: there is the right hand still
Beckons me hence.
Sir, you were burnt for heresy, not for treason,
Remember that! 't was I and Bonner did it,
And Pole; we are three to one. Have you found mercy there,
Grant it me here: and see he smiles and goes,
Gentle as in life.
   Alice. Madam, who goes? King Philip?

Does it need turn to Shakespeare to see why this is not what it might
be? The wonder is how the poet, in face of "Macbeth" and "Hamlet,"
should have dared such a flight. Through it all, the woman is commonplace and really sees and feels no more in her hallucination than
in her most practical daily life. And what is worse, her attendants see
no more in it than herself. But at least Mary is respectfully dealt with,
whereas her husband Philip is absolutely maltreated by the poet, who
is not content with making him unamiable, but actually makes him
vulgar, and in doing so, necessarily to the same extent makes the
drama vulgar. What can be said of verses like these?

   . . . . I am sicker staying here
Than any sea could make me passing hence,
Tho' I be ever deadly sick at sea.
So sick am I with biding for this child.
Is it the fashion in this clime for women
To go twelve months in bearing of a child?

If it be said that Philip was really vulgar as well as morose, and mean in intellect as narrow in sympathy, not only can this be no good reason for degrading the poetry, but in reality the drama is hardly consistent with itself. Nothing could be more kingly than his answer to Mary's innuendo:

> *Philip.* .... Many voices call me hence.
> *Mary.* Voices,—I hear unhappy rumors,—nay,
> I say not I believe. What voices call you
> Dearer than mine that should be dearest to you?
> Alas, my Lord! What voices and how many?
> *Philip.* The voices of Castile and Aragon,
> Granada, Naples, Sicily, and Milan,
> The voices of Franche Comté, and the Netherlands,
> The voices of Peru and Mexico,
> Tunis and Oran, and the Philippines,
> And all the fair spice-islands of the East.

Another difficulty rises from the fact that many important characters disappear before they are half delineated. Courtenay and Wyatt, even Gardiner himself, and Bonner, vanish just as the reader is learning to understand and take interest in them. The material for many tragedies is crowded into one, and the controlling interest is not strong enough to reduce all the details to a proper subordination.

Of refinements of language such as the reader of Mr. Tennyson's poetry habitually expects, of harmonies of expression, there are, as has been already said, comparatively few. The whole first act contains hardly more than one. When Mary is told that Philip is earnest to set foot in England, she bursts out:

> God change the pebble which his kingly foot
> First presses into some more costly stone
> Than ever blinded eye. I'll have one mark it
> And bring it me. I'll have it burnish'd firelike;
> I'll set it round with gold, with pearl, with diamond.
> Let the great angel of the church come with him;
> Stand on the deck and spread his wings for sail.

This is fine, more especially the two concluding lines, which are in deep harmony with Mary's fanatical union of human and heavenly devotion. But, at the risk of hypercriticism, one might perhaps suggest a doubt whether the use here indicated for wings is altogether poetical. Birds use their wings to soar upon, to beat the air with, and so, it is presumed, do angels. A bird, even the most stately, if it stood on a log and spread its wings for a sail, would be an amusing but hardly a poetic object. Why should an angel be permitted to use his wings in a manner that would be ludicrous in an eagle? Besides, to sailors, such a simile must inevitably raise associations with another kind of wing-and-wing navigation,—associations that are fatal to gravity.

Cardinal Pole's figure is perhaps on the whole more pleasing:

> .... Who lights the fagot?
> Not the full faith, no, but the lurking doubt.
> Old Rome, that first made martyrs in the Church,
> Trembled for her own gods, for these were trembling,—
> But when did our Rome tremble?

Paget.   Did she not
> In Henry's time and Edward's?

Pole.   What, my Lord!
> The Church on Peter's Rock! never! I have seen
> A pine in Italy that cast its shadow
> Athwart a cataract; firm stood the pine,—
> The cataract shook the shadow. To my mind
> The cataract typed the headlong plunge and fall
> Of heresy to the pit; the pine was Rome.
> You see, my Lords,
> It was the shadow of the Church that trembled.

Many real admirers of Mr. Tennyson who are yet not quite convinced of his tragic power will frankly own that they find their old friend at his best in the pretty song of the milkmaid, which contrasts so gracefully with the cares and anxieties of Elizabeth:

> Shame upon you, Robin,
> Shame upon you now!
> Kiss me would you? with my hands
> Milking the cow?
> Daisies grow again,
> Kingcups blow again,
> And you came and kissed me, milking the cow.

> Robin came behind me,
> Kiss'd me well I vow,
> Cuff him could I? with my hands
> Milking the cow?
> Swallows fly again,

Cuckoos cry again,
And you came and kissed me, milking the cow.
Come, Robin, Robin,
Come and kiss me now;
Help it can I? with my hands
Milking the cow?
Ringdoves coo again,
All things woo again,
Come behind and kiss me, milking the cow!

Finally, if it is necessary to sum up the result of the impressions produced by Mr. Tennyson's drama, it must be conceded that "Queen Mary" contains nothing which will change the opinion of those who had already made up their minds that Mr. Tennyson was a master of form, but not of thought, that he could express, but not invent. On the other hand, it cannot be denied that as a study of life, "Queen Mary" is not only an advance, but a considerable advance, upon anything the poet has yet done. He is not losing, but gaining, ground. He has descended into the arena and fought for the prize without the assistance of his own natural weapons, and he has at once, if not achieved a great victory, at least escaped defeat. In spite of its defects, "Queen Mary" is a higher type of work than anything Mr. Tennyson had done before. No doubt there are natural limits to the poet's power of self-development, but he seems not yet to have reached them. If he writes a drama of Queen Elizabeth, it will probably be better than "Queen Mary"; and, questionable as the success of "Queen Mary" is, there is still enough in it that is excellent to make the world ask for more.

22

WALKER'S 'STATISTICAL ATLAS
OF THE UNITED STATES'

Until another claimant arrives, which may never happen, this sketch, previously attributed to no one, should be attributed to Adams, who certainly was its editor, is readily held to have thought every idea and felt every sentiment it expresses, and wrote in the style it displays. And even if on the basis of new evidence the sketch were assigned to another writer, it would retain a decided importance for persons interested in its editor.

In his writings of the 1870s, Adams refers in varying ways to science, the scientific method, and the historical method without saying explicitly what he has in mind. The last sentence of the second paragraph of this sketch fills the void. It admirably states the idea of scientific (or historical) inquiry to which his historical practice consistently adhered.

Historians were usually thought of as persons interested in stating their conclusions in words. This sketch, in response to one of the colored maps in Walker's *Atlas,* says of this graphic representation, "Nothing can more clearly and impressively epitomize the history of the United States." It is an Adams response; for, in his work as a historian in the 1870s and 1880s, Adams showed as much interest in maps and statistics as in words. The opening line of his *History of the United States* would read, "According to the census of 1800, the United States of America contained 5,308,483 persons"; and in the later pages of his nine-volume narrative he would strive relentlessly to establish valid historical measurements and quantifications.

Much work done in the 1870s by Walker, King, and others which

Adams regarded as especially valuable was conducted under the aegis of the federal government and paid for with national monies. Two years after this sketch was published, Adams would move to Washington and—in company with Bancroft—would go to the State Department to begin research in its archives. Adams would pay his own expenses. Firms in Philadelphia, Boston, and New York would publish his books. None the less, his work would be a national service; and the fact would be mirrored in such details as his being accorded a desk at the State Department and deliveries and recoveries of books at his door by the Library of Congress, for all the world as if he were a senator or a member of the cabinet.

For him, such things were not new. He was an Adams, indeed an exceptional Adams. Never in office, he was always in office. A permanent insider in the government, he spoke the language his position entailed. The language is very distinctive. Its accents are audible throughout this orphaned sketch, now hopefully returned to its writer.

—*North American Review* (October 1875); unsigned—

Statistical Atlas of the United States, based on the Results of the Ninth Census, 1870, with Contributions from many eminent Men of Science, and several Departments of the Government. Compiled under Authority of Congress, by FRANCIS A. WALKER, M. A., Superintendent of the Ninth Census, Professor of Political Economy and History, Sheffield Scientific School of Yale College. Julius Bien, Lithographer. 1874.

GENERAL WALKER is one of the few American soldiers who, leaving the army for the civil service at the close of the war, have not rested upon a creditable military record, or betaken themselves from the camp to the caucus, but have achieved fresh distinction, and established new claims to popular confidence and gratitude by the display in administrative affairs of scientific method, enthusiastic industry, and practical skill. As chief of the Bureau of Statistics, he exhibited the qualities which almost forced his appointment to superintend the Ninth Census; and in this position his executive ability led to his appointment as Commissioner of Indian Affairs,—an office which he resigned, after too brief an occupancy, to accept the professorship at New Haven which he now fills. The civil service can ill afford to lose officers who combine literary and scientific culture with practical experience; but, on the other hand, institutions of learning are doubly blest in obtaining instructors who possess the knowledge of men and affairs, as well as of books and theories.

There is no science which more imperatively requires to be studied and handled with common-sense than the new science of statistics, particularly in its applications to vital, social, and political problems. The chemist, astronomer, or pure mathematician may pursue his inquiries in cloistered seclusion, and remain a child, in his ignorance of the world around him, outside of his special department. But the statistician must be able to combine the strictness and conscientiousness of minute inquiry with the power of wise generalization, including in his calculations incalculable elements, divining the reasons of variable phenomena, and patiently following out to demonstration the clews of his own insight. Obviously the first necessity of this process is the collection of trustworthy data; then comes the critical recognition of their incompleteness; and finally, highest and most difficult of all, the scientific discussion of the facts known, with the scientific interpolation, in due provisional measure and weight, of the facts half known or unknown.

It is matter for ever-fresh regret that Congress fell into a politicians' wrangle over the new law proposed for the taking of the Ninth Census, and, not being able to agree upon the needed reforms in the system, left it in a form which was universally known to be bad. But the good workman is known by his performance with imperfect tools; and the results of the Ninth Census were obtained, under all the defects and discouragements of the law, with surprising rapidity and accuracy. As far as they go, they are trustworthy: which is the first great point. Moreover, their shortcomings are clearly recognized and pointed out in the volumes themselves: which is the second great point. And their significance has been elucidated in so many fruitful and suggestive applications by Professor Walker and his co-laborers as to confer upon the work itself an unexampled practical and popular value.

In the publication of the quarto volumes of the Census, Professor Walker obtained authority to introduce twenty-four plates, all of which, we believe, were geographical in form; that is, they were maps of the United States, upon which certain physical, vital, and industrial relations were indicated by the use of different shades of color. The experiment of reducing in this way the tables of population, nationality, disease, industry, and wealth to graphic form was very successful; and Professor Walker was authorized in 1873 to prepare—what we cannot better describe than by using the words of the Secretary of the Interior, in recommending the measure—"A Statistical Atlas of the United States, based upon the results of the Ninth Census, to contain a large number of maps, with appropriate text and tables, ... for distribution to public libraries, learned societies, colleges, and academies, with a view to promote that higher kind of political education which has hitherto been so greatly neglected in this country, but toward which the attention of the general public, as well as of instructors and students, is now being turned with the most lively interest."

The result of this measure is the work before us, a magnificent folio Atlas, containing sixty full-page plates, with a series of monographs from expert hands upon special topics. The typography of the text is very handsome; and the lithographic work reflects much credit upon Mr. Bien, who has in this publication equalled or surpassed all former achievements of American lithographic map-makers. The colors are well chosen, and the registering and printing in the copy before us are worthy of high praise.

We can scarcely do better than enumerate the contents of the work, by way of giving some notion of its scope and value. To follow out the innumerable suggestions of a single one of its charts would lead us into themes too profound and too extensive for our present purpose.

The work is divided into three parts, devoted respectively to the Physical Features of the United States; Population, Social and Industrial Statistics; and Vital Statistics.

Under the first head the plates comprise maps illustrating the river systems, forest areas, rain-fall, frequency of storm-centres, mean and extreme temperatures, barometric conditions, altitudes, etc., of the United States. There is also a map of the coal-measures, by Professor Hitchcock, including all the areas east of the Missouri; but not covering the immense and but partially explored lignitic coal-fields of the Rocky Mountain system, or those still farther west, in the Pacific States and Territories. The geological map of the United States, by Professors Hitchcock and Blake, which also accompanies this part, does not throw light upon the coal-resources of the Far West, because the coal-fields of Colorado, New Mexico, Wyoming, Montana, Utah, Idaho,

Oregon, and California, being Tertiary or Cretaceous in age, are colored like all the rest of the Tertiary or Cretaceous formations. The Carboniferous period is indeed largely represented in the Interior Basin, but mostly by deep-water formations. The only true Carboniferous coal reported from that region is mined on a small scale near Eureka, Nevada. But these resources are too little known or developed as yet to be tabulated or graphically represented; and we do not wonder that Professor Hitchcock has let them alone, just as Professor Blake has wisely forborne to attempt any representation in colors of the shifting and inchoate industry of gold and silver mining. Some years ago, an ambitious Commissioner of the General Land Office at Washington issued a map of the country on which the localities in the Far West, producing gold, silver, and other metals, were indicated by spots of appropriate color. But those who were acquainted with the region failed to discover why the Commissioner's spots should occupy the precise localities he had chosen for them. Spots were vanishing and new spots breaking out, every season; and the freckled map was merely laughed at. The time had not come for such a generalization. Perhaps it may be near at hand now; but the work involves a careful discussion of the observations of King, Wheeler, Hayden, and Raymond, to say nothing of earlier explorers, by some one who is familiar with the history and the latest phases of the mining industry of the West. In the present volume, we find a very general survey of the subject from the pen of Dr. R. W. Raymond, the United States Commissioner of Mining Statistics, the most important parts of which are the tables of estimated production of gold and silver by years. Professor J. D. Whitney contributes an article on the Physical Features of the United States; Professor W. H. Brewer discusses the Woodlands and Forest Systems of the country; and Professors Hitchcock and Blake furnish appropriate text in elucidation of their geological maps. We seriously miss from this part a botanical chart of the United States, such, for instance, as Professor Porter of Lafayette College has published. It would be useful for comparison with the geological, hypsometrical, and climatic maps.

Part II contains many of the plates with which the Census volumes have already made us acquainted, illustrating the political divisions; the various relations of population (density, birth, parentage, distribution, illiteracy, occupation); the church accommodations provided

by different denominations; the characteristic crops of the country
and their distribution; the relations of wealth, debt, and taxation per
capita in different sections, etc. Here, as in all the plates of the Atlas,
most ingenious use is made of forms and colors to represent gener-
alized relations. The different shades of color represent on each map
different degrees of the element or proportion under consideration.
In the geometrical charts color has another function. For instance, in
those of church accommodations and occupations, the color indicates
the denomination or occupation; and the area of the diagram so colored, the proportion represented. The map illustrating the political
history of our territory shows still another use of color, to indicate the
successive acquisitions of territory by which the country became what
it is as a whole, and the phases of political change through which each
of the present political divisions (States and Territories) has passed.
Thus we can trace at a glance the early struggle between England and
France; the foothold of Spain in Florida and Mexico; the results of
the Revolution; the settlement of the disputes between New York and
Vermont, Massachusetts and Maine; the cession of Western colonial
grants to the general government by many of the original States; the
formation of Territories and States from these; the acquisition of
"Louisiana," under which modest title we got what is now Louisiana,
Arkansas, the Indian Territory, Kansas, Missouri, Nebraska, Iowa,
Minnesota, Dakotah, Montana, Idaho, Washington, and Oregon, with
more than half of Wyoming and nearly half of Colorado; the acquisition of Florida from Spain; the annexation of Texas, then including
part of New Mexico and Colorado; the conquest of California, including Utah and Nevada, with parts of Wyoming, Colorado, New Mexico,
and Arizona; the purchase under the Gadsden treaty of the remainder
of the two latter Territories; and, finally, the purchase of Alaska. An
enlarged copy of this map, similarly colored, ought to hang on the
wall of every American school-room. Nothing can more clearly and
impressively epitomize the history of the United States. Mr. S. W.
Stocking, the maker of the map, accompanies it with a full text of
explanation; but its great features, which are also its best, require
nothing further. Mr. S. A. Galpin, in an article on the Minor Political
Subdivisions of the United States, describes the political system based
on the township as a unit, and characteristic of New England; the
county system, characteristic of the South; and the combination of the

two, or "compromise system," as he calls it, which is followed in the Northwest and larger Middle States. The article is not cumbered with argument or reflection; it gives clear distinctions and descriptions, and then stops.

The article on the Progress of the Nation gives a tolerably good example, and the article in Part III. on the Relations of Race and Nationality to Mortality in the United States gives a very good one, of the method in which Professor Walker deals with statistical material. He is at home among the figures he has marshalled together. They march at his command. But he does not parade them in mere display or exhaust them in sham manœuvres. The article last named is specially valuable as furnishing a hint to the student of the way in which profitable use may be made of the rich material here accumulated.

Mr. E. B. Elliott, of the Bureau of Statistics, contributes some estimates of the probable population of the country in 1880, and of the population in every year since 1780, arrived at by a system of interpolation by "second differences." Mr. Elliott's estimate for 1880 is a little over 54,000,000. He also appears in Part III. as the constructor, on the basis of the very deficient vital statistics of the Census, of an approximate life table for the United States. The plates in this part comprise graphic illustrations of the local predominance of sex, of birth and death rates, and their relations to age, sex, and nationality, and to four principal classes of disease; and of the afflicted classes, namely, the blind, deaf-mute, insane, and idiotic. In the treatment of these subjects, Mr. F. H. Wines, who constructed the diagrams, has devised a new and ingenious method of using ordinates, so as to indicate three relations at once. For instance, to represent the distribution of the blind between the two sexes and among the several periods of life, a vertical line is divided into ten equal parts, each standing for a ten-year period. At the points of division ordinates are drawn to right and left, perpendicular to the vertical. Those to the right indicate females; those to the left, males. The length of each ordinate is proportioned to the number of blind of that sex at that age. The ends of the ordinates on each side are connected with a curve which forms the boundary of the figure; and finally, the sex which predominates on the whole is indicated by the shading of that side. The numerous little figures of this character, each occupying less than a square inch, which occupy several of the charts of vital statistics, bear witness to the compendious nature of this device.

In concluding this hasty survey of Professor Walker's admirable work, we desire to say of many of these charts what we have said already of one. They ought to be copied and enlarged and used for purposes of instruction in schools. There is much in them that cannot fail to impress even children with correct general ideas concerning the physical resources and distributed population and industries of the country; while any one of them would furnish a text for the profoundest comment on the part of the accomplished teacher or professor, in the presence of a class of advanced students. We trust some enterprising publisher will consider the feasibility of such an undertaking. A series of selected charts of this kind, especially if accompanied with a manual of explanations and additional information, references to authorities, etc., for the use of the teacher, ought to be both successful and beneficial. Indeed, the principal use of such a work should be rather the stimulation of thought and the facilitation of inquiry on the part of beginners. The true statistician maps and pictures his subjects in his head. For him rows of figures have color and voice and form. Yet even the most practised veteran in this "scientific use of the imagination" may find strange and unexpected suggestions and discoveries to spring from the contemplation of a few ingenious diagrams, in which, by a skilful use of simple symbolism, the various elements of numerous social problems are exhibited in juxtaposition or in superposition, so that their relations may be clearly seen. Indeed, without such assistance many interesting questions would scarcely be solved, and many others would never have been raised at all.

23

PALFREY'S 'HISTORY OF NEW ENGLAND'

In winter, when a boy, Adams spent many hours in the library of his parents' house on Beacon Hill, at 57 Mount Vernon Street. There he frequently saw one of his father's friends and political associates, John Gorham Palfrey. The boy and Palfrey formed a relationship which later had a serious consequence. Aware that Henry was interested in history, Palfrey, in 1861, challenged him to attempt a historical investigation at the British Museum. After some delays, Henry took up the challenge, and in doing so became a historian, although of a very limited kind. (See appendix C.)

Palfrey all the while was pushing forward through a *History of New England* in several volumes. In 1875, he published volume 4. As a matter of course, he had a copy sent to Henry, as editor of the *North American*. Adams by then had reviewed Bancroft's last volume and a key volume by Parkman. Wanting to review Palfrey's volume also, he read it (using a copy he appears to have purchased) and made a judgment possibly as unexpected to himself as it was startling to Palfrey: his lifelong friend was a better historian than his American rivals.

In the sketch that follows, Adams writes as if this opinion had been the judgment of the *North American* always—a pretense perhaps intended to help the judgment register and stay in memory. Yet he writes with an enthusiasm which must be new, for it grows dramatic. Palfrey had done something in volume 4 which Adams could honor beyond all ordinary achievements. The historian had taken for his subject a dispirited and miserable segment of human experience, had squarely faced its dreariness and monotony, and had written a narrative so unflinchingly honest that a reader could find it irresistible.

Volume 4 touched Adams where he was acutely sensitive, for it concerned democracy and resistance to misrule. Palfrey told a story in which leadership, or something better, is provided by average persons doing what they feel they have to do—"village Hampdens who came up to Boston year after year and voted solidly to disobey the royal orders."

Disobedience in Massachusetts! That is where these sketches took their start. There they also find an end. Having returned to a theme so heartfelt and familiar, Adams could know he had done enough. His book of sketches was complete.

—*North American Review* (October 1875); unsigned—

History of New England. By JOHN GORHAM PALFREY. Vol. IV. Boston: Little, Brown, and Company. 1875.

DR. PALFREY introduces his fourth volume by an intimation that illness and age have shaken his powers so that he must expect to fall short of his ideal, and must be content to produce what may not bear a rigorous criticism. The rigorous critic, with his attention sharpened by this warning, may perhaps succeed in detecting the signs of age and failing powers which have escaped our notice, but on a first reading we must confess to having failed in discovering any reason for placing this volume below its predecessors. Whether further study will alter this impression remains to be seen; but as yet the qualities which in our opinion have hitherto placed Dr. Palfrey absolutely first in the ranks of American historians, the strong good-sense, the thorough study, the sober and finished style, the contempt for sentimentalism and affectation either of thought or manner, the lurking humor, and, above all, the thoroughly healthy and manly insight into the morals of his subject, seem as evident in this volume as in any that have gone before. Nothing is more striking in the early society which he has described, than the individuality of character which in comparison with our own time seems to stamp each actor on the scene with a sharpness of outline as different from modern vagueness as a portrait of Holbein from a chromo-lithograph. In this era of diluted morality and popular history, Dr. Palfrey's great work has caught something of that strong quality of mind and thought which was so characteristic of the Puritan age.

The period covered by this volume, between 1689 and 1740, furnishes little either in Europe or America that can elevate or inspire the historian. The world, weary of convulsions and religious enthusiasm, was glad to rest. The Church fell into contempt. Political development ceased. Gross immorality or cynical indifference, such as were without a parallel in modern times, succeeded the long sway of religion. From this corruption France and Germany could only recover by a convulsion that destroyed the continuity of their history, and the reader of English annals is actually at a loss to understand what preserved the English Constitution and the English Church from the same fate. Chatham did indeed save the one and Whitfield the other, but the danger for a time was extreme.

During these fifty years of reaction, corruption, and indifferentism, the Puritan colonies of New England were an anachronism in the world. Virginia or Pennsylvania could flourish in such an atmosphere, but New England slowly perished. The descendants of Winthrop, Endicott, and Dudley found themselves in a new order of things. Their fathers' great experiment of a religious commonwealth had broken down. The past had to be abandoned. To shape a new future was a work of time, and the leaders were no longer men of heroic stature. It is sad to watch how literature gradually declines, how men's acts and motives become petty, how their religion grows hard and formal, their temper becomes sour, their very persons seem to grow thin and sharp, during this period of arrested development. It is this half-century of small things and small men with which Dr. Palfrey's fourth volume is filled, and naturally such a subject can hardly be enlivening. Beginning with the sombre picture of the witchcraft delusion, the author's style rises for a moment, as it is apt to do in dealing with these deeply marked characteristics of New England, into an elevation that is not far from pathos:

If any may be specially excused for being led astray by gloomy superstitions, it is they who are surrounded by circumstances, and pressed by griefs and anxieties, such as incline to sad and unhealthy meditation. The experience of the three heroic generations of English exiles in Massachusetts had been hard and sorrowful. Of those who were living when the provincial charter came into effect, the memory of the oldest went back to the primitive times of want and misery; the middle-aged men had been out in arms in the most dreadful of the Indian wars, and the middle-aged women had passed years of mourning for the husbands, lovers, and brothers whom it had swept away. The generation just entered upon the stage had been born and reared in melancholy homes. The present was full of troubles and forebodings. The venerated charter had been lost. Social ties had been weakened. Social order was insecure. The paths of enterprise were obstructed. Industry had little impulse. Poverty was already felt. There was danger of destitution. A powerful foreign enemy threatened, and the capacity for defence was crippled by penury. A people in the mood to which such surroundings naturally lead could scarcely be expected to set the example of a release from gloomy visions which bewildered the rest of mankind. Nor would it be fanciful to ascribe some influence on the spirits and the imagination to the austere environments of the settlers, and the harsh aspects of the scenery amid which their temper had been educated and their daily life was passed. An ocean divided them from the old seats of civilized life. Almost in the primitive nakedness of existence they were waging a contest with the awful elements. Their little settlements were isolated and unjoyous. The scene all around,—river, rock, covert, mountain, forest,—almost as wild and sombre as creation left it, invited to stern and melancholy musing.

The administrations of Phips and Bellomont (1692–1701) were marked by no strong indications of renewed longings for independence. Massachusetts was cautious and new to the situation, nor were either of these governors men to alarm her pride. But with the return of her hated child, Dudley, to power, in 1702, began that sullen and dogged resistance, varied on either side by outbursts of ill-temper, but always restrained within the limits of constitutional action, which slowly led on to the popular explosion of 1765. Under Dudley's successor, Shute (1716–1727), the Legislature no longer contented itself with resistance, but began a systematic and persistent policy of encroachment upon the royal prerogative, and seemed disposed to exclude the royal governors from all share in the internal control of the colony. Burnet was then sent to bring them to order after they had worried Shute out of the country, but the unfortunate Burnet fell a victim to his persecutors, and died without gaining a single step. Belcher, who succeeded Burnet in 1730, was, like Dudley, a native New-Englander, and knew how to manage his countrymen better than the Shutes and Burnets of an English court could ever have done. By yielding what had to be conceded, and persisting as doggedly as the Legislature in what was feasible, Belcher won the honors of a drawn battle. Dr. Palfrey's account of this long constitutional struggle is apparently candid, and as interesting as so petty a quarrel can easily be made. During the first half of the period he has the advantage of a certain degree of personal interest lingering about the sharply defined figures of a few remnants of the Puritan age. Stoughton, Dudley, and the Mathers are characters that can still be recalled to life. Dr. Palfrey's summing up of Stoughton's career is an excellent example of his style:

He had filled many offices, and performed their duties with a surly assi-duity, which commanded a certain sort of esteem. He perhaps loved nobody, though the winning as well as commanding powers of Dudley may have blended something of affection with the deference into which he was subdued by the genius of that highly endowed man. On the other hand, if he was not loved, Stoughton was not of a temper to be made uncomfortable by isolation, while it was a pleasure to him to feel that he had some command of that confidence which men repose in such as they see to be indifferent to their good-will, and independent of it as coveting nothing which it has to be-stow. . . . . The prosecution of the witches was a proceeding quite to his mind; the "stern joy" of inflicting great misery under the coercion of an unflinching sense of duty was strangely congenial with his proud and narrow nature; he had a morbid relish for that class of duties which, bringing wretchedness on others, may be supposed to cost the doer a struggle against the pleadings of pity. When, sympathizing with the almost universal sorrow and remorse that succeeded the witchcraft madness, his gentle associate Sewall publicly be-moaned his sin, and in agony implored the divine forgiveness, Stoughton professed that, whatever mistakes might have been made, he saw "no reason to repent of what he had done with the fear of God before his eyes." . . . . If the people did not want him, he could be content; at all events, he would not complain or solicit. If they did want him, he would serve them without fraud and without ambition, but it must be after his own grim fashion. . . . . He meant to be excellently firm; he excelled in being churlish, morose, and ob-stinate, in a style of the most unimpeachable dignity.

Towards Dudley, on the other hand, Dr. Palfrey measures out a sterner judgment:

It is needless to multiply words on the character of Dudley. It was not a mystery, nor was he a monster of turpitude. There is no necessity to regard him as having been destitute of all moral sense, nor even to set down his religious professions as merely hypocritical and false. . . . . For aught man can know, this man, like many others more famous and many less famous than he, had tampered with his better mind till the distinctions which make the world's security were obscured to his own view; and with a certain sort of sincerity he could call evil good and good evil as often as only evil would suit his domineering aim. At all events, he had no purpose to be true and useful. He meant to get power, and all that power brings with it, and with gay arrogance placed his unimportant self above the rights and the welfare of the community, which, with honest affection, had empowered him to do it grievous harm. . . . . From his early awakening to the consciousness of uncommon powers, he seems to have considered with a confident disdain what an unwise part his father had chosen when he undertook to be a witness and a sufferer for liberty and right. Though he never knew his father, who died in his early childhood, he had heard from his nursery-days of the hardships which Christian heroism had brought on that lofty-minded, if narrow-minded, man; and in his own bosom he found nothing that promised compensation for the sacrifices of such a career. . . . . When his power to wrong and distress the native country which had confided and taken pride in him had been well ascertained, he had no reluctance to this more lucrative service; for the lust of gain had silenced all misgivings, and by constitution he had sufficient courage to be not only without scruples but without shame. Thomas Hutchinson, two generations later, was so like him as to be quite unconscious of the condemnation which he was pronouncing when he said of Dudley, that "he had as many virtues as can consist with so great a thirst for honor and power."

If anything could make us quarrel with Dr. Palfrey, it would be that he has omitted to give an equally careful estimate of the Mathers. These personages have hardly yielded to the History all the enlivenment or instruction which they could have been made to supply, and, in a dreary waste like this, the humor which the Mathers can furnish should be utilized to the utmost. With Cotton Mather the old clerical influence ran out in absurdities, and henceforward the new class of lawyers were to give another aspect to society. But in the interval the wilderness is miserably barren. Dudley, Stoughton, Phips, the Mathers, and the royal governors aside, Dr. Palfrey's fourth volume has almost no personal interest to offer. The Legislature had leaders, and we know their names, but no more. In 1728, Governor Burnet made a sharp and effective attack on the Legislature, as follows:

I may appeal to the consciences of such gentlemen as have been concerned in the public affairs here, whether the allowance for the governor's salary has not been kept back till other bills of moment have been consented to, and whether it has not sometimes depended on the obtaining such consent. These matters, which are well known, leave no room to wonder why his Majesty thinks this method of supporting the governors a design to make them dependent on the people. And as you have given me no reason at all against this opinion, I must believe it is the real view intended to be pursued.

To this direct thrust the House riposted thus:

If we resemble the British Constitution, as your Excellency has done us the honor to declare, we humbly apprehend that no part of the Legislature should be independent. We have ever conceived that it was the peculiar distinction and glory of the British Constitution, that every part of it had a mutual relation to and dependence on each other. . . . . If your Excellency intends that we do not put so much confidence in the governor as the Parliament do in our most gracious sovereign, to whom the civil list is granted for his life, (which God long preserve!) we freely acknowledge it. Is it reasonable or possible that we should confide in any governor whatsoever so much as in our most gracious king, the common father of all his subjects, who is known to delight in nothing so much as their happiness, and whose interest and glory, and that of his royal progeny, are inseparable from the prosperity and welfare of his people, whereas it is most obvious that neither the prosperity nor adversity of a people affect a governor's interest at all when he has once left them? . . . . As to the past conduct of Assemblies in making the support of the government conditional, it is not easy to say what men may have had or had not in their own views and thoughts; but this we can say, that to have done so, as the case might have been circumstanced, would not have been unreasonable in itself nor without precedent from the Parliaments of England, when some of the greatest patriots and most wise and learned statesmen have been actors in them. . . . We are constrained, in faithfulness to the people of this Province, to say that we cannot pass any Act to establish a fixed salary for the governor, according to your Excellency's instructions from his Majesty.

This paper, admirably compounded of audacity and skill, can be the work of no ordinary man. Yet of such documents we learn only what Hutchinson can tell us, that they were "supposed to have been drawn by Mr. Cooke, ... and in the latter part of the controversy they were generally drawn by Mr. Wells." What manner of men were these? What was their conversation, their reading, their mode of life? We know as little of them as though they had flourished in the Middle Ages. "The greatest part of them [the House of Representatives]," writes Shute, "are of small fortunes and mean education." There are, indeed, few more curious spectacles in the history of constitutional government than this, of the people of Massachusetts, with no authoritative leader, with neither wealth nor social position, with very defective education, and with no clearly defined fundamental principle of government which they dared avow, carrying on a long, arduous, and successful constitutional struggle against the influence of the crown, and establishing precedents of which no one else in the whole world then understood the value. But the peculiarity of the phenomenon itself renders the subject the more difficult to enliven.

These village Hampdens who came up to Boston year after year and voted solidly to disobey the royal orders, were the offspring of town-meetings and the Puritan church-system. They have left no record of their own personality. They can only be dealt with in mass, as a tendency, a force, which belonged to the soil and the atmosphere. Dr. Palfrey is loyal to them in the best sense. He confesses that, "at first view," the jealousy entertained by Massachusetts of her royal governors seems captious. This is certainly a kindly view of the subject. Most readers would readily enough agree that the manifestations of that jealousy not only seemed, but often were captious, and calculated to do more harm than good. The pettiness of the points which the Legislature sometimes chose to dispute, does not indicate leadership of the first class. The contemptuous or indolent good-nature of the home government in its treatment of the stiff and crabbed Puritan colony might, if it had not at last been abandoned for force, be now a monument of British wisdom. As it turned out, the wisdom is on the side of the colonists, and Dr. Palfrey's summing up is convincing:

Extreme as may appear some of the measures of the patriot legislators of Massachusetts in their opposition to the royal governors, it is striking to observe how they were justified by later events. To the end that executive and judicial officers may do their duty without fear or favor, undoubtedly it is true that they ought not to be dependent for their living on grants made by a legislature from time to time. . . . But, most unfortunately, the constitution of government under the provincial charter of Massachusetts was such that the people could not make their governor and judges independent of themselves without throwing them into the adverse interest and making them the partial and powerful dependants of the crown. . . . But as soon as, by the overthrow of foreign authority, it became possible to place the administrators of the chief executive and the chief judicial powers in a position of absolute independence, the importance of that arrangement as a condition of good government was cordially recognized in the constitution of the free commonwealth of Massachusetts which imposed the unalterable law that the salaries of her governors and of the judges of her Court of Final Appeal should not be liable to reduction during their term of service.

In one respect this volume might perhaps have been made more complete. Dr. Palfrey has hardly thrown so much weight on the financial history of the period as its importance demands. The Province was not only harassed by wars which forced it during the whole of this half-century to the emission of large sums of depreciating paper;

it was also a victim to every species of popular financiering. The delusions of English bubble-companies had their little counter-types in Boston. The patriots fell into the grave mistake of adopting as a part of their patriotic system the establishment of a land-bank and other financial experiments, the manifest dishonesty of which is only excusable on the ground of inexperience. All the most radical financial theories of 1875 were put in full practice a century and a half ago, in New England. The nature of these experiments, their effects upon the industry, and more especially upon the morals of the Province, their relation to the politics of the patriots, are points in our colonial history that have never yet been thoroughly investigated. Even the materials for such a sketch have not yet been collected, though they probably exist in abundant quantity in the confused archives of the State House. The financial policy of the General Court and the popular party came into sharp collision with that of the home government. The interference of Parliament hastened the collapse. Litigation and ruin were spread wide through the community, and the bitterness engendered by the suppression of the patriots' hair-brained financial schemes was not without a direct influence in keeping alive that hatred of the Crown and Parliament which subsequently burst out with such fury in the political career of Samuel Adams and his friends. If only in its general relations to the development of New England society, and as an indication of the change in men's morals and interests, this subject deserves a special study and a prominent place.

The reader breathes more freely at last as he finds this long half-century of cold religion, disjointed and bickering government, blundering and desolating wars, wild and ruinous finance, stagnating intellectual life, and stationary or declining economical interests, behind him. The period was sad and monotonous. Its history can hardly be otherwise than sad and monotonous also. Dr. Palfrey's next and concluding volume will at least be illumined by some gleams of triumph and sunshine. Even in our own day the story of Louisburg and Quebec makes the blood of a New England man run faster, and, at the moment, Massachusetts must have felt a joy that had never been her share since the fall of Andros. Shirley was a far more attractive character than any of his predecessors, while the statesmanship of the elder Pitt is still a subject for honest enthusiasm. A sketch of the social and intellectual condition of New England at the close of the French wars, marking the alterations which time had brought about, and the extent to which Puritanism had been modified by circumstances, would be of no small interest and of permanent value. New England shows no sign of producing any new historian so competent to this task as Dr. Palfrey; she can never produce one who stands by training and experience in such close sympathy with his subject. His work is an honor to our time, and that he may complete it as it was begun must be a most earnest hope and wish among all literary New-Englanders.

APPENDIX A

Adams's Copies of Works to Which the Sketches Respond

The twenty-three sketches respond to thirty works—specified at the start of the individual sketch. In twelve instances, copies are in the Henry Adams Library at the Massachusetts Historical Society. On various grounds, each appears to be indubitably his copy, used while writing the relevant sketch.

[SKETCH 2] Freeman, Edward A. *Historical Essays.* London: Macmillan & Co., 1871. Bears the Henry Adams Library bookplate (printed date: January 9, 1919). On p. 190, "Charles" is underscored and "Louis" is written in the margin in Adams's handwriting. No other markings.

[SKETCH 3] Maine, Sir Henry Sumner. *Village-Communities in the East and West.* London: John Murray, 1871. Signed "Henry Adams" on the title page. The words "writers in the" appear in the margin on p. 168 in Adams's handwriting, apparently because the sentence would be clearer if the words were added. No other markings.

[SKETCH 3] Sohm, Rudolph. *Die Altdeutsche Reichs- und Gerichtsverfassung.* Erster Band. Weimar: Hermann Bohlau, 1871. Bears Adams's bookplate. Notes and/or scorings appear on pp. 34, 124, 128, 130, 132, 150, 162, 168, 179, 219, 264–65, 290, 347, 350–51, 371–72, 375, 500, 503, 535, 555, and 562. An extended note or outline in Adams's handwriting appears on a folded sheet of thin paper loosely inserted at pp. 100–1. See appendix B.

[SKETCH 8] Freeman, Edward A. *History of the Norman Conquest.* Revised American edition. Volumes 1–4. Oxford, at the Clarendon Press, for Macmillan & Co., New York, 1873. Together with volume 5, 1876. All five volumes bear the library bookplate. In vol. 1, paper slips inserted at pp. 32–33, 344–45, and 478–79. In vol. 2, some pages uncut. In vol. 3, small vertical scoring on p. 13 opposite "the great Gemot of London"; paper slips at pp. 264–65 and 400–401; some pages uncut. In vol. 4, vertical scorings on pp. 16–17. In vol. 5 (published two years after sketch 8 appeared), annotations in Adams's handwriting on pp. 1, 2, 203–4, 206, 214–15, 226, 228, 265, 298, 299, 302, 309, and 311. (The Library also contains the second edition, revised, Oxford, 1869–1877.)

[SKETCH 10] [Gaskell, Charles Milnes]. *Sketches and Essays reprinted by permission from the Saturday Review.* Edinburgh and London: William Blackwood and Sons, 1873. Bears the library bookplate. Inscribed "With Mr Milnes Gaskell's compliments" in copperplate at the top of the half-title page. Scorings on pp. 70, 76, 78–79, 81, 97–98. No other markings. Uncut pages at the back.

[SKETCH 14] Parkman, Francis. *The Old Regime in Canada.* Boston: Little, Brown, & Co., 1874. Bears the library bookplate. Inscribed "Henry Adams / kind regards of / F. Parkman / 25 Sept. 1874." No other markings. Paper slips at pp. 136–37 and 320–21.

[SKETCH 15] Holst, Hermann von. *Die Administration Andrew Jackson's in ihrer Bedeutung fur die Entwicklung der Demokratie in den Vereinigten Staaten von Amerika.* Dusseldorf: Verlagshandlung von Julius Buddeus, 1874. X-shaped marks on pp. 7, 9, 23, 32, 43–45, and 51. No other markings. Accompanied by a note from the publisher to the editor of the *North American Review.*

[SKETCH 17] Bancroft, George. *History of the United States.* Boston: Little, Brown, & Co., 1874. Volume 10. Bears the library bookplate. Annotations in Adams's handwriting on pp. 533, 535, 547–48, and 551.

[SKETCH 18] Maine, Sir Henry Sumner. *Early History of Institutions.* London: John Murray, 1875. Signed "Henry Adams / Harv: Coll:" on the title page. No other markings.

[SKETCH 19] Palgrave, Francis Turner. *Lyrical Poems.* London and New York: Macmillan, 1871. Bears Adams's bookplate. No markings.

[SKETCH 19] Palgrave, Francis Turner. *A Lyme Garland. etc.* Lyme Regis, 1874. No markings.

[SKETCH 23] Palfrey, John Gorham. *History of New England.* Volume 4. Boston: Little, Brown, & Co., 1875. Bears the library bookplate. Note in Adams's handwriting on p. 237. Slips of paper at pp. 128–29, 132–33, 196–97, 242–43, 278–79, 320–21, 342–43, 406–7, 410–11, 428–29, 504–5, 544–45, 562–63, and 594–95.

Scores of books owned by Marian Hooper (Mrs. Henry) Adams were inherited by her brother Edward's children. One—now the property of Faith Thoron (Mrs. Robert) Knapp, daughter of Louisa Hooper (Mrs. Ward) Thoron—corresponds to sketch 5 and should perhaps be assumed to have been used by Henry Adams.

[SKETCH 5] Howells, William Dean. *Their Wedding Journey.* Boston: James R. Osgood and Company, 1872. Inscribed "Henry Adams / & / Clover Hooper / Feb. 27th / 1872" in the latter's handwriting. No other markings. (The meaning of the date is uncertain. It could be taken to record that Henry Adams and Clover Hooper became joint owners of the book on that date. It could be taken to commemorate their engagement, which occurred in the evening of that day, without also meaning that the book was already in their possession. And it conceivably was written to express some other meaning not readily conjectured.)

Adams gave part of his library to Western Reserve University, including two works to which the sketches respond. The copies reportedly "show no trace of marginalia, nor do they bear Henry Adams' signature or bookplate."

[SKETCH 16] Quincy, Josiah. *Memoir of the Life of Josiah Quincy, junior, of Massachusetts, 1744–1775.* 2d ed. Boston: Press of J. Wilson & Son, 1874.

[SKETCH 23] Palfrey, John Gorham. *History of New England.* Volume 4. Boston: Little, Brown, and Company, 1875. Bears a bookplate: "From the Author." (Adams appears to have treated this copy as a chance duplicate and the copy listed above as more fully his.)

APPENDIX B

"Earliest Constitution."[1]

At an unknown date, Adams wrote a set of notations in ink on a sheet of thin paper. The sheet was found by the editor at pp. 100–101 of Adams's copy of the first volume of Rudolph Sohm's *Die Altdeutsche Reichs- und Gerichtsverfassung* (Weimar: Hermann Bohlau, 1871) in the Henry Adams Library at the Massachusetts Historical Society.

Opinions may differ about certain questions. Is one to suppose that the first words, *"Earliest Constitution,"* and the last, *"Constitution of the Lex Salica,"* are equivalents, and the text runs in a circle? Or were the last words intended to head a new, improved, or corrected draft which Adams did not get to write?

Also, are the notations an early statement by Adams of his understanding of what the prevailing forms of government were in northern Europe in the middle ages and how they changed? Or are they a late statement by Adams meant to summarize such an understanding in a minimum space?

Earliest Constitution.

The race (Stamm)
The people. (state)
The hundred. (pagus)

The Stamm is the nation.
The nation had a yearly assembly, by representatives, for religious purposes, and no other.
The People, civitas, or state
The power of the state belonged to its free citizens. It was exercised by its concilium. The concilium was the political authority.
The concilium made peace or war.
It had full competence as a judicial tribunal.
coming of age[2]
It declared the majority of citizens.

---

[1]Published by permission of the Massachusetts Historical Society.
[2]Written above "majority" in half-sized letters.

It nominated officials.
The Hundred was the judicial district of the state.
It had a court for judicial purposes.

~~The pressures of war and emigration carried away the Stamm, and it disappeared. The King, as military leader, rose in power. The Stamm became the~~

The exigences of the folk-wanderings raised the
King, as military leader, to power.
The people (civitas) was forced into closer union, and the Stamm
became a close union of states, and so *the* State.
The struggle between King and Stamm is the political history of
Germany till the 12th century when both perished together.

The Gau (pagus, hundred) became the basis of the German constitution.
What Tacitus knew as a people, became in the Frank kingdom a
gau. (Brueteri. pagus Boroetra. Batavii. peigus Batua. Chattuarii,
pagus Hattuarias. Chamavi, Hama land &c.)
The Lombards, Goths, Anglo-saxons &c developed their political
systems as gau-systems. The Frankish kings developed their system
over the gaus. The constitution of the Lex Salica was still a gau
constitution. That of the Merovingian kings was not in the interests
of the gau.

Constitution of the Lex Salica.

APPENDIX C

The Suppressed Paragraph of "Captain John Smith"

Sometime before March 1861, Charles Deane, a Boston businessman who collected and read old books relating to the American colonies, made a discovery. He found what he thought clear evidence that a celebrated chapter of American history was a lie—a mere fabrication. The chapter was the rescue of Captain John Smith from imminent execution by Indian captors through the sudden intercession of Pocahontas, an Indian princess.

Deane mentioned his discovery to John Gorham Palfrey; and Palfrey, learning that Henry Adams was going to England with his father, told him that the story of Smith's rescue by Pocahontas was false and that its falsity could be affirmed by a researcher using the resources of the British Museum. He urged Henry to weigh the chance that, by investigating the falsehood, he might write and publish an article.

In 1862, independently of Deane, though not of Palfrey, with whom he corresponded, Adams conducted just such an investigation and ascertained to his satisfaction that the incident was a lie, indeed Smith's own, spun in his last book, *Generall Historie of Virginia, New-England, and the Summer Isles* (1624). Adams promptly wrote the suggested article but then hesitated and decided against immediate publication.

Four years later, wanting to offer the article to the *North American Review,* Adams reworked the manuscript, making excisions, revisions, and expansions. His labors were both helped and complicated by investigations conducted since 1861 by Deane.

Very quietly, Deane had been bringing out annotated reprints of old books of exploration and colonial settlement. One was a reissue (twenty copies, privately printed) of Smith's earliest book about America, *A True Relation of Virginia* (1608). Appearing in London, he gave Adams a copy. The copy made clear to Adams that he and Deane had come to the same conclusion but supported it with divergent, rival proofs.

The first thought that occurred to Adams was that Deane had left him nothing to do. Reconsidering, Adams so changed his article that it would seem much less a report of an investigation of his own and much more an elaborate, anonymous response to the esteemed investigations of Mr. Deane. In addition, Adams inserted a passage showing that George Bancroft, in his *History of the United States*, had credulously parroted Smith's story and romantically heightened it.

Perhaps at a separate moment, shortly before sending the manuscript to Palfrey for possible forwarding to the *North American Review*, Adams wrote a concluding paragraph which poised those who value history for its truth, should it have some, against those who think it expedient to repeat romantic lies which have gained wide acceptance. Palfrey approved "Captain John Smith" and passed it to the editor of the *North American Review*, Charles Eliot Norton. He published it, unsigned, as the first article in the issue for January 1867. As published, the article was shorn of its concluding paragraph, meant, it seems, as an afterword, a final defense by Adams of what he knew was an incendiary venture.

Of the manuscripts of Adams's extremely numerous publications, few survive. One is the manuscript of "Captain John Smith" which Norton accepted in 1866. The manuscript is complete and thus includes the paragraph which the editor suppressed.

Lest the paragraph be misconstrued, it must be noted that, according to Adams, Smith was saved by Indians, but by many acting together, rather than by one, Pocahontas, interceding against the rest.

The paragraph says:[1]

No one can have any ill-natured disposition towards the memory of either Smith or Pocahontas, for their fame has never been a subject for sectional jealousies, and their lives seem to have had far less permanent influence on the national history than it has been usual to attribute to them. Yet it is the inevitable result of these investigations to place the person who makes them in apparent hostility to the pride which the nation feels in its annals, and in proportion to the boldness and force of the criticism will be the ill-will that it excites against the critic. It may be urged that both Stith and Burk, the two historians of Virginia, knew and recognised the general inaccuracy of Smith's works, and yet neither of them thought it expedient to vary from his statement of facts. Why then at this late date attempt to cast down from his pedestal a man whom for two centuries all Americans have agreed in admiring as a model of manly courage and heroic virtues? We may answer, for the same reason that we expunge from the history of Rome the inspiring fables of Livy, or remind the student who asks only for a great ideal, that the Greeks were the most mendacious people of antiquity, and that the Persian account of Thermopylae has never been received. This reply can only be convincing to those who believe that the value of history depends on its truth, and that the one great literary triumph of our century has been its bold and brilliant application of the laws of criticism to historical composition. But at least we may say in our defence that every undeserved panegyric upon one person is to a certain extent an injustice to his rivals or associates. If the result of Mr[.]

[1]Published by permission of the Houghton Library, Harvard University.

Deane's publications is the destruction of Smith's reputation, at all events it will compel the future historians of Virginia to make a tardy reparation to the men whom he calumniated; to the real founders of the Colony who succeeded him, and to the Indians whose kindness and forebearance saved his own life and preserved for a time the lives of his unhappy companions, in spite of the most flagrant misgovernment among themselves.

ABBREVIATIONS

CFA2   Charles Francis Adams, Jr. (1835–1915)

Cushing's   William Cushing, *Index to the North American Review, Volumes I–*
Index   *CXXV, 1815–1877, I. Index of Subjects, II. Index of Writers* (Cambridge, Mass.: John Wilson and Son, 1878). Reprinted in Kenneth Walter Cameron, *Research Keys to the American Renaissance* (Hartford: Transcendental Books, 1967).

ES   "The Writings of Henry Adams / 1855–1877," in Ernest Samuels, *The Young Henry Adams* (Cambridge, Mass.: Harvard University Press, 1948), pp. 313–21.

F or Ford   *Letters of Henry Adams (1858–1891)*, edited by Worthington Chauncey Ford (Boston & New York: Houghton Mifflin Company, 1930). Another volume appeared in 1938.

HA   Henry Adams (1838–1918)

HCL   Henry Cabot Lodge (1850–1924)

JTA   "Bibliography of the Writings of Henry Adams," in James Truslow Adams, *Henry Adams* (New York: Albert & Charles Boni, 1933), pp. 213–29. William A. Jackson, when head of Harvard's Houghton Library, told me he wrote this bibliography; and I saw an offprint signed by him. James Truslow Adams was not related to Henry Adams.

L or   *The Letters of Henry Adams, Volumes I–III*, edited by J. C. Lev-
Levenson   enson, Ernest Samuels, Charles Vandersee, and Viola Hopkins Winner (Cambridge, Mass. and London: Harvard University Press, 1982).

NAR   *North American Review*

YHA   Ernest Samuels, *The Young Henry Adams* (Cambridge, Mass.: Harvard University Press, 1948).

ATTRIBUTIONS

L iterary attributions, it would seem, should be made only when warranted and should be dropped when shown to be not warranted. Henry
Adams has been said to be the writer (or cowriter) of four articles and twenty-
eight critical notices published in issues of the *North American Review* of which
he or Perry was editor. Of these thirty-two attributions, I believe twenty-two
are valid beyond a doubt; nine are impossible on present evidence; and one,
for special reasons, is perhaps better placed in abeyance. Also I suggest that
a new attribution of a notice to Adams should be tentatively adopted.

It may save confusion if I fully explain the grounds for my judgments.
Literary attribution seems to me a serious undertaking, involving risk that
credit (or blame) due to one person may be affixed to another. To my mind,
attributions, to deserve acceptance, should be supported by good evidence
and valid reasons coupled with declared assumptions. I have made a three-
part assumption: that, to compile his *Index to the North American Review,* Cushing requested and was supplied the magazine's writers-of-record for unsigned
or initialed articles and notices; that he did not try to test or get behind the
names that were given to him, whether by the issues themselves or by the
editors and publishers; and that, when given no writer-of-record, he was prepared to leave blanks in the relevant entries of the *Index.* I think it important
that this assumption be kept in mind; for the problem of Henry Adams's
contributions to the *North American Review* subsequent to his becoming its
editor has claims to being the most difficult problem of attribution in American literature. If not solved by my efforts, the problem perhaps can be solved
by new efforts guided in part by other assumptions.

The difficulty of the problem bears insisting upon. People who venture
attributions, while entitled to enjoy their successes, are accountable for their
errors. In the pages that follow, I shall point to errors where I think they have
been made. But it may be that errors should be excused in connection with
difficult problems which would seem hard to excuse in connection with simple
ones. (I have caught myself in several major errors while studying this problem, and would be happy to be freed from self-criticism for having made

them.) So it should not be imagined that I point to the errors of others in an accusing spirit. I do so in the hope that the difficulty of the problem will be recognized and that someone, in time, will put the problem entirely to rest.

Undisputed attributions

Attribution of an article or notice to Adams, to my mind, is definitive when one or more of the following conditions are met: (1) when HA makes hand-written attestation that he is the writer, using the form "By Henry Adams"; (2) when printed attestation of *sole authorship* by HA appears in the form "Henry Adams" at the end of an article; and (3) when Cushing attributes an article or notice to HA in the Index of Writers and the entry is not crossed out by HA in his copy. (If marked with * below, the attribution meets the third condition. No. 26, as I show, is an exceptional case.)

On this basis, one article and twenty-one notices can be attributed to HA definitively. All except no. 4 are attributed to HA by JTA. All are attributed to HA by ES. None has been disputed.

1. "HARVARD COLLEGE. 1786–87."*
Article V. *NAR* 114 (January 1872):110–47. Signed "Henry Adams." At-tributed to HA by Cushing under Everett and Harvard in the Index of Subjects.
2. "FREEMAN'S HISTORICAL ESSAYS"*
Notice 3. *NAR* 114 (January 1872):193–96. Unsigned.
3. "MAINE'S VILLAGE COMMUNITIES"*
Notice 4. *NAR* 114 (January 1872):196–99. Unsigned. Attributed to HA by Cushing under Maine in the Index of Subjects.
4. "TAYLOR'S FAUST"
Unknown to Cushing and JTA. First attributed to HA by ES. When fully ready for publication as notice 7, *NAR* 114 (April 1872):441–50, the sketch was suppressed. (See *YHA*, 229, 342n2.) A copy of the page proofs, bound in a volume titled *Critical and Literary Papers* in the Henry Adams Library at the Massachusetts Historical Society, is signed "By Henry Adams" in HA's handwriting (p. 441). A second copy of the proofs, in Harvard's Houghton Library, is marked "[Suppressed]" by HA on p. 441 and bears a note on p. 450:[1]

This notice, written originally by a strong admirer of Mr[.] Taylor, but much changed by me in tone, led to a protest from the author [of the notice?], and a request from Mr[.] Osgood that the notice should be suppressed. Which was done.

Henry Adams.

In the one case, HA fully asserts authorship. In the other, he only asserts having "much changed" a notice "in tone." I take his declaration of authorship

[1]Published by permission of the Houghton Library.

as definitive. I suggest that the note on the Harvard proofs must be taken as evidence that HA, wanting the truth not known to the person(s) the note was meant to reach, was willing to state in writing that there had been a modification of a notice when instead there had been a replacement of a notice. This, I realize, is a way of saying that HA created records of two opposed sorts, true and false. It may be urged in extenuation that he was not a wholly free agent but something very different, editor of a long-established, great magazine. In my view, he clearly made opposed true and false records in connection with nos. 25, 28, 29, 30, 31, and 32 below.

5. "HOWELLS'S THEIR WEDDING JOURNEY"*
   Notice 8. *NAR* 114 (April 1872):444–45. Unsigned. Attributed to HA by Cushing under Howells in the Index of Subjects.

6. "KING'S MOUNTAINEERING IN THE SIERRA NEVADA"*
   Notice 9. *NAR* 114 (April 1872):445–48. Unsigned.

7. "HOLLAND'S RECOLLECTIONS OF PAST LIFE"*
   Notice 10. *NAR* 114 (April 1872):448–50. Unsigned.

8. "FREEMAN'S HISTORY OF THE NORMAN CONQUEST"*
   Notice 1. *NAR* 118 (January 1874): 176–81. Initialed "H. A." Attributed to HA by Cushing under Freeman and Norman Conquest in the Index of Subjects. (Perry edited the issue.)

9. "COULANGES'S ANCIENT CITY"*
   Notice 2. *NAR* 118 (April 1874): 390–97. Unsigned. Attributed to Marcel Thevenin by Cushing, in error, under Coulanges in the Index of Subjects.

10. "SATURDAY REVIEW SKETCHES AND ESSAYS"*
    Notice 4. *NAR* 118 (April 1874): 401–5. Unsigned. Attributed to HA by Cushing under Saturday in the Index of Subjects.

11. "SOHM'S PROCEDURE DE LA LEX SALICA"*
    Notice 6. *NAR* 118 (April 1874): 416–25. Unsigned. Attributed to HA by Cushing under Lex Salica and Sohm in the Index of Subjects.

Under Sohm in the Index of Subjects, Cushing lists HA as writing about "Die Altdeutsche Reichs, etc." in vol. 113, p. 198. The entry is readily explained. HA wrote some of his sketches (nos. 1, 3, 16, and 19) in response to more than one publication. Sohm's *Die Altdeutsche Reichs- und Gerichtsverfassung* is listed as a third publication at the head of no. 3, "Maine's Village Communities." On p. 198 of no. 3, as indexed, HA comments on Sohm's book. But Cushing in this instance is guiding the reader to a passage, not a notice. Also the volume number should be 114, not 113, as given.

12. "STUBBS'S CONSTITUTIONAL HISTORY OF ENGLAND"*
    Notice 12. *NAR* 119 (July 1874): 233–44. Unsigned. Attributed to HA by Cushing under England, History of, and Stubbs in the Index of Subjects. (See no. 26 below, for related errors.)

13. "KITCHIN'S HISTORY OF FRANCE"*
    Notice 7. *NAR* 119 (October 1874): 442–47. Unsigned. While listing the notice under Kitchin in the Index of Subjects, Cushing omits HA's name

as the writer—leaves a blank. But HA's authorship is given in the Index of Writers.

14. "Parkman's Old Regime in Canada"*
Notice 1. *NAR* 120 (January 1875): 175–79. Unsigned. Attributed to HA by Cushing under Canada and Parkman in the Index of Subjects.

15. "Von Holst's Administration of Andrew Jackson"*
Notice 2. *NAR* 120 (January 1875): 179–85. Unsigned. Attributed to HA by Cushing under Holst and Jackson in the Index of Subjects.

16. "The Quincy Memoirs and Speeches"*
Notice 14. *NAR* 120 (January 1875): 235–36. Unsigned. Attributed to HA by Cushing under Quincy in the Index of Subjects.

17. "Bancroft's History of the United States"*
Notice 1. *NAR* 120 (April 1875): 424–32. Unsigned. Attributed to HA by Cushing under Bancroft and U.S., History of, in the Index of Subjects.

18. "Maine's Early History of Institutions"*
Notice 2. *NAR* 120 (April 1875): 432–38. Unsigned. Attributed to HA by Cushing under Maine in the Index of Subjects.

19. "Palgrave's Poems"*
Notice 3. *NAR* 120 (April 1875): 438–44. Unsigned. Attributed to HA by Cushing under Palgrave in the Index of Subjects.

20. "Green's Short History of the English People"*
Notice 7. *NAR* 121 (July 1875): 216–24. Unsigned. Attributed to HA by Cushing under Green in the Index of Subjects.

21. "Tennyson's Queen Mary"*
Notice 2. *NAR* 121 (October 1875): 422–29. Unsigned. Attributed to HA by Cushing under Tennyson in the Index of Subjects.

22. See *A tentative new attribution* below.

23. "Palfrey's History of New England"*
Notice 11. *NAR* 121 (October 1875): 473–80. Unsigned. Attributed to HA by Cushing under Palfrey in the Index of Subjects.

A tentative new attribution

Cushing's *Index* names writers for all the articles and all but three of the notices published in the eighteen issues HA edited. Two of the notices for which no writer is listed are "Mistral's Mireio" and "Ralston's Songs of the Russian People" in the July 1872 issue, the last HA edited before leaving on his wedding journey. Authorship by HA may be ruled out in both cases, I believe, on grounds of content and style. The third notice for which no writer is listed is one which HA *could* have written. The notice is:

22. "Walker's Statistical Atlas of the United States"
Notice 5. *NAR* 121 (October 1875): 437–42. Unsigned.
The notice nowhere appears in Cushing's Index of Writers. It appears in the Index of Subjects under United States, the, Statistical Atlas, and under

Walker, Statistical Atlas. Each of the entries names no writer. In the space where a writer's name would normally appear, each entry leaves a blank (e.g., see Facsimile C).

Above, in connection with no. 13, Cushing, although given HA's name as writer of a notice, provides no name in an entry in the Index of Subjects. In this instance, differently, Cushing provides no entry in the Index of Writers and provides a name in neither entry in the Index of Subjects. To my mind, this indicates that *Cushing was given no name*: the writer's name was withheld. In such a case, I believe, the suspected withholder must be HA, who, as editor, had first rights in the case.

It may help if attention is directed to an article, "The Political Campaign of 1872," in the October 1872 issue, started by HA but completed by William Dean Howells. Here again Cushing could not obtain, or at least nowhere gives, the name of a writer. The article concerns the campaign in which HA's father, Charles Francis Adams, narrowly escaped being nominated against Grant. And this notice, no. 22, reviews a book compiled by Francis A. Walker, one of HA's political associates. In short, both article and notice involve political considerations.

Until evidence is found to the contrary, I think it best to assume that HA arranged the writing of the article on the campaign of 1872 for the October 1872 issue and wrung an agreement from Howells that the writer's name would not be disclosed; further, that HA wrote the Walker notice for the October 1875 issue and withheld his authorship from Cushing to shield Walker—and Clarence King, who is mentioned in the notice—from political penalties in Washington for having been touted in print by one of the Adamses. In my opinion, content and style very strongly support the tentative attribution of the *notice*—not the article—to HA.

Eight attributions held impossible on present evidence

Attributions to HA of an article and seven notices in issues of the magazine edited by him and Perry are in my judgment clearly impossible. They appear in Cushing's Index, JTA, ES, the Ford edition of HA's *Letters,* and the Levenson/Samuels *Letters of Henry Adams.* They are most easily considered in groups.

Three simple cases

24. "INGERSOLL'S FEARS FOR DEMOCRACY"
    Notice 8. *NAR* 121 (July 1875): 224–28. Unsigned. Attributed to Brooks Adams by Cushing in the Index of Writers, and under Ingersoll in the Index of Subjects. Also attributed to "H. Adams" (rather than "B. Adams") under Democracy, Fears for, in the Index of Subjects.
    In my view, attribution to HA is cancelled definitively by HA, who, in his copy, crossed out the "H" in the Index of Subjects and wrote "Brooks" in the margin (see Facsimile A). JTA and ES take no note of this attribution to HA.

That Brooks Adams was the writer is affirmed by his biographer (see Arthur Beringause, *Brooks Adams* [New York, 1955], 395).

The explanation of the mistaken attribution to HA seems obvious. It is either a one-letter slip of Cushing's pen or a one-letter misprint Cushing failed to catch and correct.

25. "Denison's Letters and other Writings"

Notice 4. *NAR* 114 (April 1872): 426–32. Unsigned. Attributed to C. Milnes Gaskell by Cushing in the Index of Writers, and under Denison in the Index of Subjects. Attributed additionally to HA in the Index of Writers.

In my view, attribution to HA is cancelled definitively by HA, who, in his copy, crossed out the attribution of the notice to himself in the Index of Writers (see Facsimile E).

JTA, apparently unaware of Cushing's complete, correct entries attributing the notice to Gaskell, and unaware, too, of HA's cancellation of the entry in the Index of Writers attributing the notice to himself, concurs with the latter entry by Cushing and attributes the notice to HA. To my mind, this mistaken attribution is decisive evidence that JTA was compiled without recourse to HA's copy of Cushing's *Index*, either through failure to learn of and consult the copy, or because access to books in the Henry Adams Library at the Massachusetts Historical Society was not yet permitted. (Also see no. 24 above and nos. 28, 29, 30, and 31 below.)

ES is based in part on HA's copy of Cushing's *Index*. Noting that HA "crossed out" the attribution of the notice to himself in his copy of the *Index*, ES says, "The review of Denison was by Gaskell," and cites a source, F, I, 226. On that page of the Ford edition of HA's *Letters*, HA writes to Gaskell: "I have received £5 on your account for your notice of Denison, the whilk [*sic*] I will pay to you on our meeting." But ES (like JTA) makes no mention of Cushing's complete, correct entries attributing the notice to Gaskell.

In my view, the likeliest explanation of Cushing's attribution of this notice to HA is that HA was the magazine's writer-of-record for all notices written by Gaskell; that the indexer was tardily informed that four notices recorded as by HA were in fact by C. Milnes Gaskell; and that one attribution to HA of a notice by Gaskell was erroneously not deleted by Cushing under Adams, Henry, in the Index of Writers. An aspect of the case which warrants noting is HA's collecting Gaskell's pay for the notice from the publisher (see no. 31 below).

A second error by Cushing may deserve attention. In the Index of Subjects, instead of the correct name of the author, Edward Denison, Cushing lists "Denison, Mary Andrews." How *Edward* turned into *Mary Andrews* is uncertain. The metamorphosis possibly has a bearing on a mysterious name elsewhere in the Index of Subjects (see no. 27 below).

26. "Stubbs's Constitutional History of England"

Notice 4. *NAR* 123 (July 1876): 161–65. Unsigned. Attributed to HA by Cushing in the Index of Writers, and under England, History of,† and

Stubbs† in the Index of Subjects. (Certain entries in the Index of Subjects left uncorrected by HA are indicated here by †. See explanation directly below.)

JTA (possibly as a result of mere oversight) takes no note of the attribution to HA. ES asserts that the attribution to HA is mistaken, citing William Francis Allen, *Monographs and Essays* (Boston, 1890), 364, where Allen's editors list the notice as his. Content and style, in my view, support the assertion by the editors and ES that the writer was Allen.

The likeliest explanation of the attribution of this notice to HA, in my opinion, is that Cushing was correctly informed that HA and Allen respectively had written notices of volumes 1 and 2 of Stubbs's book; that Cushing lost track of Allen's being the writer of the second notice; that Cushing then credited HA in the Index of Writers with any notice concerning Stubbs; and that Cushing replicated the error while making the pertinent entries for the Index of Subjects.

In this instance, Cushing's error resulted in the addition of six digits to an otherwise correct entry in the Index of Writers (also to otherwise correct entries in the Index of Subjects) concerning HA's no. 12. Thus the chance that HA would notice the error was minimal. In his copy of the *Index*, HA read the entries in the Index of Writers under Adams, Henry, and crossed out five complete entries (title, volume number, page number) attributing notices to himself. But he failed to cross out the added digits (volume number, page number) attributing no. 26 to himself (see Facsimile E).

To my mind, this failure by HA to cancel what seems a proven error by Cushing in the Index of Writers is of a piece with HA's failure to cancel numerous errors by Cushing in the Index of Subjects. By my count, in his copy of Cushing's *Index*, HA allowed ten entries in the Index of Subjects to stand uncancelled which mistakenly attribute an article and four notices to him as sole author. It is no wonder that he did not cross out the ten entries. They are scattered under different headings on widely separated pages of an index 116 pages long.

Two linked cases, one complex, one simple but
precipitating extremely un-simple consequences

Because the cases are linked, I shall present some considerations relating to the first, proceed to some considerations relating to the second, and then deal with considerations relating to both.

27. "Dr. Clarke's 'Sex in Education.' "
        Article 5. *NAR* 118 (January 1874): 140–52. Unsigned.
        Perry edited the issue. The article nowhere appears in Cushing's Index of Writers. It is attributed to HA under Clarke, Edward Hammond,† and Education, Sex in. E. H. Clarke,† in the Index of Subjects.
        In addition, the Index of Subjects contains a one-line entry which seems—

and possibly is—very strange: "Lippincott. Sarah Jane (Clarke). Sex in Education. H. Adams. 118. 140."†

Strangeness begins with the fact that Sarah Jane (Clarke) Lippincott did not write the book, *Sex in Education,* which the article reviews. (The author is correctly named in two places in the Index of Subjects—see above.) Also *Sarah* is a misspelling. Sara Jane Clarke (apparently no relation of Edward Hammond Clarke) edited a children's magazine and wrote literary works and travel books, often under the pseudonym Grace Greenwood. She married Leander K. Lippincott of Philadelphia. How her name got into Cushing's *Index* is uncertain. Finally, this is another instance in Cushing's *Index* of a masculine name yielding to a feminine (see no. 25 above).

JTA takes no note of the attribution of the article to HA. ES lists six "additional ascriptions" to HA gleaned from Cushing's *Index,* makes "Dr. Clarke's 'Sex in Education'" item 2, and says: "It is quite unlikely that Item 2 is by Henry Adams. As he was not responsible for getting out the January, 1874, issue, he would hardly have been tempted by Clarke's book. He was moved, however, to write a review of Freeman for that issue." ES further notes that HA, in his copy of the *Index,* did not cross out Cushing's attribution of the article to himself; but ES fails to mention that the *Index* contains two indexes, and neglects to say what sort of index HA would have had to comb, to find the relevant entries he could have crossed out.

28. "CLARKE'S BUILDING OF A BRAIN"
Notice 3. *NAR* 120 (January 1875): 185–88. Unsigned. Attributed to HA by Cushing in the Index of Writers, and under Clarke, Edward Hammond,† in the Index of Subjects.

In my view, attribution to HA is cancelled definitively by HA, who, in his copy, crossed out the attribution of the notice to himself in the Index of Writers (see Facsimile E). JTA, lacking recourse to HA's copy of the *Index,* and thus unaware of HA's cancellation, attributes the notice to HA. (Also see nos. 24 and 25 above and nos. 29, 30, and 31 below.) ES notes that HA "crossed out" Cushing's attribution of the notice to himself in his copy of the *Index* but neither explicitly concurs with nor explicitly overrides HA's cancellation.

One sentence in HA's writings relates to this notice. It appears in his letter to HCL, 31 October 1874, first published in 1930 in the Ford edition of HA's *Letters* (I, 265). It reads: "If Weir Mitchell refuses Clarke, don't write to Dalton or anyone else till further notice." As republished in 1982 in the Levenson/ Samuels *Letters of Henry Adams,* the sentence occasions a footnote (L, II, 212n1) which says about the development of no. 28 for the January 1875 issue: "When S. Weir Mitchell . . . declined [to do so], HA reviewed Edward H. Clarke, *The Building of a Brain* . . . pp. 185–188. HA had earlier reviewed Clarke's *Sex in Education* (. . . *NAR* 118 [January 1874], 140–152). . . ." [No evidence is cited that Mitchell declined to review no. 28. How the attributions to HA of nos. 28 and 27 are arrived at is not explained. No reference is made to Cushing's *Index* or HA's copy thereof, and none to JTA or ES.]

Here are two new attributions. I think both are important. If mistaken, the attribution to HA of "Dr. Clarke's 'Sex in Education'" (no. 27) burdens him with an article in Perry's last issue which he, HA, did not edit and did not write. In my view, attribution to HA of "Clarke's Building of a Brain" (no. 28) assuredly is mistaken and burdens him with a notice he did edit but did not write (see above).

Of the new attributions, that of no. 28 to HA is pivotal. It also is methodologically dubious. It overrides HA's cancellation in his copy of Cushing's *Index* of the entry attributing no. 28 to himself. Obviously, such overriding is better avoided; for it carries with it one or another of the following allegations about HA: (1) that he did not know what he wrote and did not write; (2) that he falsified while marking his copy of Cushing's *Index*; (3) that he made a slip of the pen while running one of five lines of exactly requisite length cancelling five complete entries in the Index of Writers (see Facsimile E).

Why attribution of no. 28 to HA is pivotal should be made explicit. Although he did not write "Clarke's Building of a Brain" (no. 28), HA made himself the writer-of-record for the notice; misleadingly, his name was given to Cushing; and Cushing proceeded to credit HA with a notice (Index of Writers, under Adams, Henry [cancelled by HA]) and name HA as the writer of a notice (Index of Subjects, under Clarke, Edward Hammond† [*not* cancelled by HA]).

It is evident that in many cases, whether at his insistence or to oblige another person, HA made himself the writer-of-record when someone else was the actual writer. But, in my opinion, the reason he became the writer-of-record in this case (no. 28) cannot, on present evidence, be so much as conjectured; moreover, the name of the actual writer is entirely uncertain, and the task of identifying the actual writer, although allegedly completed, is yet to be undertaken.

Misleadingness was one thing, error another. Unfortunately, in 1878, the writing of indexes was not an error-free process. Once his name was given to Cushing misleadingly as writer of "Clarke's Building of a Brain" (no. 28, edited by himself), HA was in danger of being listed in error as also the writer of "Dr. Clarke's 'Sex in Education'" (no. 27, edited by Perry). The risk of Cushing's making that exact error was the greater because he had to index three Clarkes. One was Edward Hammond Clarke, a physician and former Harvard overseer, author of the books reviewed by nos. 27 and 28, also once a writer for the *North American Review,* and thus a candidate for inclusion in both the Index of Writers and the Index of Subjects. The second was James Freeman Clarke, a well-known Transcendentalist and Unitarian minister. He had been four times a writer for the magazine and was author of a book reviewed in the magazine, so he, too, would have to appear both in the Index of Writers and the Index of Subjects. The third was Sara Jane (Clarke) Lippincott. Her maiden name was known to Cushing, and her full name (misspelled) appears in the Index of Subjects.

With all the above factors in mind, the question can be asked, was HA the magazine's *writer-of-record* for "Dr. Clarke's 'Sex in Education'" (no. 27)? I believe present evidence suggests he was not.

Of the two parts of Cushing's *Index*, the Index of Writers is evidently to the larger extent primary and the Index of Subjects is proportionally secondary. This explains why errors in specifying what the writers wrote are seldom in evidence in the Index of Writers, and errors in naming the writers of what was written are fairly often in evidence in the Index of Subjects.

In the more primary and accurate Index of Writers, HA is not entered as having to his credit an article titled "Dr. Clarke's 'Sex in Education.'" Neither is anyone else. The persons responsible for giving Cushing a writer-of-record for no. 27 were Perry, its editor, and/or Osgood, the publisher. They may have given Cushing (1) no name, (2) the misspelled name Sarah Jane (Clarke) Lippincott, (3) a different name not HA's, or (4) HA's name. In any of the cases, Cushing could lose track of what he was given.

If they gave Cushing no name, indexing errors could easily generate the attribution of no. 27 to HA under Clarke, Edward Hammond,† and Education, Sex in.† in the Index of Subjects, but not under Lippincott, Sarah Jane [Clarke].† (The errors would somewhat parallel the errors noted in connection with nos. 9 and 26.)

If they gave Cushing the misspelled name Sarah Jane (Clarke) Lippincott, indexing errors could easily generate the attribution of no. 27 to HA under Clarke, Edward Hammond,† Education, Sex in,† and Lippincott, Sarah Jane (Clarke)† in the Index of Subjects. (Again the errors would somewhat parallel those noted in connection with nos. 9 and 26.) If they gave the indexer a different name not HA's, no trace of it appears in either part of Cushing's *Index*.

If they gave the indexer HA's name, Cushing should have entered "Dr. Clarke's 'Sex in Education'" under Adams, Henry, in the Index of Writers. No such entry appears under Adams, Henry, in that Index. So a choice is forced: either Cushing was given HA's name, erred, and failed to enter the article to HA's credit in the Index of Writers; or Cushing was not given HA's name and correctly did not enter the article to HA's credit in the Index of Writers. The second alternative is by far the more probable and so must be preferred.

My conclusion is that, in view of the errors in Cushing's Index of Subjects noted above in connection with nos. 9 and 26, in view of the unexplained Lippincott entry, in view of Cushing's having to index three Clarkes, and in view of the forced choice above, it is best to suppose, as a first hypothesis, that the magazine's writer-of-record for "Dr. Clarke's 'Sex in Education'" (no. 27) was "Lippincott, Sarah Jane (Clarke)," and that Cushing lost track of the information, failed to list her in the Index of Writers, and fell into errors involving HA.

The further question must be asked, was HA the *actual writer* of "Dr.

Clarke's 'Sex in Education'" (no. 27)? One piece of evidence which might relate to the question is a book owned by HA's wife, *Recollections of My Childhood* (Boston, 1852), by Grace Greenwood (pseudonym for Sara Jane Clarke). Preserved at Harvard's Houghton Library, the copy is signed "Marian Hooper Feb 8 1852" and inscribed "Clover fr. Alice." It contains no other markings.

A second piece of evidence which might relate to the question is a copy of *Sex in Education*, by Edward H. Clarke, preserved in the Henry Adams Library at the Massachusetts Historical Society. It bears the bookplate of the Library (dated 9 January 1919, after HA's death) but contains no signature or markings, and shows no signs of wear. That it was read and used by the writer of "Dr. Clarke's 'Sex in Education'" seems the more unlikely because it contains a "Preface to the Second Edition," whereas the article appears to respond to a copy supplied from the first edition. A possible explanation of the book's presence in the Henry Adams Library, in my opinion, might be that HA acquired it after the publication of "Dr. Clarke's 'Sex in Education'" (no. 27), while arranging the publication of a notice (no. 28) relating to Dr. Clarke's next book, *The Building of a Brain*.

The main evidence, of course, is the unsigned text of "Dr. Clarke's 'Sex in Education'" (no. 27). The article presents itself as the work of an experienced American physician, or just as possibly a parent conversant with medicine; and it mainly offers parents advice about possible dangers to their daughters. HA, it happens, was neither a physician nor a parent. The style of the article differs widely from HA's, most obviously in lacking its brevity and directness. Thus the article seems not to support HA's being the actual writer.

Persons anxious to break paths through the complications relating to no. 27, "Dr. Clarke's 'Sex in Education,'" with a view to identifying its actual writer, have the advantage of knowing where they might start. Though not a doctor, Mrs. Lippincott must be considered. Similarly, persons interested in identifying the actual writer of no. 28, "Clarke's Building of a Brain," have a place to start. They know that, in circumstances involving a possibility that the famed Dr. S. Weir Mitchell of Philadelphia would write the notice (or recommend another writer in his place), HA eventually learned the name of a person willing to write the notice. Further, at some point, HA misleadingly made himself the notice's writer-of-record. This means it might help to look into all the cases in which HA misleadingly made himself the writer-of-record (or cowriter-of-record), shielding an actual writer. These cases, I believe, are nos. 25, 28, 29, 30, 31, and 32.

Three cases somewhat parallel to No. 28

29. "FROTHINGHAM'S TRANSCENDENTALISM"
      Notice 1. *NAR* 123 (October 1876): 468–74. Unsigned. Attributed to HA by Cushing in the Index of Writers, and under Frothingham† and Transcendentalism† in the Index of Subjects.
      In my view, attribution to HA is cancelled definitively by HA, who, in his copy, crossed out the attribution of the notice to himself in the Index of

Writers (see Facsimile E). JTA does not attribute the notice to HA and presumably is guided by material in Ford (quoted below). In my view, this avoidance is decisive evidence that JTA, although written without recourse to HA's copy of Cushing's *Index*, shows awareness that the *Index*, while reliable in the main, is in some places flawed and is exceptionally often in error in its entries relating to HA. But how often JTA views the *Index* as in error is hard to guess. See nos. 24, 25, 26, 27, and 28 above and nos. 30 and 31 below.

ES notes that HA "crossed out" Cushing's attribution of the notice to himself in his copy of the *Index* but does not explicitly concur with or override HA's cancellation. Also, without comment, ES cites a page in the Ford edition of HA's *Letters* (I, 287). On that page, in a letter to HCL, 12 June [1876], HA makes two statements: "I suppose Lowell will not do Transcendentalism. I shall ask Mrs. P. to do it."

The statements in no way disturb the view taken here, that HA became the writer-of-record but was not the actual writer. The statements are republished in the Levenson/Samuels *Letters of Henry Adams* and occasion a footnote (II, 274n4) which says about "Mrs. P.": "Mary Eliot Dwight Parkman (1821–1879), widow of Dr. Samuel Parkman, contributor to the *Nation* . . . was a neighbor and friend of the Adamses at Beverly Farms. She probably reviewed O. B. Frothingham, *Transcendentalism in New England, NAR* 123 (Oct. 1876), 468–474." Of course, to infer from HA's saying he "shall ask Mrs. P. to do it" that she "probably" (as opposed to possibly) did write the notice is logically fallacious; the qualified attribution to "Mrs. P." of no. 29 must be rejected; and the name of the actual writer remains uncertain. But the question may be asked, why in this instance did HA make himself the magazine's writer-of-record?

An answer can be conjectured—merely as a conjecture. No. 29 reviews a book by Octavius Brooks Frothingham, one of HA's cousins. HA may have suggested to the writer of the notice that the writer's name should be kept permanently secret and he should himself be the writer-of-record because the cousin was expected to dislike the notice, or had already seen the notice as published and was known to dislike it. If this conjecture were supported by new evidence, the case would become one of secrecy suggested by the editor, and the idea of the arrangement would be to insure that all of Frothingham's pique or wrath would fall on the shielding editor, none on the actual writer.

When the notice is read with the above conjecture in mind, its content and style can quite easily suggest authorship by James Russell Lowell; that is, suggest that HA never did ask Mrs. Parkman, because HCL had already arranged that Lowell would write the notice. If that indeed happened, HA, by making himself the writer-of-record, shielded a writer who was one of the magazine's former editors.

30. "LATHROP'S STUDY OF HAWTHORNE"

Notice 4. *NAR* 123 (October 1876): 478–80. Unsigned. Attributed to HA by Cushing in the Index of Writers, and under Hawthorne† and Lathrop† in the Index of Subjects.

In my view, attribution to HA is ruled out definitively by HA, who, in his copy, crossed out the attribution of the notice to himself in the Index of Writers (see Facsimile E). JTA, although presumably quite aware of Cushing's entries attributing the notice to HA (and unaware of HA's cancellation in his copy of the *Index* [see no. 25]), takes no note of Cushing's entries and does not attribute the notice to HA. This seems to me a correct judgment, but I have no idea how it was reached.

ES notes HA's cancellation and somewhat overrides it, saying: "The authorship of the review of Lathrop's book was a closely guarded secret. Possibly Adams *was* its author." In support of this qualified attribution of the notice to HA, ES cites an "allusion to the review" in a letter from HA to HCL, 24 June 1876. The asserted allusion (F, I, 289) begins, "I presume you saw on the MS. . . ." But the passage does not concern the Lathrop notice (no. 30). It concerns a Ticknor notice (no. 31). To my mind, this error of reading revealed in ES is important. It is the basis of a mistaken qualified attribution to HA of no. 30 which has remained unchallenged until challenged here, and it is a factor in an unqualified attribution to HA of no. 31 (see below).

Who actually wrote no. 30 is at this point wholly unknown. Why HA became the writer-of-record also is wholly unknown.

31. "TICKNOR'S LIFE, LETTERS, AND JOURNALS"
Notice 10. *NAR* 123 (July 1876): 210–15. Unsigned. Attributed to HA by Cushing in the Index of Writers, and under Ticknor in the Index of Subjects.

In my view, attribution to HA is cancelled definitively by HA, who, in his copy, twice crossed out attributions of the notice to himself, in the Index of Writers and in the Index of Subjects (see Facsimile E and Facsimile B).

JTA, although presumably quite aware of Cushing's entries attributing the notice to HA (and unaware of HA's cancellations in his copy of the *Index* [see no. 25]), takes no note of Cushing's entries, does not attribute the notice to HA, and presumably is guided by material in Ford (quoted below). ES notes that HA "crossed out . . . a review of Ticknor's *Life, Letters and Journals*" in his copy of Cushing's *Index*, asserts that HA's making the cancellation was "clearly an error," makes an unqualified attribution of the notice to HA, and lists it as one of his indubitable works.

In support of overriding HA's cancellation and making the unqualified attribution, ES cites two pages of the Ford edition of HA's *Letters* (F, I, 286, 287). On the first, HA writes to HCL, "I hope to have five or six pages of Ticknor ready by Monday or Tuesday." On the second, HA writes to HCL, "Let a check for $20 for the notice of Ticknor, be made out and sent to *me*."

But even when ES was published (1948), it was an obvious fair question whether the "five or six pages of Ticknor" that HA hoped to have "ready by Monday or Tuesday" were his manuscript, someone else's manuscript, galley proofs of the one or the other, or page proofs. It also was an obvious fair question whether HA in this case had directed that a check be sent to "*me*," not because he was the actual writer, but because he had secretly obtained "the notice of Ticknor" from a writer to whom payment was to be made only by the chief editor, and only in cash. (That he had previously collected pay for a writer in order to pass it to the writer is stated by HA in a sentence cited by ES in connection with no. 25.)

Even then, too, it was clear what later occurred. The pertinent evidence is the passage (F, I, 289–90) described by ES (see above) as alluding to the Lathrop notice (no. 30). The passage explicitly relates to "the Ticknor" (no. 31). HA says:

> I presume you saw on the MS. that the printers were ordered to send that proof and MS. to *me*. I am preparing a letter to them—not civil. Meanwhile please bear in mind that the author of that notice made it a condition that *no* one, not even you, should know the authorship. Therefore please send me the MS. and never hint that you know anything. . . .
>
> Moreover I wish the printers to understand that my orders are to be taken notice of and obeyed. I shall therefore stop everything, and oblige them to send me the Ticknor . . . in proof, with a sharp intimation to them to be more exact next time.

Read as it was written, meaning as conversational English, this passage makes clear that "the Ticknor" is a case of two persons, an editor (HA, "*me*") and an actual writer ("the author of that notice"). Also the passage makes clear that no. 31 is a case of secrecy required by the actual writer, not the editor.

The passage has the further value of documenting a situation in which HA, then or later, to shield the actual writer, made himself the magazine's writer-of-record.

My conclusion is that JTA (evidently on the basis of correct reading of the passages above) rightly avoided attributing the notice to HA; that ES erred in asserting that the third passage relates to the Lathrop notice (no. 30); that ES was in error in attributing "the Ticknor" (no. 31) to HA and was the more in error because HA had cancelled in his copy of Cushing's *Index* both the Ticknor entry in the Index of Writers and the Ticknor entry in the Index of Subjects; that HA's cancellation cannot be a slip of the pen because it is a two-fold cancellation crossing out separate entries on different pages of his copy of Cushing's *Index* (see Facsimile B and Facsimile E); and that attribution of no. 31 to HA is definitively impossible.

The three passages by HA quoted above appear in three letters to HCL dated 7, 12, and 24 June 1876. The three letters were selected for inclusion in the Levenson/Samuels *Letters of Henry Adams,* vols. 1–3, published in 1982. Dealing with the letters, the editors had many options. One was to prepare a footnote designed to serve four purposes: (1) explain the connections between the "pages of Ticknor," the "check," and what HCL "saw"; (2) point to an error in ES, alleging an "allusion" in the third passage to no. 30; (3) say something to counteract the erroneously-based qualified attribution of no. 30 to HA by ES; and (4) say something explicit about HA's being or not being the actual writer of no. 31. Alternatively, two or three footnotes were possible, worded to achieve the same ends.

Whether the editors considered writing such a footnote (or several notes) is not apparent. What matters is that they published a footnote of an opposite sort. The footnote (L, II, 273n1) is directly tied to the first passage, the one that reads, "I hope to have five or six pages of Ticknor ready by Monday or Tuesday." In its entirety, the footnote says (inaccurately): "*Life, Letters, and Journals of George Ticknor, NAR* 123 (July 1876), 210–215." [The inaccuracy is in the title of the notice.]

The footnote is ambiguous. It can be read as indicating that a connection of some sort exists between the "pages of Ticknor" and a work of the noted title in the noted magazine, in the noted volume (and issue), on the noted pages. Equally and by most readers more probably, it can be read as an attribution by the editors of "Ticknor's Life, Letters, and Journals" (no. 31) to HA.

For reasons given above, I think the attribution of no. 31 to HA in the footnote (if one is meant) must be rejected. To my knowledge, the task of identifying the actual author of no. 31, although allegedly completed, is yet to be undertaken.

An assertion of coauthorship by HA unwarranted by present evidence

32. "The 'Independents' in the Canvass"

Article V. *NAR* 123 (October 1876): 426–67. Unsigned. Attributed to Charles Francis Adams, Jr., by Cushing in the Index of Writers, and under "Independents" in the Index of Subjects. (Reprinted in HA, *The Great Secession Winter of 1860–61 and Other Essays*, edited by George Hochfield [New York, 1958].)

Content and style throughout, in my view, strongly corroborate sole authorship by CFA2. The entry in the Index of Writers, being the last under Adams, Charles Francis, Jr., is readily seen. It appears on the same page as, and only seven lines above, the start of entries under Adams, Henry. That HA saw the entry and had every chance to correct it, if there were need to, seems a fair assumption. Yet he did not make any mark, either to cancel or modify the entry (see Facsimile D).

The Ford edition of HA's *Letters* (I, 287) includes a sentence in a letter from HA to HCL, dated 12 June [1876], which ends, ". . . my brother Charles and I mean to concoct a political article together." HA's declaring an intention does not warrant an inference that the intention was carried out. (Also see no. 29, above.)

In connection with the above twelve words, Ford supplies a footnote (F, I, 287n4) which says in its entirety, "'The "Independents" in the Canvass.'"

The footnote is ambiguous. It can be read as indicating that a connection of some sort exists between the words "my brother Charles and I mean to concoct a political article together" and a work bearing the indicated title.

Equally and by most readers more probably, it can be read as an attribution of "The 'Independents' in the Canvass" to both Charles Francis Adams, Jr., and Henry Adams.

JTA, presumably affected by Ford's footnote, attributes the article to HA "and" CFA2. ES attributes the article to HA "with" CFA2. Hochfield, editor of the collections of essays in which the article was reprinted (see above), says HA wrote the article "in collaboration with his brother Charles" (p. 289).

Counting the footnote in the Ford *Letters*, we here have four attributions of the article to HA and, or HA with, his brother Charles. Implicitly or explicitly, all four draw from HA's saying on 12 June 1876 that "Charles and I mean to concoct a political article" an unwarranted inference that the article published the following October is by both brothers. In my opinion, these attributions, obviously incautious and precipitous, should never have been given credence. None alludes to Cushing's *Index* or to HA's copy thereof. Silently the *Index* is thrust aside and attention shifted to twelve words by HA in a letter to HCL. What can be learned from the twelve words is decided without due attention to all their possible meanings.

That CFA2 was sole writer is affirmed by him and by his biographer. See Edward Chase Kirkland, *Charles Francis Adams, Jr.* (Cambridge, Mass., 1965), 163. Kirkland quotes a statement by CFA2 in his unpublished diary: "My political manifesto seems to have made a roar and burst the N. American."

The editors of the Levenson/Samuels *Letters of Henry Adams* turned up new evidence, three letters from HA to Moorfield Storey, relating in some measure to the authorship of the article. In the first, 24 August 1876 (L, II, 287), HA says: "I shall let you know how my draft is formulated, so as to have it fortified by your valuable legal advice. My views on the political situation will appear in due course." In the second, 21 September 1876 (L, II, 288), HA continues: "I enclose you the passage in our forthcoming manifesto, of which I spoke to you. Please return it to me with any alteration that occurs to you. . . . I think . . . the election is going to strengthen us. . . . My October North American will . . . express all I have to say." In the third, 25 September 1876 (L, II, 296–97), HA ends: "I have yours of Saturday and have altered the passage so as to accord with your views."

An expression which might seem to warrant a footnote is HA's "our" in "our forthcoming political manifesto." The word could signify authorship by more than one author (no other is named). It could signify collective utterance by the "Independents," meaning a faction organized to affect the centennial election (HA, CFA2, HCL, and Storey were all Independents). It could signify both.

The editors supply a footnote (L, II, 296n1) which says that HA enclosed with his second letter to Storey a brief "Outline" for a proposed federal law. The footnote gives the text of the outline and, apparently taking the "our" to signify authorship by a certain pair of brothers, says: ". . . HA's and CFA2's 'The "Independents" in the Canvass,' *NAR* 123 (October 1876), 464–465."

Here is a fifth attribution of the article to HA "and" CFA2, only different from the four previous attributions in being presented in connection with a letter from HA to Storey, not a letter from HA to HCL. Once again, no allusion is made to Cushing's *Index* or HA's copy thereof. Kirkland (1963) is silently thrust aside, together with the words "My political manifesto" quoted from the elder brother's diary.

The diary of Charles Francis Adams, Jr., is preserved among the Adams Papers at the Massachusetts Historical Society. Qualified inquirers have long been permitted access to the volumes. The entries explicitly pertaining to the writing of the articles are as follows:[2]

26 Aug. 1876: "Began to write a political manifesto for the Octr N. American and got through the beginning of it."

27 Aug. 1876: "Wrote most of the day and got thoroughly warmed to it, making the paper fly."

28 Aug. 1876: "To town and morning at office, out at 1:45 and before dinner at 6:30 had finished the rough draft of my N. A. political manifesto."

29 Aug. 1876: "To Beverly with Minnie & Lizzie Ogden, where I dined, took a walk with Henry—got home at 7 o'cl and in the evening began to wash out [i.e., edit] Wingate's last paper of the series in the N. A. Review."

7 Sept. 1876: "At home all day and furbished over my draught of the political article, getting at the work of copying and completing 8 pages."

9 Sept. 1876: "Hard at work copying till 3 o'cl, getting to p. 26."

10 Sept. 1876: "A tremendous day's writing,—kept at it all day except an hour's walk in afternoon—did not stop till 12 o'cl and got to p. 60—33 pages in one day, or 11 hours writing."

11 Sept. 1876: ". . . finished my article and went to town to correct it at the Athenaeum. Left it with the printer at 5 o'cl."

14 Sept. 1876: ". . . writing something for my manifesto. . . ."

21 Sept. 1876: "Corrected the proofs of my political article."

23 Sept. 1876: "In town[,] Henry & Cabot Lodge came to office about N. Amer. articles. . . ."

13 Oct. 1876: ". . . my political manifesto seems to have made a row [my reading] and burst the N. American."

These diary entries by CFA2, in my opinion, solidly affirm that CFA2 was sole writer of "The 'Independents' in the Canvass" (no. 32). They show that CFA2 (1) wrote a first draft, (2) lent the magazine a hand by editing a Wingate article for the issue, (3) wrote a second draft, (4) took his manuscript to the printer, (5) "wrote something" additional for the article, (6) corrected the proofs, (7) conferred with HA and HCL about his own article and the one

[2]Published by permission of the Massachusetts Historical Society.

by Wingate, and (8) learned of a "row" about his article which had "burst" the magazine.

My opinion is that the case of no. 32 is both simple—CFA2 wrote the article—and complex—HA used expressions in letters to HCL and Storey which, read incautiously by modern authorities, resulted in the article's being half or more-than-half removed from its writer and proportionally attributed to HA, although he at most was its editor. I suggest that interest in the matter should center, not in the attribution to CFA2, which seems definitive, but in HA's conduct, which, at least as I see it, needs explanation.

Attention perhaps should again be directed to the unsigned article mentioned above in connection with no. 22. That article, "The Political Campaign of 1872," in the October 1872 issue, closely resembles "The 'Independents' in the Canvass," in the October 1876 issue, except in one very striking respect. In Cushing's *Index*, the earlier article is attributed to no one. I believe that in such a case, if the article is political, the first conjecture must be that the article was highly dangerous to its writer.

There seems no possibility that HA coauthored the 1872 article (he had been five months abroad when it appeared). There seems every possibility that HA arranged that CFA2 would write the article, but in absolute secrecy, and further arranged that Howells would keep the secret permanently.

If the earlier article was written by CFA2 at HA's suggestion, and was highly dangerous, HA had a strong reason to tell HCL misleadingly four years later that "a political article" would be concocted, not by CFA2 alone, but by two brothers jointly. That is the precise move that HA interpolated on 12 June 1876, writing to HCL about a planned "political article" for a "very political" October issue.

During August and September, writing to Storey, HA used expressions which could make it seem that he, HA, was sole author of the Independents' manifesto. Also, writing to Storey, HA made no allusion whatever to his elder brother. So again HA chose behavior which could have the effect of shielding CFA2 from possible suspicion concerning a dangerous political article published four years in the past.

The above line of argument can be disputed. The elder brother's diary for 1872 shows that CFA2 during the campaign wrote an ambitious speech about the campaign and delivered it at Quincy, but the diary nowhere records that CFA2 wrote an article about the campaign for anonymous publication in the October 1872 *North American Review*. To some minds, the diary's silence may seem definitive proof that CFA2 did not write the unattributed 1872 article.

All the same, the argument has strengths. It at least faces up to the necessity of accounting for HA's leading people to think in 1876 that he was half-writing or solely writing what clearly was being solely written by CFA2. Also, in my view, it lends the case of no. 32 a marked resemblance to five other cases, nos. 24, 28, 29, 30, and 31; for, to shield an actual writer (CFA2), HA speaks as a prospective cowriter (in his letter to HCL) and a current sole writer (in his letters to Storey).

The argument, too, points to an interesting possibility. If the publishers of the magazine objected to the political drift of "The 'Independents' in the Canvass" on the basis of unsigned printed proofs and supposed that the author was HA (or conceivably both HA and HCL), and if HA did not disabuse the publishers of their misconception, the publishers' notice at the start of the October issue would reflect the publishers' honest opinion that their political quarrel was with HA (or both HA and HCL); and CFA2 may have been kept out of the fracas.

Two parts of the story seem to me wholly clear. HA all along knew who would write no. 32.[3] And at some moment late in 1877 or early in 1878, HA (or HCL or both) gave Cushing the truth for his *Index.*

An attribution perhaps better placed in abeyance

33. "VON HOLST'S HISTORY OF THE UNITED STATES"
   Article 3. *NAR* 123 (October 1876): 328–61. Signed "Henry Adams and H. C. Lodge." Attributed to HA and HCL by Cushing in the Index of Writers, and under Constitution and Holst in the Index of Subjects; also attributed to HA and "H. C. Lea" under U.S., History of, in the Index of Subjects. (Reprinted in HA, *The Great Secession Winter of 1860–61 and Other Essays,* ed. by George Hochfield [New York, 1958].)
   In his copy of Cushing's *Index,* HA crossed out the "Lea" and wrote "Lodge" in the margin but otherwise let the pertinent entries stand (see Facsimile C). That HCL "collaborated with Adams" to produce the article is affirmed by HCL's biographer. See John A. Garraty, *Henry Cabot Lodge* (New York, 1953), 38. The Ford edition of HA's *Letters* (F, I, 295n3), JTA, ES, and the Levenson/Samuels *Letters of Henry Adams* (L, II, 285n1) repeat the attribution to HA and HCL.
   This river of agreement owes some of its impetus to passages in two letters from HA to HCL. HA says in the first, 5 August 1876 (F, I, 295) (L, II, 285): "I too have just finished von Holst, and will make you a proposition. If you will write one notice of it, I will write another, and then we will take what is best out of each and roll them into one. . . . Perhaps we could make an article for October. . . ." He says in the second, 23 August 1876 (F, I, 296) (L, II, 286): "I enclose you the review of v. Holst into which I have tried to work all

[3]HCL seems gradually to have acquired the same knowledge. By mid-summer 1876, in his dealings with HCL about the article, HA was using "our" and "ourselves" to mean, not two brothers, but the Independents as a body. See HA to HCL, 2 August 1876 (F, I, 295) (L, II, 284): "Our political manifesto must go in last. We shall want to have all the information possible on the course of the canvass. I think we shall have to cut down to four articles this time, for Boynton will need space. Then we shall have Read, Hazen, Boynton and ourselves." Footnoting this passage (L, II, 285n3), the editors of the Levenson/Samuels *Letters of Henry Adams* attribute no. 32 to HA and CFA2 but without giving a reason name the elder first. Their note reads, "The manifesto was CFA2 and HA, 'The "Independents" in the Canvass. . . .'"

the material. I like it. . . . The last two pages are *my* centennial Oration. If you are satisfied with it, send it to the printers. . . ."

An instance of what has been inferred from these passages is a comment by Hochfield, editor of the collection of essays in which the article was reprinted (see above). Hochfield says (pp. 253–54): "Though the review was intended as a collaboration of sorts for which Adams and . . . Lodge . . . were to write separate pieces and then 'take what is best out of each and roll them into one,' Adams had the final and decisive hand in its composition. The last two pages, furthermore, which he called 'my centennial oration,' are entirely his own. . . ." The comment insists that HA was the principal writer, yet also seems to insist that, out of the thirty-three pages of the article, HA wrote two which when published were "entirely his own." This seems possibly nonsensical, and Hochfield can be viewed as beginning to sense a problem.

Attribution is dangerous. Like fliers and mariners, attributors can engage in their enterprise because they are bold, yet are likely to succeed enduringly only if they are cautious.

To me, of the thirty-three cases, this one (no. 33) seems the case most likely to crash or wreck an attributor. I assume that Cushing made his attribution of the article to HA and HCL on the basis of the printed names "Henry Adams and H. C. Lodge"; that is, I assume Cushing asked no questions. I agree that the printed names at the end of article can easily appear to be tantamount to handwritten attestations by HA and HCL that they are the writers of the article. But I have the problem that authorship attested in print by two persons seems to me something extremely different from authorship attested in print by one person. When there are two printed names, I think either or both can mean—and commonly do mean—almost anything. So my opinion is that the attribution of "Von Holst's History of the United States" to HA and HCL should be placed in abeyance until the case is reviewed by interested inquirers: a jury, if one can be found.

I wish to suggest as well that something interesting happens when the printed names are ignored and attention is confined to the two passages quoted above. Without violence to any syllable they contain, one can find the passages suggestive of a five-stage occurrence:

1. HA made HCL a "proposition" of separate, simultaneous authorship of rival notices, to make possible joint authorship of a single notice—or even "an article for October"
2. HCL reacted by immediately completing a full-length article, sending it to HA, and then sending added "material"
3. HA, withdrawing his proposition, became purely an editor
4. HA fitted the supplementary material into the article and returned it to HCL for approval and printing
5. HA simultaneously extended two expressions of praise to his industrious associate: one emphatic (that he liked the article), and one extravagant and

hyperbolic (that he liked it so much that, although he had written none of it, and possibly agreed with none of it, its last "two pages," meaning its last paragraph, could stand as *his*, HA's, "centennial Oration").

If the article is re-read with this conjectured occurrence in mind, its content challenges reappraisal. From beginning to end, the text sustains the thesis that the Constitution of 1787 "made a nation." But the question whether the Constitution made a nation was one of *Lodge's* current concerns. (See HCL, *Early Memories* [New York, 1913], 247.) And, in my opinion, present evidence shows that HA, far from subscribing to the thesis, believed in 1876 that it is human beings that make nations, and make and remake constitutions.

The style of the article seems to indicate sole authorship by HCL. In the one sentence in the last paragraph in which clear evidence of HA's style might be alleged, I, for one, see instead an admirer's imitation of HA's style; and I notice that a metaphor in the sentence involves a geological absurdity which HA, as editor, might charitably have permitted to stand, but which he could scarcely have written.

A possibility broached in the preface of this book is that HA and HCL signed no. 33, not because both were its writers, but to display in the issue the names of the retiring "editors" mentioned in a publishers' notice in the front of the issue. It might equally be urged that the two men signed their names with an added motive. By my count, while editing eighteen issues, HA contributed an article and twenty-two notices (excluding no. 33); and, while helping edit eleven issues, HCL contributed two articles and eight notices (conjecturally including no. 33). Present evidence indicates that they served gratis—were paid not a dime for their work, whether as editors or as writers, after consenting to edit the magazine. Their main recompense was not money; it possibly was not reputation; it may have been sheer satisfaction. I can believe they published their names together in their last issue partly to identify themselves as the retiring editors and also to express a deep satisfaction each knew they both were feeling.

FACSIMILES*

In his *Index to the North American Review,* Cushing positioned his Index of Subjects first, his Index of Writers second.

In the Index of Subjects, there are thirty-eight entries attributing to HA articles and notices published in issues of the magazine subsequent to his becoming editor (including three entries which identify him as coauthor of an article). The entries appear on pages 8, 16, 21 (2), 24, 28, 32, 34 (2), 36, 39, 40, 46, 48 (2), 51 (2), 52, 56, 61, 63, 64, 68 (2), 78, 81 (2), 82, 90, 95, 100, 104 (2), 106 (2), 107, and 109 (2). (Of two entries on p. 100, one merely concerns a passage, not a notice. See no. 11 above.)

In his copy, HA made marks on three pages of the Index of Subjects: 28, 106, and 109. Facsimiles A, B, and C reproduce the pages.

HA cancelled two entries attributing notices to himself in the Index of Subjects, but failed to cancel ten which are equally mistaken, in my view, as explained above in connection with nos. 26, 27, 28, 29, and 30. The ten entries I believe mistaken appear on pages 21 (2), 32, 34, 40, 48, 61, 64, 104, and 107.

In the Index of Writers, twenty-eight attributions of notices to HA and one attribution of an article to HA as coauthor relate to issues of the magazine published subsequent to his becoming editor. All appear on page 118. In his copy, HA made marks on two pages of the Index of Writers: 118 and 135. Facsimiles E and G reproduce those pages. Two additional pages of the Index of Writers which warrant special notice are reproduced by Facsimiles D and F.

*Facsimiles have been abbreviated to accommodate explanatory captions.

FACSIMILE A

Page 28 of the Index of Subjects in Adams's copy of Cushing's *Index,* showing HA's cancellation of an "H" and his writing "Brooks" in the margin. See no. 24 above. (Courtesy of the Massachusetts Historical Society.)

FACSIMILE B

Page 106 of the Index of Subjects in
Adams's copy of Cushing's *Index*, showing
that HA cancelled the attribution to him
of "Ticknor's Life, Letters, and Journals."
See no. 31 above. (Courtesy of the
Massachusetts Historical Society.)

Loc

FACSIMILE C

Page 109 of the Index of Subjects in
Adams's copy of Cushing's *Index*, showing
that Adams crossed out a misprint, "Lea,"
and wrote "Lodge" in the margin. See
no. 33 above. (Courtesy of the
Massachusetts Historical Society.)

INDEX OF WRITERS.

FACSIMILE D

Page 117 of the Index of Writers in
Adams's copy of Cushing's *Index*, showing
that HA could easily see the attribution of
"The 'Independents' in the Canvass" to
CFA2. See no. 32 above. (Courtesy of the
Massachusetts Historical Society.)

FACSIMILE E

Page 118 of the Index of Writers in Adams's copy of Cushing's *Index,* showing the entries HA cancelled and did not cancel. See nos. 25, 26, 28, 29, 30, 31, and 33 above. (Courtesy of the Massachusetts Historical Society.)

HEDGE, FREDERICK HENRY. *Lewes's* Life and Works of Goethe. **82** 564. *Madame Ossoli's* At Home and Abroad. **83** 261. *Shedd's* History of Christian Doctrine. **98** 567. The Method of History. **111** 311.

HEDGE, LEVI. Essay concerning Free-Agency. **13** 384.

HEILPRONN, M. *Saulcy's* Étude d'Esdras et de Néhémie. **109** 272.

HEMANS, HENRY W. France under the Second Empire. **111** 402. Prussia and Germany. **112** 113.

HENRY, CALEB SPRAGUE. Among the Pines. **95** 534. *Spear's* Religion and the State. **124** 318.

HEYWOOD, JOSEPH CONVERSE. *Duer's* Constitutional Jurisprudence. **86** 464.

HIGBEE, JAMES M. Steamboat Disasters. **50** 19. Illinois. **51** 92.

HIGGINSON, HENRY. Explanation of the Musical Scale. **4** 19.

HIGGINSON, THOMAS WENTWORTH. Portugal's Glory and Decay. **83** 456. Children's Books of the Year. **102** 236.

HILL, ADAMS SHERMAN. *Greeley's* American Conflict. **104** 238. *Walt Whitman's* Drum Taps. **104** 301. *Cutler's* War Poems. **104** 306. Charles Lamb and his Biographers. **104** 386. The Character of Jonathan Swift. **106** 68. Laurence Sterne. **107** 1. The Chicago Convention. **107** 167. Causes of the Commune. **116** 90. *Forster's* Life of Jonathan Swift. **123** 170. *Salter's* Life of Grimes. **123** 186.

HILL, CLEMENT HUGH. Peerages and Genealogies. **97** 36.

HILL, HAMILTON ~~ALPHONSO~~. Ocean Steam Navigation. **99** 483.

HILL, THOMAS. The Imagination in Mathematics. **85** 223. *Peirce's* Analytic Mechanics. **87** 1.

HILLARD, GEORGE STILLMAN. Clarence. **32** 73. Life of Sebastian Cabot. **34** 405. Chief Justice Marshall. **42** 217. *Everett's* Orations and Speeches. **44** 138. *Hoffman's* Course of Legal Study. **46** 72. *Lieber's* Essay on Penal Law. **47** 452. *Dwight's* Versions from Goethe and Schiller. **48** 505. *Lowell's* Poems. **52** 452. Margaret Miller Davidson. **53** 139. Common School Education. **54** 458. Recent English Poetry. **55** 200. *Bremer's* Neighbors. **56** 497. The School and the Schoolmaster. **57** 149. *Sears, Edwards,* and *Felton* on Classical Studies. **57** 184. *Prescott's* History of the Conquest of Mexico. **58** 157. *Cushing's* Parliamentary Practice. **60** 494. *Bethune's* Sermons. **63** 262. *Greenleaf's* Edition of Cruise on Real Property. **69** 376. *Felton's* Memorial of Dr. Popkin. **75** 473. *Appleton* on the Rules of Evidence. **92** 515. *Hurd's* Law of Freedom and Bondage. **96** 148. *Story's* Roba di Roma. **97** 247. *Ticknor's* Life of Prescott. **98** 1.

HILLEBRAND, KARL. Herder. **115** 104, 235; **116** 389.

HITCHCOCK, CHARLES HENRY. The Antiquity of Man. **97** 451.

HITCHCOCK, EDWARD. *Dr. Webster's* Manual of Chemistry. **23** 349. The New Theory of the Earth. **28** 265.

HITCHCOCK, M. S. *Carpenter's* Mesmerism, Spiritualism, &c. **125** 390.

HITCHCOCK, THOMAS. Soul and Substance. **124** 404. The Functions of Unbelief. **125** 462.

HODGSKIN, JAMES B. The Financial Condition of the United States. **108** 517. Our Currency, Past and Future. **111** 78.

HOLLAND, FREDERICK MAY. *Tischendorf's* Discoveries in the East. **92** 250. CRITICAL NOTICES. **193** 1–4; **194** 4–7.

HOLLEY, HORACE. On the Pleasure derived from witnessing Scenes of Distress. **2** 59.

FACSIMILE F

Page 134 of the Index of Writers in Adams's copy of Cushing's *Index,* showing a correction not in HA's handwriting. The same correction seems to appear in all copies of the *Index.* (Courtesy of the Massachusetts Historical Society.)

HOWELLS, WILLIAM DEAN. Recent Italian Comedy. **99** 364. Italian Brigandage. **101** 162. Ducal Mantua. **102** 48. Modern Italian Poets. **103** 313; **104** 317. Henry Wadsworth Longfellow. **104** 531. *Francesco Dall Ongaro's* Stornelli. **106** 26. George William Curtis. **107** 104. *Fambri's* Free Press and Duelling in Italy. **108** 299. The Florentine Satirist, Giusti. **115** 31. *Niccolini's* Anti-Papal Tragedy. **115** 333.

HOWES, FREDERICK. British and American Shipping. **32** 422.

HOYT, JOSEPH GIBSON. The Phillips Family and the Phillips Exeter Academy. **87** 119. Educated Labor. **89** 358. Popular Fallacies. **96** 87.

HUBBARD, FORDYCE MITCHELL. Robert Herrick. **84** 484. *Hawks's* History of North Carolina. **91** 40. The Venerable Bede. **93** 36.
    CRITICAL NOTICES. **185** 14, 15; **187** 2, 3; **190** 1–3; **191** 12–15; **192** 14.

HUBBARD, GARDINER GREENE. Proposed Changes in the Telegraphic System. **117** 80.

HUDSON, HENRY NORMAN. *Furness's* Shakespeare. **117** 475.

HURLBUT, WILLIAM HENRY. The Poetry of Spanish America. **68** 129. Henry Heine. **69** 216. The French Revolution of 1848. **80** 273.

INMAN, JOHN. *Stephens:* Incidents of Travel in Yucatan. **57** 86.

IRVING, WASHINGTON. *Wheaton's* History of the Northmen. **35** 342.

IRWIN, AGNES. *Tenot's* Coup d'État. **110** 377.

JACKSON, CHARLES, JR. The Great Exhibition. **75** 357.

JAMES, HENRY. Faith and Science. **101** 335. *Stirling's* Secret of Hegel. **102** 264. *Bushnell's* Vicarious Sacrifice. **102** 556. *Swedenborg's* Ontology. **105** 89. *Foster's* Swedenborg's Angelic Philosophy. **106** 299.

JAMES, HENRY, JR. *Senior's* Essays on Fiction. **99** 580. *Miss Prescott's* Azarian. **100** 268. *Trollope's* Lindisfarn Chase. **100** 277. Emily Chester. **100** 279. *Arnold's* Essays on Criticism. **101** 206. *Miss Alcott's* Moods. **101** 276. The Gayworthys. **101** 619. *Higginson's* Works of Epictetus. **102** 599. *Mrs. Howe's* Later Lyrics. **104** 644. *Morris's* Life and Death of Jason. **105** 688. *Howells's* Italian Journeys. **106** 336. *Hamerton's* Contemporary French Painters. **106** 716. *Falloux's* Madame Swetchine. **107** 328. *Morris's* Earthly Paradise. **107** 358. The Spanish Gypsy. **107** 620. Theophile Gautier. **116** 310. *Cherbuliez's* Meta Holdenis. **117** 461. Iwan Turgéniew. **118** 326. *Gautier's* Posthumous Works. **119** 416. *George Eliot's* Legend of Jubal. **119** 484. *Taylor's* Prophet. **120** 188. *Howells's* Foregone Conclusion. **120** 207.

JAMES, ISABELLA. *Darlington's* Memoirs of Bartram. **70** 210. *Michaux's* North American Sylva. **86** 359. The Aquarium. **87** 143. *Gray's* Botanical Text-Books. **87** 321. Prince Gallitzin. **88** 349.

JAMES, WILLIAM. *Huxley's* Comparative Anatomy. **100** 290. *Wallace's* Origin of the Human Race. **101** 261. *Bernard's* Rapport. **107** 322. *Darwin's* Variation of Animals and Plants. **107** 362. *Bushnell's* Women's Suffrage. **109** 556. *Carpenter's* Principles of Mental Physiology. **119** 225. ~~Urkunden zur Geschichte des deutschen Rechtes. 121 193.~~ Grundzuge der Physiologischen Psychologie. **121** 195.

JARVIS, EDWARD. Causes of Mental Disease. **89** 316.

JENCKES, THOMAS ALLEN. Civil Service of the United States. **105** 478.

JOBSON, D. WEMYSS. The Clubs of London. **81** 1.

FACSIMILE G

Page 135 of the Index of Writers in Adams's copy of Cushing's *Index*, showing HA's cancellation of an entry attributing a notice to William James. Possible writer: Marcel Thevenin. (Courtesy of the Massachusetts Historical Society.)

ACKNOWLEDGMENTS

I wish to acknowledge the unfailing helpfulness and expert guidance extended to me at the Massachusetts Historical Society by Louis L. Tucker, director; Stephen T. Riley, director emeritus; John D. Cushing, librarian; Peter Drummey, associate librarian; Richard A. Ryerson, editor, Adams Papers; and Celeste Walker, assistant editor, Adams Papers. J. C. Levenson and Charles Vandersee of the University of Virginia, editors of the *Letters of Henry Adams* (Cambridge: Harvard University Press), very obligingly provided immediate help relating to books owned by Adams and letters to Adams from Charles Milnes Gaskell. Eleanor L. O'Sullivan supplied needed information and photocopies from the Freiberger Library, Case Western Reserve University. At Harvard University, Erica Chadbourne, curator of manuscripts at the Law School Library, provided information concerning books possibly once owned by Adams; and Melanie Wisner traced an uncatalogued source, the Houghton Library copy of the proofs of "Taylor's Faust." Frederick M. Keener, Barbara Kaars, and Earl N. Harbert made invaluable criticisms and suggestions concerning the Preface and Attributions; and Eleni Chalfant suggested specific improvements in the Preface and Attributions at every stage in their preparation. Manuscript material is published by permission of the Massachusetts Historical Society and the Houghton Library, Harvard University.

INDEX OF NAMES

This index embraces Adams's sketches 1–23
and all prefatory and appended material.
Italicized numbers indicate a whole sketch.

INDEX OF SUBJECTS

This index covers subjects touched on by Adams or writers he quotes or translates in sketches 1–23 and appendixes B and C.

necessity of removing distortions, fictions, & legends from, 48, 219
necessity of scientific training in, 114
overbroad study of, 182
statistical methods; "scientific use of imagination"; maps, charts & "simple symbolism" in, 127–28, 196, 199–201
to be reconstructed entirely, 45
tone of impartiality in, not actually meritorious, 79
valuable in proportion to its truth, 219
History, a survey of[1]
American Revolution
diplomatic triumph; provisional treaty of 1782, 153–59
military campaigns of 1778–81, 151–53
ancient Egypt
Nile tombs emanations of most intense faith that ever existed, 89–91: religion a form of ancestor worship based on belief that father was sole author of child, 89–91; social organization & law possibly depravations of archaic social organization & law, 92–93
ancient Germany
family a loose, flexible, almost indefinite association, 92: ancestors not worshipped; rights of fathers not inordinate; rights of wives, sons, &

daughters roughly equivalent to fathers', 92
inhabitants lived in villages, owned land in common & had strong family ideas, but organizational unit was not family or group of families, 45–46, 91–92, 94, 117, 166
inhabitants long assumed to have been organized tribally, under tribal chiefs empowered by primogeniture, 164–65: alleged to have lost archaic features (including chiefs & primogeniture) during tribal wanderings, 92–93
tribes may never have existed; no evidence of tribes or tribal ideas; no evidence of primogeniture; loose, flexible, almost indefinite family possibly *was* archaic, 162–66
unexpected new evidence that all inhabitants were organized three ways at once, as *nation, states, & hundreds,* 162, 216–17: family powerful but subordinate to the *state,* 162; individual full-grown man, associated with other men in artificial groups, constituted the *state,* 162: existence of individual's rights & individual's ownership of property affirmed by Salian legal procedure, 103–12; power of the *state* belonged to its free citizens; power

---

[1]Users of this entry are advised that Adams's writings show evidence of fairly consistent accuracy, in combination with occasional apparent hesitation, doubt, or confusion in the use of terms. The following terms may be differentiated, interchanged, or confused on the indicated pages: *ancient,* 94, 123; *still more ancient,* 166; *very ancient,* 93; *archaic,* 89, 92, 94, 103, 114, 116, 124, 161–62, 167; *early,* 87, 112, 117; *very early,* 45; *oldest,* 93, 166; *original,* 89, 93; *pagan,* 114; *prehistoric,* 86, 89; *primeval,* 179; *typical,* 92; & *undeveloped,* 45.

Aryan, 89, 91–94, 166, is clearly equivalent to *Indo-European,* 94, 161, 166. *Depravations,* 93, is clearly equivalent to *perversions,* 94. *Gau, hundred, pagus & soke,* 178, 216–17, are statedly equivalent. *Folk,* as used on 217, appears to coordinate with *nation, race & Stamm* as used on 163, 216. *Union of states & the State,* as used on 217, appear to be equivalents of *nation* as used on 116. *National & popular,* as used on 119, may be near-equivalents.

Confusion centers in the word *tribe,* 162, as compared with *civitas, people,* & *state,* 162, 216–17; *district,* 162; *free kingdom,* 178; *province,* 118, & *shire(s),* 117, 178; in the expressions *tribal,* 162–66, & *old tribal,* 118, as compared with *local,* 119, & *sectional,* 120; & in the term *tribal chief,* 164–65, as compared with *ealdorman,* 118; *lord,* 118; *petty kings,* 118; *prince,* 118; & *viceking,* 118. The manifest source of confusion is Adams's initial acceptance of, and eventual disbelief in, the reality of Germanic tribes. His near-conviction that Germanic tribes never existed (that what existed were Germanic states) fully emerges only in sketch 18.